More Than Meets the Eye

AN INTRODUCTION TO MEDIA STUDIES

Third Edition

GRAEME BURTON
Lecturer in Media and Cultural Studies,
University of the West of England

A member of the Hodder Headline Group
LONDON
Co-published in the United States of America by
Oxford University Press Inc., New York

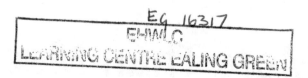
First published in Great Britain in 1990
Second edition 1997
Third edition published in 2002 by
Arnold, a member of the Hodder Headline Group,
338 Euston Road, London NW1 3BH

http://www.arnoldpublishers.com

Co-published in the United States of America by
Oxford University Press, Inc.,
198 Madison Avenue, New York, NY10016

British Library Cataloguing in Publication Data
A catalogue record for this book is available from the British Library

Library of Congress Cataloging-in-Publication Data
A catalog record for this book is available from the Library of Congress

ISBN 0 340 76204 7 (pb)

1 2 3 4 5 6 7 8 9 10

Production Editor: Anke Ueberberg
Production Controller: Bryan Eccleshall
Cover Design: Terry Griffiths

Typeset in 10pt Sabon by Phoenix Photosetting, Chatham, Kent
Printed and bound in Malta by Gutenberg Press

What do you think about this book? Or any other Arnold title?
Please send your comments to feedback.arnold@hodder.co.uk

More Than Meets the Eye

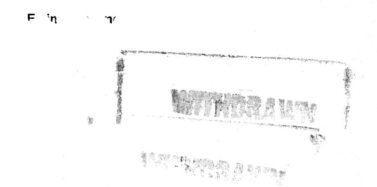

Contents

Acknowledgements

I would like to thank my students for helping me to attend to the missing bits of the picture. I am grateful to my editors for their perseverance, and to Lesley Riddle in particular for her nurturing influence. Finally, thanks to the family that tolerates a sometimes grumpy author, some of whom have gone on to be media students themselves.

The author and publishers would like to thank the following for permission to use copyright material in this book: Twentieth Century Fox for Figure 6.5; Advertising Association for Table 7.1 and Figure 7.3; Audit Bureau of Circulation for Tables 1.1 and 1.2; © 1994 BBC Education for Figure 6.2a (*Middlemarch*); British Phonographic Industry for Figure 10.4; the Broadcasters' Audience Board for Figure 9.4; © Crown Copyright for Figures 9.2, and Tables 1.3, 9.4, 9.5, 9.6, 9.7, 9.8 and 10.1; DaimlerChrysler UK Ltd for Figure 1.1; Datamonitor for Figure 4.7; the Department of Health and Social Services for Figure 5.6; Egmont Fleetway Ltd, 1997 for Figure 2.1; HarperCollins Publishers Ltd for the front cover of *The Mirror Crack'd from Side to Side* by Agatha Christie, Figure 5.3b; Hutchinson for the front cover of *Going Wrong* by Ruth Rendell, Figure 5.3c; the Independent Television Commission for Table 5.1 and Table 1.4; the International Institute of Communications for Table 4.2; Manchester University Press for the pie charts from *Mass Communication* by Roland Lorimer, Figure 4.6; MORI for Figure 10.3; Mysterious Press UK for the front cover of *The Neon Rain* by James Lee Burke, Figure 5.3a, and *The Big Nowhere* by James Ellroy, Figure 5.3d; the National Meningitis Trust for Figure 7.1; the National Readership Survey for Tables 4.4 and 9.2; NTC Publications for Figure 7.3; Pearson Education for Table 5.2; Procter & Gamble for Figure 2.3; Sage Publications for Figures 3.6 and 10.2; and Take2Games for Figure 3.1.

Introduction

TO THE READER

The third edition of this book hopefully remains true to my original intentions, however much rewritten and expanded in places. It is not a book about practical work: it is designed to help make sense of the media, to explain how the media communicate with us, and to give you an understanding of how they operate and of who runs them.

I assume that you like reading, watching and listening, and that you are curious about what goes on in the media world, because it is a part of all our worlds, of all our experience. The following chapters should cause you to think about the media and media products in new ways.

THE AIMS OF THIS BOOK

I want to help you make sense of what is going on in the media, and to add to your interest in and enjoyment of what you watch, listen to and read. The following chapters should help you organize your own ideas about the programmes you watch, about the newspapers you read and about all the media that are part of our everyday lives. You should come to understand that there are reasons why we have the kind of media that we do have in Britain, and why it is important to study them.

This book will explain how media organizations put their messages together, why they do this in the way they do, and what effects their output may have on us. In particular I want to clarify some of the terms that are commonly used to make these explanations. Indeed, I want to explain why these terms and ideas matter anyway. So I hope that – by the time you have finished this book – you will understand more about the media in relation to your life, your thinking and your world.

Most of all, as a student of media and of communication, you should be encouraged not to take things for granted. Books, records, programmes do not just appear from nowhere for no reason. The reasons why they appear in the way that they do are important, because they help shape our view of the world. This book aims to help you understand this process of shaping.

THE STRUCTURE OF THIS BOOK

This book is organized into ten chapters. The first three deal with basic ideas about the study of media in general. The rest work their way through media communication, from where it starts – with the owners of systems and makers of programmes – through to where it ends, in the heads of ourselves, the audience.

Chapter 1 asks the basic question, why bother to study the media at all? It gives you some pointers to what you may get out of media study besides straightforward enjoyment.

Chapter 2 gives you some particular ideas about how you can study: how you can analyse media material, and avoid the trap of just chatting about papers and programmes in a rather general way.

Chapter 3 presents the media as examples of communication like any other – this book, for instance, or even talking. So it looks into the idea of communication as a process that has various parts. The remaining chapters will help you to understand the parts of this process.

Chapter 4 deals with the organizations that make the media material. They decide to pay for and to manufacture media material in the first place, so we need to see why and how they do this.

Chapter 5 is about the way that this material is made and about the sort of material that gets made. It asks why so much media product is basically the same, why we get so many stereotypes in this material, and how this affects us.

Chapter 6 looks at media product in terms of what makes it seem real in different ways, and of how it seduces us with its story-telling.

Chapter 7 is an extension of Chapter 5, looking at news and advertising in particular. It explores how we are led to understand news material in one way rather than another. It talks about some basic aspects of advertising and about devices of persuasion that appear in adverts.

Chapter 8 looks at the messages in the programmes and magazines, and other examples of product. Something is being communicated to us, so what is it? Even casual entertainment, even the most fun shows are telling you something, whether you realize it or not. And what you are being told really matters because it goes inside your head.

Chapter 9 focuses on the audience. We need to look at ourselves as consumers of the media products. Many of the media makers certainly regard us in this way. So how exactly do they see us? How does this affect what they put out?

Chapter 10 picks up on the possible effects of all this material upon us, on the way that we think.

So this is what you are in for if you read on. The book is not just a lot of facts about the media, but more about ways of using those facts, about ways of making sense of the media.

HOW TO USE THIS BOOK

Basically, you should use it to find out what you want.

I have written the book in certain chapters in a certain order because I think that it makes sense. But it is your book. So you should use it the way that you need to – the way that you should use any book.

If you aren't bothered about reasons for taking a media course then skip Chapter 1. If you don't want to be held up by the introduction to study methods, then leave it until the end. If the explanation of key terms as a basis for Media Studies looks too heavy, then refer back to it when you need to.

Most of all, you should learn to pick out bits to suit your own interests and study needs. If you are on a taught course, then your tutor will have organized a course plan, with topics in a given order. Look at the chapter details. Look at the table of contents. Look up the key words for the topics that you are dealing with. Go to the parts that you need.

Do use the reading list, which might help you chase up ideas and topics.

Do use the glossary: it will help you find out the meaning of the special words and phrases used in the text (these appear in small capitals).

By the end of it all you really should have a better idea of what is going on behind the act of watching a programme or reading a newspaper. For factual details about how a newspaper is made or how special effects on television are done, then there are other books – and your tutor – that can deal with such matters. This book focuses on your ideas and understanding. It will enable you to study how and why the media create the things that they do.

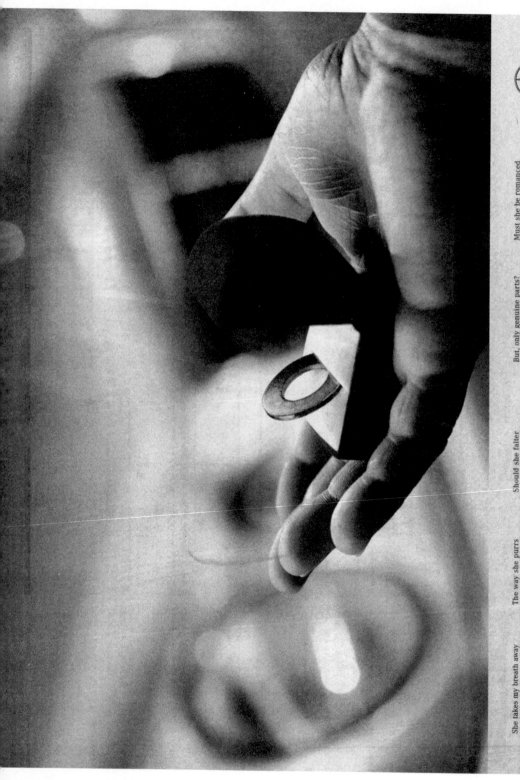

She takes my breath away
The way she moves
Sleekly turns the road to silk

The way she purrs
A lyrical lullaby
To my hardened heart

Should she falter
Should she err, I will go to
The ends of the earth for her

But, only genuine parts?
The best of engineers?
The whole silver service?

Must she be romanced
To the letter?
Must she be so scrutinized?

Passionate about Parts and Servicing.

She's worth it.

 Mercedes-Benz

1

Why Study the Media?

There should be reasons why you study anything. These reasons should be ones that you understand and believe in. You should know why you are doing anything, in fact. And those reasons should answer that big question – SO WHAT? This is Media Studies – so what?

There are also those who argue that the study of the media is such a grand enterprise in all its detail that it is too great a task. John Hartley (1990) was actually talking about the 'impossibility' of Television Studies when he said that there were three big problems:

1 the dispersal of the object of study
2 the specialization of modes of analysis
3 the inability of people working in the field to understand what the others are doing.

He would be talking about:

• what we actually mean by study of the media
• the different and particular approaches to analysing media
• the problems that come from needing to understand and put together these different approaches.

I would argue that Media Studies is indeed a subject of great scope. Indeed, it has many parts and many implications to be followed up. It is true that researchers need to make better efforts to understand what each other is doing, how and why. There is a huge amount of material to be synthesized. But I believe that it is worth the attempt because, as Roger Silverstone (1999) says: 'it is because the media are central to our everyday lives that we must study them ... as social and cultural as well as political and economic dimensions of the modern world'.

Fig. 1.1 Mercedes Benz ad

Mercedes Benz are typical of multinational corporations (the cars are made by Daimler Chrysler) that use the media to reach into our lives. This advert brings romance to the car business and to technology. It also invokes music and another advert. See if you can work out where all these elements are.

I go along with that, but I would like to add some answers of my own to the big question. I hope they will convince you, and that you will agree with at least some of them.

1 YOUR INTERESTS

In the first place, you may be personally interested in certain types of magazine or programme, so you want to look into these further. You may also find it interesting how the material is created, you may like reading about the practical side of media making. Again, you may feel that you want to study media because it is something you know about, something you feel confident with, a subject where you have a head start because you already have some background in it and some opinions.

2 MEDIA POWER AND INFLUENCE

Many of the main arguments for studying the media come down to this: everyone believes that they do have some power, though it is surprisingly difficult to establish exactly what kind of power this is. The main power of the media lies in the fact that they can shape what we know about the world and can be a main source of ideas and opinions. They may influence the way we think and act. This power is the greater if we take the media together rather than looking at one individual medium such as television. And it is most obvious when we look at examples of media use such as an advertising campaign. Such campaigns do use media together, and thus repeat and reinforce any message they are putting across. Some people argue about how much power the media really have. But the continuous and public arguments suggest that it must be worthwhile studying the media in order to see whether or not they really do have this power and influence.

3 ECONOMIC POWER

In particular, the sheer economic power of the media makes them significant and worth studying. The media industries employ thousands of people directly and make the employment of thousands of others possible (for example, in terms of the production of equipment). The income and expenditure of the media are vast. The amount spent on making programmes or producing a magazine is colossal. For instance, the income of the UK ITV (Channel 3) companies from advertising was £2.725 billion in 1999, plus £590 million for Channel 4 and £187 million for Channel 5. The licence fee income of the BBC was £2.3 billion in 1999, of which £114 million was spent on collecting the fees.

And then what about advertising in general? In 1999 Britain spent £12 billion on advertising. People do not spend this sort of money on making messages and sending communication unless they believe it has some effect. So the sheer financial clout of the media is an argument for studying how and why they work in the way that they do.

4 SCALE OF OPERATIONS

This is also huge. It provides an argument for looking at what is going on. One may measure this scale in all sorts of ways. One could talk about it in terms of size of audience. Peak-time audiences for television run to about 19 million people – that's over a third of the population of this country. *Coronation Street* and *Who Wants To Be A Millionaire?* hit this in 1999. One could look at it in terms of geographical scale of operations. So what about satellite channels like Sky, spraying down their programmes over Britain and most of Europe? Or what about scale in terms of proportion of the particular media industry controlled? The news gathering companies AP, Reuters, AFP and UPI totally dominate the sourcing of world news stories for newspapers across Europe. This shows that when we talk about 'operations' we are not just talking abut production. If you want to launch a new magazine on a national scale in Britain, then you need to be sure of the retail support of WH Smith, with its dominance of prime-site outlets, let alone its control of nearly 50 per cent of the distribution business. However we measure this scale – this massness of the mass media – it is so great that, again, it must make the media a subject worth looking into.

Institutions and Influence
Is it the size and wealth of a given media company that matters, in terms of its potential influence?
Or is it the nature of the material put out by that company that matters more?

---

5 ACCESS TO THE AUDIENCE

This is about the ability of the media to get to their audience. It is notorious that radio and television are special in the sense that they get into the living room. They have access to every household in the land. But, then again, there is the *Sun*, which reaches nearly four million people every day; or the *News of the World*, which gets to five million people every Sunday (and both papers are owned by the News Corporation). This ability to get to us, sometimes in huge numbers, also makes the media special as communicators. A total of 60 per cent of UK homes now have access to the Net. Digital television is proliferating channels and interactivity. Our homes have more direct access to information and to the rest of the world than at any time in history.

Table 1.1 Four newspaper groups control 89 per cent of national circulation

Dailies	Jan–Jun 00	Jan–Jun 99	Change
1 *Sun*	3,563,803	3,730,466	−4.47%
2 *Daily Mail*	2,376,468	2,350,241	1.12%
3 *Mirror*	2,258,950	2,313,063	−2.34%
4 *Express*	1,065,273	1,095,716	−2.78%
5 *Daily Telegraph*	1,033,680	1,044,740	−1.06%
6 *Times*	722,642	740,883	−2.46%
7 *Daily Record*	620,103	665,313	−6.80%
8 *Daily Star*	607,649	615,038	−1.20%
9 *Financial Times*	457,653	385,025	18.86%
10 *Guardian*	396,534	398,721	−0.55%
11 *Independent*	224,224	223,304	0.41%
12 *Scotsman*	84,716	79,925	−5.99%

SUNDAYS			
1 *News of the World*	4,041,987	4,209,173	−3.97%
2 *Mail on Sunday*	2,297,915	2,279,430	0.81%
3 *Sunday Mirror*	1,939,513	1,981,059	−2.10%
4 *Sunday People*	1,538,991	1,643,310	−6.35%
5 *Sunday Times*	1,369,461	1,374,436	−0.36%
6 *Sunday Express*	977,791	1,003,287	−2.54%
7 *Sunday Telegraph*	811,408	816,653	−0.64%
8 *Observer*	415,004	404,859	2.51%
9 *Independent on Sunday*	248,564	250,034	−0.59%
10 *Scotland on Sunday*	105,277	120,644	−12.74%
11 *Sunday Business*	68,436	55,494	23.32%

Source: ABC, July 2000 © Audit Bureau of Circulation

6 INFORMATION AND ENTERTAINMENT

These two things are very important to most people. So where do we get most of this from? Right: the media. Thousands of hours of television are pumped out through all channels: there are 200 satellite channels; 90 per cent of people polled say that they get their news from television, and that they believe it for the most part; 13 million people read the three main tabloid and four main quality newspapers every day; there were 139.75 million cinema attendances in 1999; 180 million CDs were sold in 1998. If you think about it, where else do you get your information and entertainment from but the media? Remember, books are as much a media industry as any other. You may spend time socializing and playing a sport. But again, statistically, you are spending an average of 25 hours a week just watching television – that's 1,300 hours a year. So if the media are the main providers of information and entertainment, again it makes sense to look at what they provide and why, because it certainly is a major part of your life.

Table 1.2 Top magazines by circulation

1 *AA Magazine*	4,246,863		26 *Chat*	490,516
2 *Skyview*	2,299,295		27 *Woman's Weekly*	483,722
3 *Cable Guide*	2,067,752		28 *Best*	461,851
4 *Safeway Magazine*	1,944,359		29 *Cosmopolitan*	460,970
5 *Boots Health & Beauty*	1,909,500		30 *Candis*	450,443
6 *What's on TV*	1,741,156		31 *Hello*	436,523
7 *Somerfield Magazine*	1,413,900		32 *Marie-Claire*	422,995
8 *Asda Magazine*	1,363,354		33 *Prima*	413,196
9 *Radio Times*	1,334,908		34 *Sugar*	395,952
10 *The National Trust Magazine*	1,319,122		35 *Now*	390,812
11 *Take a Break*	1,218,915		36 *Good Housekeeping*	384,541
12 *Voila*	1,200,000		37 *People's Friend*	383,149
13 *Reader's Digest*	1,131,273		38 *Sainsbury's*	382,161
14 *Saga Magazine*	1,019,629		39 *National Geographic*	378,976
15 *TVTimes*	790,603		40 *Loaded*	353,640
16 *Debenhams*	742,350		41 *Top of the Pops*	349,813
17 *FHM*	674,836		42 *Motoring & Leisure*	337,731
18 *Woman*	653,045		43 *Official PlayStation mag*	337,186
19 *TV Quick*	638,855		44 *Know Your Destiny*	332,755
20 *Birds*	579,876		45 *Auto Trader*	326,388
21 *Bella*	564,104		46 *Computeractive*	325,751
22 *Woman's Own*	552,916		47 *My Weekly*	324,216
23 *IN2Film*	525,500		48 *BBC Gardeners' World*	312,252
24 *That's Life*	521,650		49 *Yours*	309,906
25 *OK!*	491,586		50 *Maxim*	304,663

Source: ABC, June 2000 © Audit Bureau of Circulation

7 REPETITION OF MESSAGES

This refers to the repeating of items of information and entertainment. The main channels of serious news in three of the media all give you more or less the same items, much of it from three main news agencies. The fact that thousands of copies of newspapers are printed means that the same messages are being reproduced thousands of times. Films appear in the cinema, a year or so later they come out on video, about two years later they appear on broadcast television. Now they are appearing on satellite and cable systems. Whatever one gets out of a particular film, this too is being repeated across various media. And there is evidence to prove that what is repeated is believed. So this, too, is a good argument for studying the media and for studying the possible effects of this repetition.

Table 1.3 Percentage of households with selected entertainment equipment 1998–99

Television	98
Telephone	96
Video recorder	85
Compact disc player	68
Home computer	34

Source: General Household Survey, Office for National Statistics © Crown Copyright 2000

8 MEANINGS AND MESSAGES

All this media material tells us something. On one level there is often a pretty obvious intention to tell us something – perhaps tell us what a new record release is like through a review. But on another level what we are told is less obvious. It is, perhaps, not so obvious that an advertisement warning against AIDS is actually suggesting that women are significant AIDS carriers (because this campaign featured a photograph of a young woman). This example is important because it is simply untrue that females are significant in this way. Statistically it is males who are more likely to be carrying the virus. So a good argument for studying the media is to dig down for these less obvious meanings and messages, and then think why they are there anyway.

There may be other reasons why one should study the media. But those already given provide some major answers to the title question of this chapter. They provide a good argument for looking into what is being said, into who is saying it, into how it is being said, into who is taking in what is being said, into what effect all this may have on readers and viewers. So I hope that you feel convinced, if you needed convincing, that what you are doing is worthwhile and important to you as an individual.

> **Media Study and Media Effects**
> Should one study the media because of a belief in media effects?
> Or is it valid to study media material and media audiences even if there isn't much evidence of influence?

Table 1.4 Why people watch what they do

	Percentage			
	Often	Occasionally	Rarely	Never
I watch the same programmes because I like them and know when they are on	72	21	5	2
I make selections from *TVTimes, Radio Times* or some other TV listings magazine	49	22	16	12
I read the TV listings that appear in the newspaper	47	28	14	10
I watch programmes picked by other family members or people in my house	25	40	18	16
I skip from channel to channel until I find something interesting	23	36	27	13
I choose on the basis of advance programme trailers shown on TV	19	52	22	7
I plan what to watch several days in advance	16	27	32	25
I follow recommendations of friends	15	46	28	10
I watch one programme and then leave the set tuned to the same channel	12	31	35	21

Base: All TV viewers. Note: 'Don't knows' have been excluded

Source: Independent Television Commission

Table 1.4 illustrates the importance of the 'why' question in any course of study. Why do we watch what we watch? Why does it matter? Why do some people have some ways of selecting media material, but not others? Item one in the table begs the huge question of why people like some programmes and not others. Study of the media involves an attempt to answer such questions.

Activity (1): Computer Games

The subject of this activity should remind you of the range of forms of communication covered by the term 'media'. At the same time, computer games may also be part of the great debate about media influence. By and large, they are marketed at young males. Games are full of male representations and discourses. They fall into genres. They can be analysed as texts, in terms of their narrative, and so on.

The computer games market is now dominated by Sony, Nintendo and Sega. EXPLORE THE IDEA OF THE POTENTIAL OF COMPUTER GAMES FOR INFLUENCE ON THEIR CONSUMERS THROUGH THE FOLLOWING TASKS.

- Use the latest edition of a source such as *Social Trends* to find out how many households own the equipment for playing computer games, and to find out what proportion of leisure time is spent on playing games.
- Use CD-Roms for one of the broadsheet newspapers to track down information about how these three companies compete with one another, and what share of the market each has.
- Look at a popular game (e.g. the latest version of *Tomb Raider*) and write down three appealing features of the game, why you think these features should appeal and to whom you think they should appeal.

REVIEW

You should have learned the following things from this chapter on reasons for studying the media.

These reasons include:
- personal interest
- beliefs in the power and influence of the media
- the scale on which they operate combined with the access they have to many people
- the great economic power of the media
- they are our main source of information and entertainment
- they construct many messages, which may influence our views of the world.

JUDGE DREDD
LAWMAN OF THE FUTURE!
The Year is 2117.
Mega-City One is a sprawling future metropolis in which unemployment is near total and everyone is a potential criminal.
Policing Mega-City are the Judges - endowed with the power to dispense both instant justice and certain punishment. The toughest of them all is Judge Dredd.
IN MEGA-CITY ONE, HE IS THE LAW.
DREDD

Fig. 2.1 Judge Dredd

The Judge Dredd image can be used to examine ideas about masculinity. The Judge Dredd stories can be used to explore ideology: ideas about the location of power in society, in particular.

2

How to Study the Media

One does not really study the media just by, for example, reading magazines and talking generally about their style or about the sort of articles that are in them. Nor is it sufficient only to seek out facts such as newspaper circulation figures, or information about how television is run. Though these activities may be useful, they are not enough. What one has to do is to try different methods through which to examine various aspects of the media (not just the material that they put out).

Three major aspects of what we loosely call 'the media' are INSTITUTIONS, TEXTS and AUDIENCES. But there are different ways of understanding what we mean by these terms and why they matter in terms of the study of media. Although texts are the obvious aspect of the media we experience, they are not the only, or the most important, part of media study. Many commentators are interested in how the media affect our understanding of the world. This involves looking at more than just texts. It also involves taking different approaches to **description and analysis**, which helps make sense of how **the media are part of our lifestyles, our beliefs and even our social relationships.** All this should become clearer as you read on.

So this chapter introduces some different approaches to studying the media. They are your tools for taking things apart, seeing how things work, seeing where meanings about our world may come from.

1 KEY POINTS

1.1 Process

Process is the subject of Chapter 3; but to make the point briefly, the aspects of the media one may look at are:

- the **institutions** (organizations) that own, run and finance the media
- the **production systems** that put together the material
- the **conditions** under which media material is put together
- the **texts** (or products, or materials) that are produced
- the **representations** (or versions of subject matter) that are in the texts

- the **meanings** that are in the representations, or in our minds, or circulating in society
- the **audiences** that make sense of the product
- the **context** in which the material is received and understood.

All this should emphasize the point that **studying the media is not just about the product,** even though it is true that this is the easiest part of the process of communication for one to get at.

1.2   Investigation

In general, investigative approaches for all subjects involve kinds of:

- **description** of the features of your object of study
- **analysis** of such features
- **application** of ideas and of analytical approaches
- **interpretation** of what one takes from analysis and description.

In media this could be, for example, about how a newspaper is produced, how the internet operates, how people watch television, how magazines represent people with disabilities.

Some of the features described will seem to be significant in various ways. This significance affects the interpretation. The reasons for features seeming to be significant will have a lot to do with the frameworks for understanding that are in your head. These frameworks are a central part of this book – how to make sense of media.

Put another way, you could say that **investigation focuses on the *how* and the *why*.** That is, for example:

- *why* do things happen the way that they do?
- *why* do we have the kinds of production systems and product that we do?
- *how* do these systems work?
- *how* does the audience make sense of what it reads and sees?
- *why* does it make a particular kind of sense of this material?

These are basic questions that you can ask yourself as you carry out close examination of, for example, a magazine or of satellite broadcasting.

1.3   Repetition and Significance

One simple fact that may help your investigations is that **anything that is repeated may well be significant.** In a sense, all study and research is looking for patterns of repetition. What this means is that if you are describing ownership of the media, and this seems to repeat some characteristics across most of the media, then those characteristics are significant in some way. To take another fairly obvious example, if you study magazines for women in a certain age band and find that certain topics are repeated again and again, then these topics must be more significant than those that are not repeated. How you interpret this significance is another matter. But in this case it is fairly obvious that such repetition means that the makers of the magazines think that these topics are important, that they think they will sell the magazine, that they think the readers will like them, that whatever is said in the articles will contribute to the knowledge and opinions of the readers.

1.4   Absence and Significance

It is worth realizing that there are other reasons why the topic that you are investigating could throw up significant evidence. **What is absent may be as significant as what is present.** So, for example, the fact that there are no teenage boys' magazines like those for girls does seem significant. The fact that there is virtually no hard political news in the most popular newspapers does seem significant.

1.5   Source and Significance

There may also be significance in the SOURCE of the information that you obtain. For example, if you read a book like *American Independent Cinema* (Hillier, 2000), then what you find out from reading the interviews with directors has the significance of being a primary or first-hand source.

If you read the BBC Charter, that is primary; if you read what I tell you about it, then that is secondary. Someone's opinion about the director's work is secondary. Both kinds of source have their own usefulness. You also have to take into account just what you are trying to study. If you are trying to study a film critically, then the film itself is more primary than a description of it in some critical work.

In general, it may be difficult to get to primary sources, but it is really useful if you can. What counts as primary rather depends on what you are trying to investigate.

1.6   Texts and Meanings

Studying the media involves looking for MESSAGES and MEANINGS in the material. There is a kind of assumption (which you need to test) that these meanings are there and can influence you. Meanings come through all forms of communication, not only words. In fact, it is arguable that they come more powerfully through pictures because these are more like real life (**iconic**) than words are (**symbolic**). That is to say, looking at a picture of a person is quite like looking at the real person, whereas looking at a set of words describing that person is not the same thing at all. It is this illusion of 'being like' that is important, and that makes IMAGE ANALYSIS important. If you are able to break into the image in a methodical way, then you are breaking into an illusion. And, let's face it, a great deal of media material is pictorial nowadays: comics, television, film. Even newspapers are very visual if you think about the graphic qualities of layout and the number of photographs that fill the popular tabloids. You can check this emphasis on pictures by using the CONTENT ANALYSIS method of study.

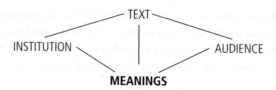

Fig. 2.2 Essential concepts in media studies

Meanings are embedded in texts by the producers who work for the institution, intentionally or otherwise. Texts yield meanings when audiences engage with them. Audiences construct meanings in their heads through interaction with the text.

Media Study
Should media study concentrate on textual material?
Or should it deal with factors that influence the making and reading of texts?

Activity (2): Content Analysis

This activity is concerned with the methodology of media study. Content analysis is, of course, only one approach and is geared towards texts. You should try other approaches from this chapter, and investigate other key areas of the subject.

Use this approach on a magazine of your choice (for example, *Just Seventeen, GQ,* or even the *Radio Times*). THROUGH CONTENT ANALYSIS, TRY TO MEASURE AND OBJECTIFY:

- the proportion of adverts compared with the rest of the copy
- the proportion of illustrations compared with all other content
- proportions of articles by type.

I suggest that you measure by pages, to the nearest quarter page, and round your figures up or down at the end. At the end of the task you should have demonstrated, in this one case at least, the importance of advertising to income in the media, the emphasis on visual material and the weight given to some types of articles above others.

2 METHODS OF STUDY

Now we can look at some specific methods that range across the media. These methods are not, of course, mutually exclusive. They can complement one another. It is also possible to adapt methods to suit particular needs.

An example of this is David Buckingham's investigation (1987) of *EastEnders* and its audience. In this case he interviewed the producers, he interviewed groups of young people as audience, he described and interpreted the marketing of the programme, he conducted textual analysis of certain episodes.

See what use you can make of the following methods of investigation.

2.1 Textual Analysis

This is something of a catch-all term for analysis of any media material. Really, it stands for a range of specific analytical approaches such as semiotic analysis, image analysis, content analysis, narrative analysis and genre analysis. All these are based on specific theories and concepts, and take a particular approach to the text in question. They try to describe and make sense of certain features of a text. Indeed, they make claims that these features (such as signs or CONVENTIONS) actually do exist. All of them lead to ideas about meanings in the text, ideas about how audiences make meanings out of reading texts, suggest something about how and why texts are produced. So textual analysis refers in general to the taking apart of a text.

It tends to look for structures and patterns of one kind or another in the text. It treats all media material, visual or otherwise, as a kind of 'book', with meanings to be read into it. It may be argued that we can only make sense of a text because it operates within a **system of meanings** that we share in our CULTURE. SEMIOTICS, with its foundation of signs and codes, is an example of such a system.

This will be discussed further in Chapter 3. But I want to point out now that you will find that there is a close relationship between concepts such as 'text', 'sign', 'structure', 'narrative', 'code' and 'convention'. TEXTUAL ANALYSIS, STRUCTURAL ANALYSIS, semiotic analysis all involve understanding of similar concepts, and are all ways of getting to the same thing: how the text is put together, how we read meanings into it.

Semiotics concentrates on the building blocks of the text to get to meanings – the words or the elements within a picture – what it calls signs.

Structuralism looks for organizing principles and at whole sections of text – for example, chunks of narrative, or the *mise en scène* (composition) of a film shot.

What you should remember is that media study is not just about texts. We tend to do a lot with texts because we can get at them. But there are dangers in, for example, assuming too much about institution or audience from reading a text. Similarly, be careful about assuming that meaning is all in the text. Texts aren't like a truck, on to which we pile some goods called meanings. Maybe texts work on your mind, but you also work on a text to make sense of it.

2.2 Semiotic Analysis (of Text)

This approach assumes that all texts are made up from sets of signs, and that these signs have meanings attached to them. (You should also look at the section on semiotics in Chapter 3.) The point is that the meanings of signs (or combinations of signs) is not fixed. So semiotic analysis is not like using a theorem or a formula to work out a problem of meaning. It is also the case that some meanings are more literal, and some are more ambivalent and cultural. The word 'cat', therefore, may mean the creature we call a cat; it may also mean ideas about 'cat-ness' – perhaps about the independent nature of the cat or about the furry warmth of a cat. The first meaning is labelled denotative, the second one is connotative. As Taylor and Willis (1999) say, 'a knowledge about the VALUES and beliefs of a particular culture is necessary if connotative readings of signs are to be successfully arrived at'. Indeed, one could also say that such readings (meanings) are ideological – they are about the particular view of the world held by that culture.

The way the word SIGN is used is quite complicated. But the essence of it for your analysis is to recognize words as signs, pictures as signs, and parts of pictures as signs (the colour of the cat or the background to the cat). The process of suggesting meaning through signs is a process of signification.

Semiotic analysis may be used on word texts. It might recognize the repetition of certain kinds of word in a story that produce a certain kind of impression or feeling in the reader. But it also works on visual texts and those many texts, like magazine adverts, that combine words and images. It has also tended to be used for the decoding of certain kinds of meaning – those that are ideological in nature, that are about the major beliefs and values that dominate the way we think about relationships, about social institutions, about the way we believe society should operate.

In the case of images, you should tie this in with my approach to image analysis below.

A semiotician would look at the following aspects.

- **Denotation** – picture elements that you describe factually and objectively. Meanings about things that are referred to from a material world, e.g. this is an image of a male kicking a round leather ball; the ball is in the foreground of the image.
- **Connotation** – meanings from those elements. Meanings from a world of ideas, e.g. this image creates a meaning of aggression because the ball and the foot seem to be kicking into the face of the viewer of the picture.
- **Anchorage** – picture elements that really pin down meaning, e.g. this is an image of X taking a penalty kick (and we know this because it says so in the caption to the photo).

Further connotations from this image might be about the game of football in general and about its place in our culture.

So this method of study involves looking carefully at what makes up a written or visual text, and looking for what might be suggested as much as for what is actually described.

2.3   Structural Analysis (of Text)

This method involves looking at how the text is organized and at what this may tell us. The patterns of organization may be within one image or in a sequence of pictures, within a short piece of writing or within a whole story.

In terms of words, of written language, one key structure that we get to by analysing a text is essentially that of grammar. This means that we are also talking about conventions or rules, which are organizing principles (see also semiotics and codes). Other organizing principles within language are the rules of spelling and the rules of word order, or syntax.

But all 'languages', all media, can be analysed for their structures. The proposition is that all texts have an underlying system of elements and rules that helps produce the meaning of a text. Genres (see Chapter 5) would be a particularly recognizable example of this. This principle of structure has caused critics to look for basic elements in a text – types of character or patterns of storyline – and then look for principles by which these are put together. Strictly, this is as much about looking for how the meaning is put in the text, as it is about clarifying what that meaning is.

This approach also has problems, it has to be said. For example, it seems attractive to suppose that many stories use the element of the 'villain' character, from the witch in *Hansel and Gretel* to those various Asian, East European and Russian villains in Bond stories. The trouble is that the meaning of villain is not necessarily 'written into' the structure of the text. It is also constructed in the head of the reader/viewer. With a given story, different cultures might read different characters as villains. So they would not see the text as being structured in quite the same way.

You should also look at further comments on structuralism in Chapter 3, and at the explanation of narrative in Chapter 5, but at this point it is sufficient to take on two main kinds of structure: the structure of opposites in a story; the structure of narrative, which affects things like building to the climax of a story.

BINARY OPPOSITIONS **are opposing concepts that one reads into the text,** usually through contrasting sets of words or of pictures. The most basic oppositions are to do with good and evil, or with male and female. One can then find words or picture elements lined up on one side or the other, to underline the opposition, and of course to suggest approval or disapproval of one element or the other. Males are tough, hard, reasonable; females are pliant, soft, emotional. Villains are filmed in shadows, in dark clothes, with unshaven faces; heroes are clean-cut, in pale clothes, in light.

Although I suggest elsewhere that there are more than two sides to every story (especially a news story), it does seem deeply ingrained in our culture that we should think in these opposing ways. Many texts do have this structure built into them. Many stories are based on conflict, and the easiest conflict to set up is that between two people or two views. There may be more than one set of oppositions in a story. To describe this structure is to describe how the text is put together. One has found a pattern. But, to make sense of the text,

IF HEADACHES PERSIST, CHANGE YOUR TABLETS.

For fast effective relief, always keep Ariel tablets in the drawer.

Fig. 2.3 Image analysis: an example

Position signs: the camera and the viewer
The camera position places one in the kitchen, as part of the scene. The viewer is in quite close proximity to the woman, so as to be (emotionally) involved in her situation.

The point of view is low, so that the viewer takes in both the pile of washing, and the despairing posture and expression of the woman. However, this also brings the copy line and the pack shot, foreground bottom, well within our field of vision. We will notice them, even if they do not interfere with the naturalism signified through the image. We are meant to understand that this woman has been caught in an unguarded (and therefore true) moment.

Treatment signs: devices of filming and of processing

The image is within a portrait frame, apparently taken with a long lens, which keeps in focus the foreground and background. This contributes to a kind of naturalism.

The lighting provides a fairly strong, even illumination, which one might associate with television treatment. It is 'fill' lights above that are illuminating her face and creating the clean, glossy surface to the table. There is nothing outside the window to locate the house – it becomes any house: the universal kitchen.

The colours, dominated by greens and browns in the original, also have a safely universal co-ordination – again, the typical kitchen. However, the artful placing of one red garment against the white of the washing machine draws the eye and signals that this is what the image is about.

The image exploits signs of perspective – the floor-tile effect and the lines of the units – to signify depth, and therefore the 'realism' of the scene.

Content signs: objects in the picture and their placing

The objects in the picture signify that this is a kitchen – units, mugs on the wall, etc. They signify a degree of female-ness – e.g. the rubber plant. They signify (cultural assumptions) female activity – e.g. washing in progress (even the curtains from the window are missing and therefore possibly in the wash). They signify a narrative in progress – e.g. she has been drinking from the mug in front of her, or is about to.

In semiotic terms the objects belong to paradigms and to codes. Most obviously we read the body language code of the woman – discomfort and despair – which is anchored by the word 'headaches', below.

In terms of the placing of elements within the frame, the woman and the pile of washing are associated by being centre frame and next to one another. We are invited to make sense of this in terms of her having a problem – the washing being the problem – and then the Ariel tablets providing the solution to the problem.

Meanings

Beyond those meanings that I have already identified, there are meanings (connotations) that refer to life outside the picture. The picture endorses the idea (and assumes) that the kitchen as a domestic space and washing as domestic labour belong to women. The woman is actually trapped by the table in front of her and by the confined kitchen space around her. The language of the caption also refers to and therefore endorses the idea that it is women who suffer from headaches. Notice the use of the words and phrases 'headaches', 'tablets', 'fast, effective relief'. These are words with which we are familiar from other adverts for pain-relieving products that are predominantly associated with women through one device or another. It is an ideological position to assume that women are in effect disempowered through suffering from headaches, not to mention the obligation to do the washing.

one has to explain what the opposition means. Usually that meaning is about the positive and the negative: one of the opposing elements being valued in terms of 'right' or 'good' or 'attractive', the other as 'wrong', 'bad', 'unattractive'. In fact, one is into what is valued and what is not, into aspects of ideology.

Narrative structures are the arrangement of the building blocks of plot and drama in a story. Describing and interpreting the structure of the narrative is another kind of structural analysis. For example, what is called **mainstream narrative** or the **classic realist text** has a developmental structure (see also narrative, p. 163). This is your average story in most media, where the plot develops from some initial problem or conflict, through various difficulties to some neat ending where everything is sorted out. Analysis of such narrative structures not only leads to understanding of how we come to see that text meaning what it does, but is also likely to help explain how we, as readers or viewers, are positioned in relation to the text. For example, autobiography depends on us being privileged to see into the mind of the story-teller and to see things through their mind.

Looking for a structure in the narrative of a text leads to more than just a description of how the 'machinery' works. It helps explain how we understand a text. It helps us understand that what we think a text means is, first, more complicated than it appears on the surface and, second, is not a matter of chance.

2.4 Content Analysis (of Text)

In this approach you simply break down (under headings) the content of, for example, a particular programme or paper, and measure it. You may express this breakdown in terms of a percentage of the total number of pages. For instance, in a given magazine it may be that 23 per cent of it is occupied by advertisements. Such an approach can also be used to objectify what is in fact treatment, not content. For example, you could add up the number of shots in a drama programme that show the heroine in close-up as compared with other female characters. You will find many more shots for the heroine. This proves that one of the reasons why we know (subconsciously) that she is meant to be a heroine is because she is given so much screen time.

The great thing about such analysis is that it stops people making generalizations such as 'there's too much violence in that thriller series'. If (and it is a big if) you measure violence in terms of the number of violent acts, as researchers have done, then you can do the counting for yourself. Find out just how many violent acts the supposedly violent programme actually contains. You could even stop-watch how long they last relative to the total programme length. It may well be that the generalization is completely wrong.

So this analysis can be used to prove or disprove snap judgements on material. Of course, it may also throw up points that you had not thought about until you saw the figures.

2.5   Image Analysis (of Text)

There are different approaches to such analysis. But in general they will seek to break down the elements of a given image (whether film shot or magazine photograph), and to find out how the meaning in the image is constructed into it. In fact, there is often more meaning in the image than there seemed to be at first.

I have found the following approach to be useful as a method for teasing out meanings from images.

I would argue that there are three main elements to any image.

■ *The Camera/Spectator Position*

Where the camera was when the picture was shot. This automatically puts us, the viewer, in a particular position relative to the objects in the image. This position may be significant because, for example, we come to realize that the camera lens centre is pointing at the bottle of perfume in the advertisement and not just at the scene in general.

■ *The Image Treatment*

Devices used to put the image together. These also affect one's view of what the image means, at all levels. For instance, a modern photograph may be sepia-toned in order to make it seem old-fashioned (and so to give it a quality of nostalgia). The use of focus, of lighting, of composition, of framing, are all devices that can affect our understanding of what is actually in the picture. It is rather like talking about *how* one says something, as opposed to *what* one says.

You may find that, elsewhere, these devices are referred to as 'technical codes'. If you are dealing with film or television then you also have to take account of devices or codes of sound, which will affect the meanings you read into the pictures. This sound is made up of three main types: music, effects noises (FX), and dialogue or voice (including voice-over or narrator). This is discussed further under narrative.

■ *Image Content*

The objects that are represented within it. And content analysis can throw up some interesting points here too, and prove that we do not usually look at images with any great care. For instance, a scene from a film may show two people fighting in a room. It is apparently just a picture of two people fighting, but the paper knife behind them on a sideboard gives new meaning to the image. It suggests that something dire may be about to happen. It suggests that the fight may turn out to be more than just a brawl. So what is in the image, where it is placed, what symbolic meanings it may have, all matter.

Other approaches to image analysis include the semiotic method described in 2.2 above. There is also that approach described in terms of *mise en scène*, developed through Film Studies, but applicable to any visual medium. In this case the image as text is looked at in terms of the composition of elements within the frame, across it and in terms of depth. The relationship of people within the frame may, for instance, tell us about their emotional relationship – a couple may be separated on either side of a the picture. Or the background in the picture may tell us something about fear and threat, as this relates to a character in the foreground. There may be symbolic elements in the picture. The juxtaposition of picture elements may be important for bringing out meaning for the viewer.

Activity (3): Image Analysis Activity

This activity is also about methods of analysis and about decoding pictures in particular. You will find that it does work on a range of photographed material in various examples of media. It can be used on film and television, especially if you have a VCR with good frame control. These media also position us through the camera, use codes of colour and composition, and incorporate devices such as symbolism and juxtaposition of elements within the frame (see Activity 6 in the next chapter).

CARRY OUT AN IMAGE ANALYSIS OF YOUR OWN, PROBABLY ALSO ON A MAGAZINE ADVERT, USING THE MODEL EXAMPLE GIVEN IN THIS CHAPTER.

At the end of the analysis, make a shortlist of all the meanings/words that you have drawn out of the advert (for example, 'romance'). Then put a number against each word to stand for the number of devices in the image that you believe have suggested that meaning. In this way, you will see that some ideas may be emphasized above others.

2.6 Tables of Information

Sometimes it is possible to study the media through published information (see the Select Reading and Resource List section at the end of this book). If you read the magazine *Campaign* in your library or look at the media pages of daily newspapers (e.g. the *Guardian* on a Monday), it isn't hard to find tables of items such as newspaper readership, or advertising expenditure by leading organizations. There are well-established sources of such tables, which you should be able to find in your library, such as *Social Trends*.

So you can study the media by studying these tables. Once more it is a matter of looking for patterns of similarity or difference. It isn't hard to spot highest and lowest circulation. But you can add factors such as comparing popular with quality press. Sometimes it is useful to turn tables of figures into graphs or bar charts so that trends and contrasts become more obvious.

On one level you may simply find out which are the most popular newspapers, or whose sales are rising or dipping. But if you also look at the cover price, and then add two-thirds again for popular newspapers and one and half times again for the quality papers, and multiply by the circulation figures, you can also work out roughly how much money they are earning. The additions allow for the proportion of income derived from advertising. Having a lower total circulation doesn't necessarily mean that your profits are lower.

So tables may cover information, for example, about audience composition or reading and viewing habits, income and expenditure figures for media, ownership of media institutions, popularity of media genres.

2.7 Other Sources of Information

If you are studying the media in order to see how they communicate and why, then another way of doing this is simply to go to sources of information which reveal facts that seem significant.

It is worth pointing out now that there are certain sources that provide useful facts and figures. Major libraries carry *Who Owns Whom*, which lists the ownership of all companies registered in the United Kingdom. This is a useful way of checking on the labyrinth of companies that own companies. For example, you will find that few local newspapers are really under local ownership. Another useful source is the year book for ITV and that for the BBC. These will tell you the broad proportions of expenditure and some facts about the range of programming. Also, every company registered in Britain is bound by law to provide a copy of its yearly report on request; if you can work your way through the soft sell and the figures, you will get some idea of how much is spent on what. You will find the *BFI Film & TV Year Book* and the *Guardian Media Guide* useful, as are web sites such as bfi.org.uk and aber.ac.uk/media/functions/mcs.html (both accessed May 2001).

Activity (4): Research Activity

This activity is geared towards using information sources and relates to audience rather than text.

Seek out a version of *Social Trends*, published by the government in book and CD-Rom formats. Look for the relevant sections and their tables, and SEE WHAT YOU CAN FIND OUT ABOUT MEDIA USAGE BY DIFFERENT SECTIONS OF THE POPULATION.

2.8 Use of Questionnaires (for Audience)

Another way of studying the media is to construct and administer some questionnaires of your own. The media and their market research arms are asking us questions every day about ourselves, and our reading and viewing preferences. You can do the same thing.

As a rule of thumb, it's a good thing to start by telling the respondent what the questionnaire is about; then ask some simple questions about the respondent and their background; then go on to ask questions with Yes/No answers (which are easy to process); then to graded questions, ending with open questions for which any answer goes. This is a useful structure to follow.

The validity of your questionnaire depends on numbers questioned as well as how tightly you have defined your audience. For example, it is useful either to ask questions of a particular age group, or of an audience (respondents) covering a range of ages and occupations, and both genders.

This method of media study is obviously useful for finding out about things like reading habits, or opinions of programmes.

If you could also persuade your local newsagent to answer a few questions about what magazines sell best in your area, or even talk to someone in the local media about programming policy, then you would have some useful information that could also be compared with what you found out from your questionnaires to the public.

Whether you fill out the questionnaire form as you conduct an interview, or whether your interviewees do this themselves, you are in fact conducting a survey.

2.9   In-depth Interviews (for Institutions or Audience)

This approach is one often used by the media themselves and by market researchers. In essence it involves a lengthy one-to-one interview with prepared questions. Such an interview could be used to elicit information, perhaps from someone who is particularly expert in their field. It is also likely to be used to find out people's opinions, perhaps about an advertisement for a certain brand of perfume. It is important to select your interviewee carefully to be representative of your audience, or because they are especially well informed. Then a long interview is like taking a core sample.

2.10 Focus Groups (for Audience/Marketing)

These are a development of the above, where one talks to a selected group about a given topic in order to gain information and opinion. Again, market researchers will, for example, show the group samples of publicity material or perhaps the pilot for a programme and ask standard questions. Certainly you could, for example, select a group of women within a certain age band and show them some television soap opera material in order to find out how they make sense of the material. This is a primary source of material, where reading someone else's research into women watching soaps would be using a secondary source.

This research methodology has been very popular for some years in the field of market research. However, it is now being realized that, like all methodologies, it has some drawbacks. The most obvious of these is that what people say in the special situation of a selected focus group may not be what they really say and do in their everyday lives.

2.11 Audience Analysis/Ethnographic Surveys

This approach is less about measuring and counting than it is about describing experience. In this case you would, for example, watch some television with your chosen group for survey. You could ask prepared and standard questions, but you would also use an open-question, conversational approach to get people to talk about how they watched, as much as what they watched. You could also observe what actually went on in terms of how viewing happened and whether people talked much when the programme was on, for example.

Necessarily this is about small samples, but it does get to the heart of an audience really behaving as an audience.

Study Methods

Is it valid to use only one method to study some aspects of the media?
Or does one have to use a variety of methods in order to come up with any meaningful
     conclusions?

REVIEW

You should have learned the following things about studying the media from this chapter:

1 KEY POINTS

1.1 One needs to look at media communication as a process that includes institutions, production systems, production conditions, texts, representations, meanings, audience, a CONTEXT to production, and reception.
1.2 Investigation of the media should be based on a careful description of these aspects, the use of analysis based on critical approaches and interpretation of their significance.
1.3 Repeated patterns in the content and treatment of media material are likely to be significant.
1.4 Items that are missing or not mentioned may be significant because of this.
1.5 There are primary and secondary sources of information to be researched.
1.6 Media material may be seen as texts to be analysed for meanings.

2 METHODS OF STUDY

2.1 Textual analysis involves looking for the meanings that are generated by media material.
2.2 Semiotic analysis is based on the premise that all texts are composed of signs that produce meanings on two levels: connotative and denotative.
2.3 Structural analysis assumes that texts have organizing principles or structures that help produce meanings.
2.4 Content analysis tries to quantify exactly the amount and nature of material.
2.5 Image analysis breaks into the meaning of visual material through careful description of where the camera is placed, of technical and other devices that contribute to the

treatment of the image, and through careful observation of elements of image content in relation to one another.

2.6 Analysis of tables of information available through various sources.

2.7 Going to reference sources of information.

2.8 Using questionnaires to investigate audience knowledge and attitudes in particular.

2.9 Using in-depth interviews to investigate attitudes and knowledge in personal detail.

2.10 Using focus groups to investigate the opinions and attitudes of a cross-section of the audience at one time.

2.11 Ethnographic surveys involve discussions with the audience at the time and point of media consumption.

Fig. 3.1 Blair Witch CD-Rom computer game cover

This cover, from a popular computer game, links with ideas about marketing spin-offs and genre intertextuality. It also raises questions about the nature of text and the nature of audience. Is a computer game a text in the way that a film is? Would the audience for the game be the same as that for the film?

3

A Basis for Media Studies: Key Words

This chapter describes the backbone stiffening this book. I have already suggested some reasons why we should study the media in the first place. I have described some methods of study that necessarily referred to concepts in this chapter. Now I want to present some ideas and terms that I believe are central to Communication/Media Studies. These ideas help us interpret our findings. They help make sense of how and why the media communicate in the way that they do.

1 THE PROCESS OF COMMUNICATION

All acts of communication are a process. This process includes a source, a message and a receiver of the message. When the media communicate with their audiences, then there is a process going on.

From one point of view, we may study the media by fastening on parts (or factors) of the process, and seeing how they affect the creation and understanding of messages. It is important to remember that any one of these factors within any communication process will affect the content and treatment of its messages. So it is also true of the media.

In describing the process of communication in the mass media, Stuart Hall (in Hall *et al.*, 1980) talks about 'a structure produced and sustained through the articulation of linked but distinctive moments – production, circulation, distribution/consumption, reproduction'. It is these 'moments', and others, that we are going to look at.

If process includes the idea of message, then the idea of message includes the notion of meaning. It is arguable that the meaning is the message. Again it is Hall who says, 'if no meaning is taken there can be no consumption'. But we certainly do consume media products, and in doing so make meanings from what we consume. I say 'make' meanings because, although some people talk about taking meanings from texts, it isn't really true that we simply swallow the meanings from a magazine like pills from a bottle. As I will explain later, some of the meanings are to an extent determined by the producer, but it is also true that we have at least some freedom to make sense of media material in the way that we want to. The nature of, the degree of, that freedom is shaped to a large extent by determining factors in the process of communication through the media.

One should understand that **the word process refers to something that is active, dynamic and that has continuity.** Communication through the media is like a continuous flow. This process involves the different media interacting with each other, as when television news editors read the early morning papers to see what their version of the news is. It involves the media interacting with society at large, as when the soap serials pick up current social issues and events, and weave them into their storylines.

The idea of process can lead one to look at the sequence of events in which meanings are created and received, and made again by the audience interpreting the text. So let's check out some of these basic factors and apply them to the media. This will help you see how the remaining chapters in this book fit in.

Media and Audience

In what ways do the media give us 'a picture of the world'?

In what ways may we, the audience, create our own picture from what the media put out?

1.1   Source (Institutions)

Media institutions are the source of many types of message that we receive. These media may be responding to events and opinions in society at large, but they are at the same time the composers and initiators of the communication. So we need to look at their characteristics, at the way they operate, at their reason for communicating, in order to understand how and why the messages are shaped.

1.2   Need (Intention)

All communication answers some need in the sender or the receiver. Institutions are driven by the need to make a profit, by market forces, and to some extent by creative forces within the production side of their organization. Audience needs for information and entertainment are discussed in Chapter 9. The degree of intention behind the encoding or making of texts as communication is another matter. The debate about what media producers do, consciously and unconsciously, and about the difference when it comes to audiences making sense of media texts, is one that runs and runs.

1.3 Encoding (the Production Base)

All messages have to be put together (encoded) in some form of communication. How messages are put together is bound to affect how they are understood. A news item on television is not the same thing as it is on radio, even though both are broadcast media and tend to cover the same topics. For example, if you have pictures of an event, they provide an immediate sense of action and background, of being there (though this is certainly not to say that television is superior to radio in any way).

It is the production side of institutions that, in effect, does this encoding, though ideas within the text may filter through from the organization as a whole. This is the point in the process where it may be argued that meanings are put into the text, intentionally or otherwise.

1.4 Message Content/Message Treatment (Texts)

All messages can be defined in terms of what they say and how they say it. Every message conveys some kind of meaning to the recipient. But how the message is handled has an enormous effect on how it is understood, and indeed on what is understood. For example, in a drama about the injustice of war, this message comes across in one way if the play relies on a narrator to make comment, and in quite another if recordings of authentic war action and war speeches are used. The basic message is the same, but the different treatment means they do not have quite the same meaning.

1.5 Decoding (Audience)

How one 'unpacks' a piece of communication to get at its meaning obviously affects the kind of meaning that one gets. To make a basic point, most of us decode communication through the filter of our own experience and indeed our prejudices. If we stick with the example of the war drama, then it should be fairly obvious that a member of the armed forces will probably decode that drama rather differently from a committed pacifist. The media communicators are well aware of our tendency to read what we want to read into communication. So, intentionally or not, many examples of media communication are structured in such a way that they push us into getting the message originally intended (see later comments on preferred readings).

1.6 Context

All communication is carried on in some kind of physical or social context. The context always affects how the communication is understood, and maybe how it is put together in the first place. On a simple level, one of the reasons why tabloid newspapers have the format they do is that they are relatively easy to open and to manage in buses and canteens – that makes them more attractive to use.

Process requires us to look at the wider social context in which the meanings of the messages are created and understood by the audience. For example,

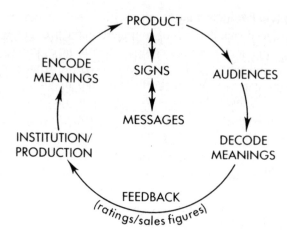

What the producers mean to say and what the audience think they mean, may not be quite the same thing.

Fig. 3.2 A model of communication through the media

analysis of young women's magazines provides ready evidence of powerful messages about the importance of appearance and image to young women. But these messages do not only appear in such magazines. Apart from other media, they are also generated through peer-group discussion, which in itself will affect how these messages are understood.

There is also the idea of **a context of 'reading'**. An example might be television, which is read in the context of our own homes. It has to compete with family chat and distractions. Children's programming is organized around the assumption that the audience will be home at a certain time to watch. The volume on advertisements is turned up at source so that they will at least be heard if people start talking between programmes or even go out to make a cup of tea.

In these cases we are talking about the contexts in which we receive or consume the communication.

One can also take account of the **context of production**, which is to do with the circumstances in which the media material is produced. In this case it matters, for example, that a film is made as a collaborative enterprise by a large group of people, and is not shot in narrative sequence. Whereas at the other extreme a novel is in its creation a solitary enterprise, probably written in sequence.

There is also the **cultural context**, which affects both producer and audience in terms of how the product is conceived and understood.

1.7 Feedback

All communication will get a response in some form, however delayed. Record and magazine producers appreciate FEEDBACK in the form of good sales. What is more interesting is that they, along with other media makers, do not encourage rapid feedback in terms of comment on the product. And, of course, it is difficult to offer such feedback compared with the example of face-to-face communication. But whatever feedback is received, in whatever form, it does affect the communication. When the British soap *Brookside* started out, its producer sought heightened REALISM by using some (authentic) bad language. But the feedback from the audience was poor: too much reality was hard to take; ratings were affected. So the scripts were changed.

Market research is an example of how the media consciously seek feedback from their audience.

2 INSTITUTION

As a concept within media study, media institutions can be seen both as businesses and as social structures. A **political economy analysis** of media would see media industries as producers and distributors of material goods and of ideas about how we should live. A more sociological and **interactionist analysis** would see the media industries as a collective social institution, rather like the various educational agencies (including schools and colleges) are part of an institution called education. The media, in this view, interact with education and with other large institutions (e.g. the law).

There are arguments, taken up elsewhere in this book, about how far the media may be a dominating force in society, and how far they are just one of a collection of major forces that interact with one another. They are frequently examined and discussed in terms of their supposed influence or their supposed power to influence society. But as I indicate in the next chapter, there are big questions about the nature of this power, and rather unfounded assumptions about how it is exerted.

As a basis for Media Studies, institutions are best studied in relation to other key terms. There are questions about how they respond to audiences, about how they may or may not produce texts with PREFERRED READINGS, about how they are changing in a global market-place.

3 TEXT

I have already suggested that one basic way of looking at media material is to regard it all as text of one sort or another. A text can be read. It will be organized or structured in particular ways, just as the text of this book has been written to a structure. The idea is that if you can work out what the organizing principle is, if you can analyse the way things are 'said', then you have a good chance of working out what the material means and what effect it might have on you.

With regard to what these meanings are, when looking at the media it is difficult not to end up talking about aspects of society and of politics. The treatment of old people in sitcoms or the reporting of the police handling of a 'traveller' convoy will both say something about social groups and about power. John Fiske (1987) says that 'every text and every reading has a social and therefore political dimension, which is to be found partly in the structure of the text itself and partly in the relation of the reading subject to that text'. So again he is saying that the sense we make of a text is both in the way that the text is put together and in the way that we choose to make sense of it.

In terms of reading meanings into a text, it is also possible to define different kinds of text:

1   a **closed text** is one where the way it is put together closes down the range of possible meanings one may get from it
2   an **open text** is the opposite – it is possible to make sense of that text in a number of different ways; even with an open text there are a lot of cultural pressures, assumptions that we make, which may limit our interpretation. Roland Barthes, who developed many ideas about semiotics in the 1960s, also talked about:
3   **readerly texts**, which were 'easy' to make sense of but which also tended to 'help' the reader into making assumptions about meaning; this links to point 1 above, and might be in the example of a popular spy novel
4   **producerly texts**, which need more work on the part of the reader to make sense of them, but which might cause the reader to think harder about what they really mean and how; this links to point 2 above, and might be in the example of an abstract painting.

Activity (5): From a Television Programme

This activity is about making deductions from the textual material in front of you. It is also about the idea that texts are part of a process in which meanings are made. It makes connections with the institution behind the text, and the audience (made up of people like you) that watches and makes sense of the text.

YOU SHOULD LOOK AT THE TITLES AND CREDITS AS WELL AS THE MAIN BODY OF THE PROGRAMME. YOU CAN USE ANY TELEVISION PROGRAMME – *Hollyoaks* would be a current example.

- Who is making this programme and why?
- What are the characteristics of this type of programme and how do they affect your understanding of it?
- Describe the audience for the programme, and identify what it is about the programme that supports your definition.
- Are there similar types of programme, and in what ways are they similar?
- What deductions can you make about how the programme and its scheduling fit in with the lifestyle of the audience?

4 STRUCTURALISM

Again, in talking about structural analysis, I have already given some explanation of this idea, which is applied to texts, and which assumes that there are organizing principles and patterns to be found in them.

One of those structures is that of oppositions. One may see opposing sets of ideas, opposing pairs of characters, opposing images. These are often related to that basic ingredient of stories – conflict. They are also (see discourses on p. 220) connected with the notion that one of the sets of ideas is 'approved' as opposed to the other. So the classic spy story will set up 'our side' and 'their side'. And through details of behaviour, appearance and author's comments, it will be made clear to the reader that our side is OK and their side is not. This is how ideological notions such as patriotism are promoted and reinforced. The possibility that the other lot believe they are being just as patriotic isn't often given space in such stories.

This idea of oppositions can also be seen in magazine adverts, for example. Sometimes it is glaringly obvious, as when they use a before-and-after photo to promote the value of a product. But often it is there in terms of a picture showing us, for example, what our life could be like, and therefore the opposite – that our life isn't like that – is implied, if not shown. You won't have to look hard to find these oppositions in the media all around you. The issue is, who benefits from the privileging of the one set of ideas in that opposition?

These points relate directly to the other idea I introduced in the last chapter: that many texts have kinds of narrative structure. In Chapter 5 I will elaborate on the fact that structuralist critics have looked for kinds of 'master plan' for stories and their organization. Whatever patterns one can see in the telling of stories, they do say something about how the organization of the text can organize the understanding of the reader. They do help explain how the ideas within a story are themselves organized and brought to the attention of the reader. For example, it is quite common for soaps to have subplots that echo the story involving the main characters. So the minor characters, like the main ones, might be having problems with an elderly relative. This would reinforce the issue raised about how one treats older people.

Structuralism is attractive as an approach to media texts because it does bring out patterns in their form, and because it offers a methodical approach to teasing out ideas. But there has been some critical reaction against being too simplistic in looking for 'a plan to explain everything'.

Graeme Turner in *British Cultural Studies* (1992) talks about a division between structuralists and culturalists (see 5.1 below). He suggests that structuralism at least has been more interested in form and structure, and producing general meanings and principles, than in coping with details of culture. Then there is a cultural tradition that is almost humanist and that resists the idea of labelling things too precisely.

Anyway, there is a danger of becoming so taken up with the hunt for structures that their significance is lost in the analysis. In relation to narrative analysis (see Chapter 6) it is possible to get so taken up with the idea of a

Fig. 3.3 From *EastEnders*: Sandra and Jack argue

These two characters from *EastEnders* are engaged in a stock situation within the soap genre – the argument. This conflict is underpinned by a sense of oppositions – those opposing elements that are common in narrative structures. Try listing examples of conflict and of oppositions within soaps that you know about. See if any common patterns emerge as to what the conflict is about. See also if you can find examples of parallelism in the narrative structure: for example, if two lead characters are in conflict over something, that there is also a subplot about a similar kind of conflict.

structural formula that one tries to make the text fit the structure. So a structuralist approach may help you make sense of a text, how it works, what its ideas may be, but it is only one approach.

I suggest to you that as a student of the media you try different approaches and that you **resist the idea that there is any one correct way to make sense of the media.** Often the differences between academic approaches say more about academic culture than they do about 'correctness'. I have found that few ideas are mutually exclusive, and that many can be accommodated within one another – semiotic analysis within process, for example.

5 CULTURE

The study of media is also partly the study of culture. As a basis for Media Studies one needs to recognize that the texts we discuss come out of our society and our culture. This means that they will contain references and meanings that are particular to our culture. For example, we can use phrases like 'working class', which will have some meaning for most people in Britain, but little meaning in the USA. This is not to say that our media products are incomprehensible to all other cultures, but it does mean that what is assumed and understood may be different: there will be different interpretations.

If you were to examine regional media in Scotland then this would also become a cultural study. This would be because you would come across different newspapers and television programmes that talked about subjects and made assumptions that are special to Scotland and to the way that people think in that part of Britain. These differences may not be huge but they are there. You only have to think of how Scottish people are represented in sitcoms to see that we are aware of those differences, and so are aware of something called culture, and of cultural values.

5.1   Cultural Studies

Cultural Studies is interested in cultural differences between:

- ways in which media institutions may be set up and run
- ways in which different cultural groups are represented in and through media texts
- ways in which different cultural groups as audiences make sense of texts
- ways in which cultural context (beliefs and lifestyles) can affect how media are run, or how their material is interpreted.

> **Culture and Media**
> Do the media reflect a culture that is 'out there' in society?
> Or do the media create new kinds of culture?

6   REPRESENTATIONS

This important idea is developed in Chapter 5. It is very much a part of Cultural Studies as well. It refers to ways in which social groups and institutions are represented through the media. It is concerned with the ideas that are put forward through, for example, programmes about schools and teachers. A recent series on BBC television (*Hope and Glory*) explored problems and conflicts involving teachers, parents and pupils.

REPRESENTATIONS usually give us a selective view of their subject matter, one that fits the dominant social and cultural view of that subject. But we don't necessarily see the representation as being selective. This is because **representations naturalize their meanings**. They make it seem natural that, for example, the institution of football stands for a decent game undermined by the behaviour of a minority of fans. They deny a less optimistic view that might point to the significant size of that minority, and to the frequent incidents of aggression on the pitch.

Representations create identities for social groups. In the case of subcultural groups these may well be negative identities. In 2001, the issue of illegal immigration to Britain was being debated in the context of negative views of immigrants in the media, as scroungers and wasters.

Representations emphasize difference between a given group and the views and values of those in mainstream culture.

Representations are more than STEREOTYPES, which are only one kind of representation.

Not all representations are negative.

Representations are bound up with the process of signification – the making of meanings through signs – and with the sets of meanings we get from those signs. It is often argued that these sets of meanings are bound to be ideological and to do with being powerful or powerless. There may be different representations of the same institution or social group, which stand for different views and values. Family life, for example, is not represented in only one way through all the media. However, the idea of representations becomes significant if, for example, a given group is represented mainly in one way – which works against their interests, and which disempowers them.

7 MEANING

The notion of process includes the notion of ideas about people and their beliefs being kept in circulation through the media. This brings us back to the central importance of meaning. These messages and meanings are both **overt** (the most obvious and apparent) and **covert** (more or less concealed and implied).

In general, the media define all sorts of meanings for us – about what is normal, what is entertainment, what is news, what is important, what is valued, what we should believe in. It is **the value messages that are most important** because what we value is what we live by. So I suggest that it is basic to study of the media that we look for what is valued, why it is valued, and what effects these values may have on us, the audience.

To study the media is to study meanings:

- where they come from
- what they are, how far they are intentional
- how they are built into media material
- how they are incorporated into our own thinking.

For example, one idea that is very much valued is that of mothers and motherhood. Pictures in advertisements, storylines in soaps, feature articles in magazines are some examples of media product where you are likely to see/read about motherhood in an approving light. In fact, approval of

Fig. 3.4 From the ITN news titles sequence

This symbolic image from the ITN news titles sequence is part of a dissolved sequence of shots. As it passes briefly before our eyes, the iconic power of the clock face of Big Ben invests the news with the authority of Parliament, above which it stands. It is a cultural icon of English-ness, as the Eiffel Tower is an icon of French-ness. In fact, the image unlocks the central beliefs of our dominant ideology. It calls up the mythologies of our culture. Of course, we believe in the rightness of Parliament, in its democracy, in the notion that London is the centre of Britain, in the idea that our world should be run by the few hundred people who do their political business below this clock. Ideology works to ensure that its beliefs are seen as being naturally true, just as news works to naturalize its own authority.

motherhood is built into our IDEOLOGY, or way of looking at the world. And to this extent you need to understand that it is basic to Media Studies that you will keep coming upon ideology, whatever concept you start with or whatever analytical approach you take.

Meaning is constructed into texts by producers and audiences. The meaning is not something like a parcel, which is wrapped and passed on to the audience. It is more like a set of blueprints for a structure the media producers expect the audience to follow and that they design quite carefully; but still the audience may build something else from this design. The audience is not a passive receptacle for what the media has on offer.

To study the media is to study how these meanings are constructed by both producers and audience. Take the example of a certain kind of television light entertainment show, which features some 'star' personality. Consider the likely beginning of this show. The star descends a grand set of stairs at the back of the stage, accompanied by triumphant orchestral music. There is canned applause or applause from a studio audience. The lighting is dramatic and, in any case, with a key light on the performer. The rest of the set dressing is theatrical. The star's clothes appear to be elaborate and expensive. The camera is on a crane and a dolly (small truck), so that it can follow the performer and can carry out elaborate movements, changing height and angle. All these signs, which are conventional within the given secondary CODE and which are used together by convention, send complex messages or meanings to us: 'this is an important person descending as if from heaven'; 'this is a production worth watching because money appears to have been lavished on it'; 'this is the beginning of a show'; 'this person has star status'; 'we are expected to treat this as entertainment and to enjoy it'; 'we should share in the approval and pleasure of the audience'; and so on.

Text and Meanings

Does a story have as many meanings as it has readers?
Does it have only one true meaning, which is what the writer intended?

---

8 | IDEOLOGY

This is a key term, which refers to value judgements and meanings that circulate in society, and that define how we understand the world. These meanings (see Section 6 above, on representations) help define for us who is important and has power, and who is not important and does not have power. The point about ideology is that it is invisible: we take its meanings for granted. We don't notice it is there unless we start thinking critically and stop taking things for granted. Ideology tells us that black people are naturally good at sport, that people with disabilities are naturally not interested in sex, that girls are naturally better at domestic tasks than boys, and so on. Ideology works through representations of these groups. Ideology promotes the idea that individuality and individual achievement is naturally a good thing.

There are some views of ideology which argue that it is entirely based on economic interests: it works in favour of those who have power and wealth. Other views place less emphasis on economic determinism. Louis Althusser, for example, talked more about how ideology affects the way we live and how we conduct our social relations (although he still believes that these relations favour capitalism). He would argue that how we live – and how ideology comes through to us – is partly defined by obvious and 'repressive' means: the police. But it is also defined through less obvious 'IDEOLOGICAL STATE APPARATUS' – what we learn through family and at school, for example. Others would point out that ideology may be about dominant views and values, but it is not total and inclusive. For example, I have recently watched the police drama *Tough Love* in which:

- one character had a disabled wife in a wheelchair, who was also attractive and managed domestic work and a social life
- the villain was not brought to justice
- the central character found that loyalty was misplaced and that senior members of the police force placed the interests of the institution above the law they were supposed to uphold; that character survived, but did not triumph in the end.

You will find this term and ideas about it, appearing elsewhere in this book, but especially in Chapter 8 on meanings and issues.

9 SIGNS: SEMIOTICS

We have said that the process of communication through the media helps create vital meanings in our heads. We have said that these meanings come to define how we see the world. Even on a simple level, our idea of what is entertainment can be so defined. Television defines all of its output, but especially comedy, as entertainment, hence the pat preview phrases such as 'That's Friday night's entertainment to look forward to on BBC1.' We come to see it as natural that television should be about entertainment, and perhaps feel that anything that is 'heavy' is somehow unnatural. That is the meaning that has been created. But it is anything but natural. **Communication is not natural: it is learned**. This happens in both the encoding and decoding stages of the process.

It may be said that the meaning in media communication is signalled to us. This signalling and signing can take place in all sorts of ways. Headlines signal to us what we should understand is priority news. News photos make signs about who and what is to be considered important.

There are specific signs that perform this signalling in whatever form of communication is under discussion. The media encompass all forms: the spoken word on radio, the photographic image in magazines, the printed word in newspapers, and combinations of all these in television. So it is a fact that recognition and analysis of specific signs is crucial to understanding of these messages and their meanings – for example, the word 'disaster' in a headline and a close-up of a grief-stricken face below it.

This view of texts as being made up from signs that belong to different forms of communication is one that was developed in the 1960s, in particular by Roland Barthes. So what follows makes a great deal of use of his ideas. Semiotics is about the study of signs and their meanings.

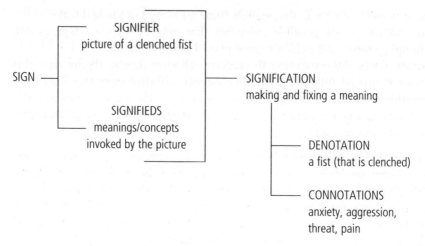

Fig. 3.5 Sign elements in the semiotic process

Activity (6): From a Film

This activity brings us back to text and meaning, and to the image. But it should make the point that approaches to meaning in the text don't have to 'belong' to one medium or another. For example, the third question below is in effect about *mise en scène* – a term that is much associated with film analysis. But television programmes also have qualities of composition, as indeed do many still images. Similarly, the camera that positions us in relation to the subject of a photograph also does this for a movie. (When doing this activity, refer back to Chapter 2, Section 2.5, for help if necessary.)

TAKE ONE SHOT OR SCENE FROM A FILM, PROBABLY USING FREEZE-FRAME IN A VIDEO COPY, AND ANSWER THE FOLLOWING QUESTIONS.

- What are the image position signs that affect one's understanding of the scene?
- What are the image treatment signs that affect one's understanding of the characters, or that affect one's sense of realism?
- What is there about the placing of objects and people within the frame that also affects understanding of character and of realism?

9.1   Signs and Meaning

The meanings of signs are learned. They do not 'naturally' belong to the sign. This separation between sign and meaning is important because it explains why people may see the same signs or material as meaning different things. Formally speaking, the sign may be seen as being composed of three elements:

- the SIGNIFIER – the thing that signals some meaning (a clenched fist)
- the SIGNIFIED – the possible meanings that may be signified (aggression, triumph, 'stone' in the child's game played with the hands)
- SIGNIFICATION – the meaning the receiver chooses to give to the sign; this choice is usually influenced by the existence of other signs that may have 'possible meanings' in common with one another; the word 'signification' is also used as a verb to describe the process of offering (signifying) meanings through signs in a text.

The word 'disaster' on a news page would be a signifier. It could mean many things. There could be a whole range of signifieds in the reader's head, including various types of possible disaster. Usually other signs (or words and pictures) will help pin down the intended meaning. There could be a picture of a smashed aircraft beneath this single-word banner headline. In this case it would be clear that an air crash is the signification.

Individual signs may signal strongly to us, but in the end it is always the collection of signs that add up to the complete meaning in a message. Ultimately, one has to read the complete sentence, the paragraph, the entire news article, in order to make sense of it.

If one looks at semiotics and the idea of meanings, then the following are well-established terms. I'm commenting on them with a magazine advertisement in mind.

Denotation describes picture content. It refers to the meanings of the image that are up front. A photograph of a mobile phone in the advert simply means on a denotative level that it is a mobile phone. In terms of analytic method, you can make a detailed description of every single item in a given advertising image in order to get to meaning on the surface level. Do this before you jump to conclusions about what the ad really means underneath.

Connotation refers to the possible deeper meanings of this content. This is the level of symbolism, metaphor and suggestion. If you look at details together then maybe your mobile phone is actually all about meanings like sociability and independence.

Anchorage describes those elements that anchor or fix the main meaning. Often it is a caption that ties down what the advertisement is about, especially when it does not have the product in it. A visual element may anchor meaning, especially if it dominates the picture in some way. Do realize that what is anchored may well not be just the name or type of product. It may be some quality of the product, such as 'soft and gentle' for a brand of soap.

The fact that pictures are different from words in that their signs are not produced in a linear form (sequence) is recognized through the concept of **polysemy** (many signs). This term is used to describe the flood of signs that we take in all at once when looking at, for example, a magazine picture. This term also leads to the idea that there are therefore many possible meanings coming at us from the picture. So it is often the case that when we try to explain the meaning of a picture it seems more ambiguous and less fixed than a piece of writing.

9.2   Codes and Conventions

Collections of signs in specific forms – such as speaking, writing and pictures – **are known as codes.** These codes are also defined through their conventions – or the unwritten rules about how the code hangs together, how it is used, how it will be understood. All examples of communication are bound by conventions. We learn these rules as part of our process of SOCIALIZATION. Precisely because of this we are often not aware that these rules exist. Once more they seem so natural that they become invisible. To study communication is to try and make the conventions (and the codes) visible.

If we consider primary codes such as writing or visuals, then some of the conventions are very basic. For example, there is one which says that we write from left to right starting at the top of a sheet. This is not, of course, what happens in some other cultures. Some of the rules of visual codes are just as basic: we learn to look for 'important' items in the middle of the frame, rather than at the edge – we have learned to accept, through documentary photography, that the scene may be cut off at the edges by the frame, so that everything is not neatly contained within it. You will see that these conventions are shared by the producers and the audience. Communication depends on agreeing these rules so that encoding and decoding are pretty well matched and at least the main meanings are put across successfully. These rules may change over a period of time as creators of communication experiment and invent. Even spelling, for instance, may change, in spite of the efforts of the dictionary makers. The rules of visual narrative have changed as people become more attuned to picture sequences. It is no longer necessary to use some conventional device such as a wave effect and dissolve to represent a shift back in time. People can take a straight cut, and pick up the threads.

Do also remember that all the visual media draw on such primary codes as non-verbal communication. We understand these, too, through conventions that organize the use of these signs. We learn how to use non-verbal communication from the screen as much as from real life. Part of the meaning of film, television and photographic material comes from our being able to decode these signs. A combination of codes and conventions can establish meaning such as a cut between close-ups of faces of two people in a group apparently looking at one another, which means that there is some connection or relationship between the two.

9.3   Secondary Codes

In addition, there may be codes within the codes, which we also learn to understand. These are SECONDARY CODES. Students of the media must learn to recognize the signs, to unravel the codes, to get at the meanings. For example, there is a secondary code of television news. An instance of this would be those special signs that 'mean' the credibility and truthfulness of the newsreaders. The signs involved include the face on close shots, the formal dress, the generally serious expressions and style of speech, the face to camera half-body shot, usually of the reader sitting at a desk. In this example, as in many cases,

the idea of a secondary code and the idea of a discourse simply overlap. If you were trying to explain the DISCOURSE of the news you would refer to exactly the same signs. You would also say that the discourse produces the same meanings of credibility and truthfulness.

These **secondary codes also operate through conventions.** Some of the rules are quite practical – such as the use of columns in newspapers and the assumption that we read down one column and then go to the top of the next. These are the rules for the production of a given format. But there are secondary codes that are to do with rules particular to a type of product. For example, women's magazines include special signs and conventions that define how we expect the models in the photographs to pose; this is very different from the way we expect people to pose in family snapshots.

Genres and modes of realism are also based on secondary codes with their own rules. To take one more example, consider the cover of a typical magazine for women (and the word 'typical' should alert you to the existence of conventions). This cover may well include elements such as a smiling female face (non-verbal code), that face centre frame of the cover (pictorial code), the head shot with titles of articles around it (magazine secondary code). All of these signs combined by convention add up to meanings such as: 'this is a magazine for women'; 'pay attention to this cover'; 'be happy'; 'read on inside'; 'this is what women are/should be interested in'.

The fact that the media communicate, in semiotic terms, through overlapping codes, each with their own kinds of sign, causes one to say that **media use multiple codes.**

10 AUDIENCE

The concept of audience is also basic to Media Studies because audiences are basic to the existence of the media. There is someone to talk to out there. There is no point in producing texts if no one buys them or no one listens. And as I indicated at the beginning of this book, a lot of critical attention given to the media turns on the idea that there is an audience out there that can be, or is being, influenced.

Since Chapter 9 is given over to audiences, I want to avoid too much repetition. But you need to understand that there are probably three main areas of critical interest in relation to the idea of audience.

1 **Conceptualizing the audience** is about how one defines audience, given that it changes so much in terms of numbers or social composition, depending on what example of text you are talking about.
2 **Problems with audience** relate to whether any meaningful definition of audience exists at all, except at the point when there are people watching, reading or listening.
3 **The relationship of audience to institution and/or text** is also problematic. One is obviously interested in how audiences read texts. But there are also questions about how media institutions conceive of audiences, as well as

about what relationship the audience stands in with respect to those institutions. In particular there are debates around whether the audience has a passive or an active relationship to texts, whether it receives ideas as given, or makes sense of the material in ways of its choosing.

11 MASS MEDIA AND SOCIETY

11.1 Models for the Media–Society Relationship

What follows summarizes views of how the media do, or should, operate in relation to society. You can use these for discussion of how you believe media should work, ideally, as well as to offer a critique of how they seem to work in practice. You will find these theories described at more length in *Mass Communication Theory* (2000) by Dennis McQuail.

Authoritarian Theory sees the media as a means of communicating authority views. This theory also suggests that they should be used to produce a CONSENSUS or agreed way of looking at things in the society as a whole.

Free Press Theory sees the media organized so that anyone can say anything at any time. All these views will, it suggests, balance each other out in the end.

Social Responsibility Theory sees the media as working to an ideal of objectivity, and on the basis of having a sense of obligation to society as whole. Media operating this system would offer diverse views, but would draw a line somewhere – not encouraging, for example, violence or criminality.

Developmental Media Theory sees the media as being there to develop national culture and language. This theory also suggests that the media should carry out tasks of social and educational development within the framework of some national policy. This view of what the media could be like and how they should work is associated with what does and could happen in developing-world countries that are trying to grow their economies and resist the cultural influence of the developed nations (e.g. not buy hours of American television!).

Democratic Participant Theory sees the media as operating through a great variety of types of media organization. This theory suggests that there should not be any centralized bureaucratic control of the media. It suggests that the media should be organized to encourage the rights of minorities and individuals to have access to the media and to use them.

You should cross-refer these ideas with the description of functions of the media within society in Chapter 4 of this book, on institutions. Such theories are based both on an interpretation of how the media do work in various societies, and on ideas about how they might work.

Of course, one's opinion about each theory partly depends on ideological perspectives. For instance, if you run the Chinese state press then you don't have much problem with some authoritarian perspective on how the media should be run. You will believe that the state authorities should control the press for the good of the people. On the other hand, if you run CBS network in the USA then the Chinese view would not be acceptable, and you would likely subscribe to a view that combines freedom with social responsibility.

It is useful to be able to take a broad view of the media in a given country and to describe them in principle. It is likely that you will tend to approve of one system or another, but still you need to be careful about instant disapproval of some systems, because it might say something about your ideological blinkers. As a media student you need to be aware of ideology and its workings, and try not to be trapped within it.

In particular it is useful to be able to look at examples other than our own in Britain, to be able to stand back from what we take for granted. In Holland, for example, the media are more libertarian than ours, with fewer controls in their broadcasting acts and in their laws. Access to broadcasting is more firmly democratic in that 'broadcasting organizations' are defined by the size of their membership and have an equally well-defined right to certain amounts of air time.

We might like to think of ourselves as belonging to the democratic participant model. We might take a pluralist view of our media, believing that we have many choices of channel or of magazine, with a range of views. But I am about to point out that our media organizations are not that different in the ways that they are set up and the ways that they work. Perhaps we don't have that great a choice of material when you consider how much of it falls under genre headings – all the same type done in much the same way. And maybe there is more of a centralized control of the media than we would like to think.

The ITC is a kind of bureaucracy, which has a great influence on commercial television. The government interferes in various ways that you will read about. A few newspaper proprietors control the output of most of our press. This isn't direct state bureaucratic control, but neither is it a great example of freedom, especially if one expects to see recognition of the rights of minorities or good access to the media for ourselves, the audience.

The advantage of thinking about the whole media system and of not taking our own for granted is that it is then possible to think about different ways of doing things. Who should run things? How should they best be run? How could we pay for our media? It isn't inevitable that our media should be dominated by financial interests in terms of control and of finance. For example, we could decide that we want alternative views in different kinds of national newspapers – views that don't fit in with those of advertisers who substantially pay for our mainstream press. We could decide that all commercial newspapers have to pay a levy to fund an alternative national press.

Media and Society
Should the media be free to provide whatever people want?
Should the media be regulated by the government, which represents the people?

11.2 Critical Views of Media and Society

The following paragraphs give you a summary account of the more important schools of thought about media and society. If you want to follow these up, or if you have an interest in sociology, then I suggest you try one of my other books: *Media and Cultural Studies* (Access to Sociology series, 1999).

In conjunction with this section you may also find it useful to refer to Figure 3.6, in which McQuail (2000) suggests that there are two opposing sets of characteristics that help define theories about media and society.

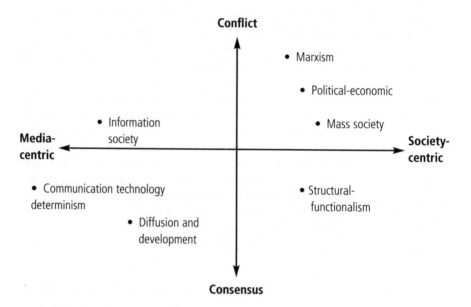

Fig. 3.6 Model for theories about media and society

Theories about the relationship between media and society are located within the tensions between the two sets of opposing forces; the pull between conflict and consensus in society, and as represented in the media; the pull between a media emphasis and an emphasis on society.

Source: D. McQuail (2000) *McQuail's Mass Communication Theory* (4th edn). London: Sage.

■ *Marxism*

Marxism takes the view that media influence society and that this helps preserve differences of power between social groups based on class, race and gender. Marxists also see the media as affecting the political process, and tending to keep power in the hands of those who already have it. The main lever of power is an economic one: those who control production and distribution control everything else, including the production of ideas through the media.

Marxists propose that we live in a capitalist society, driven by the belief in producing and consuming goods. This belief in goods (or commodities) then affects the way we value everything else. So that even our views of social relationships end up being based on the value of wealth – how much we earn and own. Marxists tend to the view that we read texts the way that the media producers want us to. It is essentially a rather pessimistic view of how things are, but there are versions of Marxism which believe that things can and do change. These versions go along with the notion of a dominant ideology – or set of views of, and values about, the world – but suggest that this ideology isn't fixed and does change to some extent. The views and values of ideology boil down to beliefs about the power relationship between social groups, which ends up supporting the position of the already powerful.

The fact that media ownership is so concentrated in few hands does tend to support a Marxist view in which control over production and distribution gives control over the ideas that are heard. It also excludes alternative kinds of material and views. However, one can also see that things are not quite that simple. So a modified view of social control (neo-Marxism) was proposed by thinkers like Antoni Gramsci. In his view, the idea of HEGEMONY was important: the idea that ruling ideas, the dominant ideology, rule because they have come to be accepted as natural by everyone. This is invisible power and rule by consent. He also accepted, however, that ideas could be contested, that there could be a struggle for control, through institutions like the media. Sometimes this struggle and consequent changes in the ruling set of ideas can be obvious, as in the case of South Africa. This country has moved from the subjugation of black people to rule by black people.

■ Political Economy Model

Contemporary critical positions out of Marxism tend to talk about a **political economy analysis** of the media. There is an underlying question about how far media influence and social structures are based on economic factors, and how far other factors (such as belonging to a subcultural group) come into play.

McQuail defines political economy theory as 'a socially critical approach that focuses primarily on the relationships between the economic structure and dynamics of media industries and the ideological content of media'.

He summarizes its main features as proposing the following:

- economic control determines what happens in the media
- media structures tend towards concentration of control and towards global integration
- there is commodification of media content and of audiences
- diversity, choice and alternative media all tend to diminish
- the private interests of media institutions predominate over any public interest of audience or of society.

■ Pluralism

Pluralism takes the view that media may influence audiences in some respects, but that, overall, the influences balance out and are not significant. Pluralists would argue that media institutions are too big and complicated for any individual or group to really use them as way of influencing the audience. Anyway, they believe that we have a plurality of institutions, products and audiences; they believe that we do have choices in respect of what we watch, read and hear – that we should have these choices; they believe that the capitalist market-place produces these choices; they associate the word 'choice' with freedom; they tend to believe that audiences read texts freely and can form their own opinions by looking at a variety of texts. So they argue that the relationship between institution and audience is one in which the audience ultimately gets its way because the producers must give the audience what it wants.

Table 3.1 Contrasting views of the media

	Media	Audience
Determinism (e.g. Marxism or Political Economy Model)	The media are driven by economic interests. These interests belong to elite groups. The views (the ideology) of these groups is embedded in media texts and practices.	Audiences become part of mass culture or are defined as market units. They are in some degree 'victims' of ideology.
Pluralism (e.g. Libertarian models)	The media are driven by market forces. These forces produce a choice of materials and of views.	Audiences may graze in the pastures of choice offered by a free media.

■ Feminism

Feminism takes the view that media are run by men in the interests of men and produce texts that reinforce those interests. Therefore gender is the key factor when making any analysis of the media. Different versions of feminism come out of Marxism, pluralism and Freudian psychology. Some are more radical and militant, some more liberal than others. Feminists are especially concerned about representations of women as offering negative and repressive ideas about what it is, and should be, to be a women in our society. They would describe the media and society as being patriarchal – dominated by the idea of the power of the male father figure. Many of them would also see this power as being economic at the base, whether or not they called themselves Marxists. One of the problems with this position, tied up with postmodern criticism of the media, is that 'women' as a concept can mean many things. Women constitute half the human race, but then they may be defined in many different ways – black women, for example – which make a lot of difference when one is trying to make sense of the media in terms of gender.

■ Postmodernism

Postmodernism takes the view that there is no provable relationship between media and society, and that it is more important to look at what audiences do with texts. A postmodernist would likely also be associated with a Cultural Studies perspective. They would be especially interested in how social groups are represented through the media. They would see cultural context as being important in understanding how we make sense of the media. Where a modernist view is associated with structural analysis and the content of texts (what they say), a postmodernist view has less belief in the importance of structures and more belief in the importance of how texts are formed and understood.

This critical position is vehemently opposed by Philo (1999), suggesting that the uncritical adoption of postmodernist approaches renders everything relative and 'unreal': 'This focus on the text and the negotiation of meaning has reduced the ability to study the real and often brutal relationships of power which form our culture.'

All the ideas, concepts and critical views outlined in this chapter should give you a basis for studying the media. What follows now develops ideas about how the media operate and especially how we make sense of them in terms of institution, product, and audience.

Activity (7): Applying Theory

This activity asks you to connect ideas about the media with what actually happens in media industries.

Look at the theories or models for different kinds of media–society relationship on page 46. Against each one, WRITE DOWN EXAMPLES OF CONTROL OF THE MEDIA, OF MEDIA MATERIAL, OF USE OF THE MEDIA BY INSTITUTIONS OR AUDIENCES, THAT YOU THINK FIT THE GIVEN THEORY. For example, where do you think educational television programmes fit in to each model?

REVIEW

You should have learned the following things in this chapter, as a basis for Media Studies.

1 PROCESS
- All communication is a process. The media are no exception to this.
- There are key factors in the process of communication through the media which one may look at; these are source, need, encoding, message content and treatment, decoding, context and feedback.
- Process also involves looking at how meanings are created and taking account of the social/cultural context in which media communication takes place.

2 INSTITUTION
- These are organizations that have different kinds of power in society.

- Media institutions include advertising agencies, news gatherers and those organizations that manufacture media material.

3 TEXT

- All media material, visual or otherwise, may be seen as a text to be read. This reading may involve a variety of approaches to get at the meanings in a text, including structural analysis.
- There are open and closed texts, readerly and producerly texts.

4 STRUCTURALISM

- All media texts have some organizing principles or structures within them. Two useful examples of these are binary oppositions and narrative structures. These help organize and produce meanings from texts.

5 CULTURE

- Texts and their meanings are very much governed by the values of their given culture.

6 REPRESENTATIONS

- This refers to ways in which the media construct views of the world, and of social groups in particular. These views may be inaccurate, but we are often persuaded that they are 'naturally' true.

7 MEANINGS

- Meanings are in messages, which may be overt or covert.
- Meanings and messages are often about values.
- The meanings we get from texts may be put there by the producers, but are also made from the text by the audience.

8 IDEOLOGY

- This is about a particular view of the world based on certain value judgements. Ideologies are powerful in their influence over people's thoughts. Ideologies provide meanings about who is and who is not powerful. Ideologies work in the interests of the powerful.

9 SIGNS: SEMIOTICS

- 9.1 The meanings in media communication are signalled to us through a variety of signs. We need to identify these in order to get at the meanings. Signification is the process through which we recognize many meanings that are signified. Meanings work on the levels of denotation and connotation; what is obviously meant and what is more obscure.
- 9.2 These signs are organized into codes covering words and pictures. How they are organized, put together and understood depends on rules or conventions that we also need to recognize.
- 9.3 There are codes within the general codes of speaking, writing and pictures. These special codes are called secondary codes. They have their own rules. They help organize categories or media material – such as genre, and treatment of media material – for example, in terms of realism.

10 AUDIENCE

- This refers to the readers and viewers of media product. There are problems with the term because audiences can have so many different characteristics that their members have nothing in common except the text they are reading or viewing.
- There are big questions about how audiences understand or read texts.

11 MASS MEDIA AND SOCIETY

- There are a number of general theories about how the media do or should operate in relation to the society of which they are a part. These may be summarized as follows: the Authoritarian Theory, the Free Press Theory, the Social Responsibility Theory, the Developmental Media Theory, the Democratic Participant Theory. These theories should be cross-referred to ideas about media functions.
- Some important critical views of the relationship between media and society are defined as follows: Marxist, the Political Economy model, Pluralist, Feminist, Postmodernist.

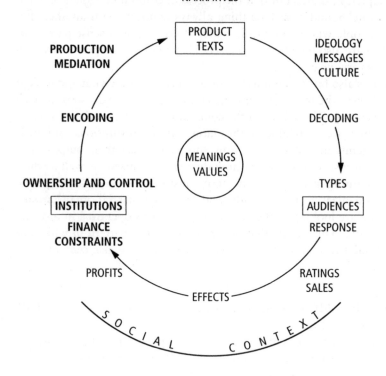

REPRESENTATION
INFORMATION AND PERSUASION
GENRES REALISM
NARRATIVES

PRODUCT
TEXTS

**PRODUCTION
MEDIATION**

IDEOLOGY
MESSAGES
CULTURE

ENCODING

DECODING

MEANINGS
VALUES

OWNERSHIP AND CONTROL

TYPES

INSTITUTIONS

AUDIENCES

**FINANCE
CONSTRAINTS**

RESPONSE

PROFITS

RATINGS
SALES

EFFECTS

SOCIAL CONTEXT

4

Institutions as Source

In the last chapter, I pointed out that the process of communication is one that ultimately has no boundaries. One thing always connects with another. For example, the people who make media material are also in a sense part of its audience. They are also members of society. They read newspapers and watch television like everyone else.

However, it is also fair to simplify the idea of process somewhat and look at it in terms of where the messages (in magazines or programmes) start, as well as where they end up. The source of the communication shapes the message.

In this chapter we will look at the nature of the institutions and their production systems, in order to see how this may affect their output. The phrase 'nature of institutions' covers how they are organized, as well as their values and operating principles. The term 'institutions' includes a public broadcasting organization like the BBC and other commercial organizations. In particular we are looking at the largest organizations operating in any one of the given media. This means that we are looking at a pattern in which, in each case, about five companies or fewer own about 70 per cent of their respective media.

Examples of this dominance are as follows:

- music (global) – MCA (Seagram), Warner (Time Warner), Sony, EMI (Thorn-EMI), Bertelsmann
- film (global) – Twentieth Century Fox (NewsCorp), Warner (Time Warner), Walt Disney Co, Universal (Seagram – also MCA), Paramount (Viacom), Columbia (Sony)
- press (Britain) – *Sun/Times/News of the World* (News International), *Daily Mail* (Daily Mail and General Trust), *Mirror* (Mirror Group Newspapers), *Daily Express* (Northern and Shell)
- television (Britain) – BBC, Carlton, Granada, United News and Media.

According to Herman and McChesney (1997), the five largest media corporations (measured by sales value) are also the most 'fully integrated global giants': Time Warner (now merging with AOL), Disney, Bertelsmann, Viacom, NewsCorp.

1 DOMINANT CHARACTERISTICS OF MEDIA INSTITUTIONS

1.1 Monopoly

The ownership of the various media in Britain tends towards monopoly. In no case does one organization have an absolute monopoly, but the **domination by a few companies is sufficient to raise doubts about choice and accountability**, as it would in the case of any monopoly. This situation could lead to what is called a cartel – where a few companies make an unofficial arrangement to carve up their particular industry for their own profit and convenience. For example, it has been proposed that the major ITV companies are such a cartel because they dominate programme purchase and production, and the remaining companies virtually have to go along with what they want. The major companies are Carlton, United News and Media (UNM) and Granada. Carlton also owns Central, Westcountry, GMTV and a stake in Meridian. UNM also runs Meridian, HTV and Anglia. Granada also controls, Yorkshire, Tyne Tees and LWT. This means that three companies control two-thirds of all British television contractors. They have access to over 80 per cent of the audience. They also control OnDigital, the major digital television channel. They also own most of the stake in ITN, the news organization.

Similarly, cable distribution in Britain is dominated by NTL and Telewest, with the possibility of a merger happening.

It also seems likely that UNM will merge with Granada to create a commercial duopoly. UNM, ironically, will have to sell off one of its companies (HTV in the west) to the remaining rival, Carlton. However, one must also remember that there are other major players in British television. ITV (Britain's channel 3) is not necessarily always that successful. By September 2000 its audience share had dropped to 25.7 per cent.

Some would argue that one cannot simply talk about monopoly in one country, as GLOBALIZATION and new media compete for the attention and the income of what is in the end a finite audience. In relation to television, David Aaronovitch has commented that an increasingly fragmented market is served by an increasingly risk averse industry (*Independent on Sunday*, 10 September 2000). The industry is chasing so many different audiences that it plays safe with what it puts out.

1.2 Size

Major media organizations are very large. They employ many people and have huge turnovers of cash. It follows that they are well equipped to produce and pay for expensive media material. It also follows that they are the better placed to monopolize in their particular field. It cost Eddie Shah £15 million to equip and launch a new national daily tabloid newspaper, *Today*, in 1987. He still failed to attract enough advertising to make it viable, and *Today* ended up being taken over by Rupert Murdoch's News Corporation. NewsCorp closed down the paper in 1995 because even with a readership of nearly a million it still wasn't making enough money. Large organizations dominate production and distribution. They achieve economies of scale and a range of industry contacts that make it nearly impossible for any other company to enter their field on a national scale. They are still going into mergers to give themselves financial muscle, nationally and globally. WH Smith, the high-street magazine and stationery retailer, has taken over the book publishers, Hodder Headline. The BBC has a deal with the US Discovery channel. Turner Communications in the US (CNN) is merged with the Time Warner Corporation, which itself is now going into a merger with AOL, the world's biggest Net server.

1.3 Vertical Integration

Vertical integration describes the way that businesses are organized. So far as the media are concerned, it refers to the way in which **functions such as the source of product, the production process, the distribution of product and the sales of product are all concentrated in the hands of one organization.** For example, Paramount can put together the package that makes up a film, including buying the rights to a book on which it is based. Then it gets the film made (though it does not own the actual studio), and acts, itself, as distributor. Viacom, which owns Paramount, also owns Blockbuster video and has a share in the well established US satellite movie channel HBO. Murdoch's Twentieth Century Fox is a comparable example. In this case he also owns the Metromedia chain of television stations and he owns Fox television, which he has more or less established as a fourth major network in the States. So Fox is also into the integration of production, distribution and exhibition, typically blurring the lines between the visual media. In the print industry, Reed International is into forestry, paper production, and then the production of books and magazines from these raw materials.

This characteristic of media company ownership reinforces the point that **a lot of power is concentrated in a few hands,** and raises questions about how answerable these organizations are to their consumers and to the public at large.

1.4 Conglomerates

Many of these institutions are conglomerates. This means that they are part of a collection of companies rolled up together, not necessarily all in the media business. Examples of conglomerates are shown in Table 4.1. Once more, we see a concentration of power, both in a given media industry and across industries. So it is that the News Corporation has interests in every sector of British media as well as in other companies. So it is that Pearsons owns the *Financial Times*, 14 per cent of Sky television, book publishers such as Longman and Penguin, educational publishers Dorling Kindersley and Simon & Schuster, the American educational software house NCS, and Thames Television (via RTL, which itself includes the biggest broadcaster in Europe, CLT–UFA).

Table 4.1 Concentration of power: media ownership

Selected book publishers

News Internat.	Holtzbrinck	Pearsons	Thompsons	Reed Elsevier	Random House
· HarperCollins	· Palgrave	· Longman	· Routledge	· Octopus	· Jonathan Cape
· Unwin Hyman	· Henry Holt & Co.	· Penguin	· Nelson	· Heinemann	· Arrow
	· Pan	· Signet		· Methuen	· Chatto & Windus
	· Picador			· Hamlyn	
	· Sidgwick & Jackson				
	· Macmillan				

Selected national newspapers

News Internat.	Mirror Group Newspapers	Northern Shell	Associated Newspapers	Hollinger	Guardian & Manchester Evening News
· Sun	· Daily Mirror	· Daily Express	· Daily Mail	· Daily Telegraph	· Guardian
· Times	· People	· Star	· Mail on Sunday	· Sunday Telegraph	· Observer
· Sunday Times	· Sunday People	· Sunday Express			
· News of the World					

Hollywood film majors

News Internat.	Sony	Disney Corp.	Matsushita	Time Warner/AOL	Viacom
· Fox	· Columbia	· Disney	· MCA/Universal	· Warner	· Paramount

Global music corporations

Bertelsmann Music Group (BMG)	Sony	Electrical and Music Industry (EMI)	Universal	Warner

1.5 Diversification

Media institutions are also characterized by a tendency to diversify into other businesses, perhaps in order to spread their risks. And other businesses will buy into the media for the same reason.

1.6 Multinationals

These institutions are multinationals. This means that **they cross the boundaries of countries and continents**. Sometimes there are simply tax advantages in this. But it is also a way to extend power and profit. Silvio Berlusconi owns major television channels in France and Italy. If he has any kind of labour, production, or finance problem in one country then he has profits from his other enterprises to fall back on.

1.7   Control and Domination

These institutions attempt to control the source of product, the means of production, the means of distribution and the outlets for their products wherever possible, because this makes their position more secure. The American film majors have started buying back into cinema chains, having been forced to sell them off 40 years ago because such all-embracing control was thought not to be in the public interest. The American majors dominate distribution and finance. Through their ability to finance films they strongly influence the kinds of films that are made, even though they do not make them all themselves. In Britain we have no film production on any scale. But there is still a powerful control over what we see because American majors such as Disney and CIC dominate the distribution of films in Britain. Exhibition of films has also come to be dominated by the 1990s phenomenon of multiplexes. Here, too, US names such as Warner and Showcase are significant. In 1999, these two, plus UCI, had 741 multiplex screens between them – all in major cities – a large slice of the market. American majors have international distribution systems – the greatest number of films in Britain are released by UIP – so they have a dominant position with regard to the four items named at the beginning of this paragraph. They have a dominant position in terms of deciding what we see, when and where. They have a secure position with regard to profitability.

This situation, which generally holds true for all the media, works against the interests of audience choice. It makes it difficult for independent media producers to find an audience. In the case of cinema it means that choice usually depends on the existence of an 'art-house' cinema in your area. Such arts complexes are subsidized through local and national grants, and some film distribution is supported by the British Film Institute (BFI).

Media Ownership

Is the apparent concentration of media ownership something to be criticized because it gives too much power to the media?

Is this concentration to be approved because it helps British media to be strong enough to compete in a global market-place?

1.8   Institutional Values

What things do these media organizations appear to value? Certainly the companies concerned would argue that they value things like the goodwill of their consumers and the quality of their products. The problem here is that the

Table 4.2 National media concentration

Company	Media use (%)	Company	Media use (%)
BBC	44.1	Guardian Media Group	0.5
Carlton Communications plc	6.9	Transworld communications	0.5
Channel Four Television Corporation	6.2	LBC Radio Group	0.5
Granada Television Ltd	4.1	CM Black Investments	0.4
Capital Radio Investments Ltd	3.4	GWR Group	0.3
News International plc	3.4	H Bauer Verlag	0.3
MAI plc	3.0	Border Television plc	0.3
Yorkshire Television Holdings plc	2.5	Thomson Investments Ltd	0.3
Mirror Group Newspapers	2.0	Time Warner International	0.3
HTV Group	1.8	Sir Peter Michael	0.3
Scottish Television plc	1.4	Grampian Television plc	0.2
Daily Mail and General Trust plc	1.1	Radio Clyde Holdings	0.2
United Newspapers plc	1.0	Ulster TV plc	0.2
Pearson plc	0.9	Metro Goldwyn Meyer	0.1
Reed Elsevier plc	0.8	Sport Newspapers	0.1
EMAP plc	0.8	Newspaper Publishing plc	0.1
Luxembourg Telecom Company	0.7	Chiltern Radio	0.1
DC Thompson and Company Ltd	0.5	East Anglian Radio Group	0.1
Television South West plc	0.5	Gruner + Jahr, Bertelsmann, Constanze	0.1
WH Smith Ltd	0.5	GMTV	0.1
		All others	9.4

Source: Shaw, 1996 © International Institute of Communications

Shaw's conclusion was:

> 'In summary, a systematic examination of media use does not disclose a market that seems to warrant concern. The market is quite unconcentrated by conventional standards.'

notion of quality is arguable, and the extent of their accountability is open to question. The media are to an extent regulated (see p. 84) to make them accountable. Television organizations are forced – through, for example, the contracts issued and monitored by the Independent Television Commission (ITC) – to provide local programming, but there is no equivalent body for other media. The values of the market-place and popular demand seem to prevail.

- They value **profits**.
  Given that most of the institutions we are talking about are funded commercially and are answerable to shareholders, then it is inevitable that the pursuit of profit is a priority.

- This also means that they value **advertising**.
  All media industries, apart from the BBC, depend, to some extent, on income from advertising to stay in business. For daily newspapers, between 30 and 60 per cent of their income comes from advertising (less for the popular press and more for the qualities). In the case of the ITV companies, about 95 per cent of their income comes from advertising. It follows that they must please their advertisers. And it is not only direct advertising that is relevant here. Indirect selling of products through product placement is very big business in American film and television in particular. Companies pay good money to have their products used and placed in shot (this is illegal in Britain). Story-telling in drama is also to some extent shaped by advertisers' or sponsors' needs, not creative interests. The most obvious examples of this are the contrived dramatic peaks in the stories that mark the advertising break and should hold the audience through it. Similarly, it may be that programmes or magazines will feature certain kinds of content and treatment (or leave things out) in order to please the advertisers. For example, fashion features in newspaper magazine supplements, or items on restaurants or entertainment in local papers, which are locked in with advertisements.
- They value **audience spending power**.
  This means that either they will pursue large audiences (popular television quiz shows) or upmarket wealthy audiences (quality Sunday newspapers). These newspapers may have a smaller circulation than the tabloids, but one can charge relatively more for the advertising space.
- It follows that they value **a social and political system that is fundamentally capitalist**.

This makes it likely that they will present such a system and its values in a favourable light. This often happens indirectly – a kind of assumption about what is 'right'. These values and assumptions add up to an ideology – a system of beliefs. It is in the interests of media companies to maintain such a system because it is the one that favours the pursuit of profit and the raising of finance through shares (among other capitalist features). So the media owners tend to favour Conservative politics. Many British newspapers (e.g. the *Mail* or *The Times*) can be shown to favour this political party and/or its politics to some degree.

1.9 Distribution

Media try to control distribution as much as production. In terms of vertical integration it makes sense to control how your goods get to your consumers. Anyway, there is a lot of money to be made out of being a distributor. So WH Smith is the leading distributor and retailer of books, newspapers and magazines, as well as music. Nynex is the dominant force in cable distribution. Sky (News International) dominates satellite distribution in terms of income and audience share. The Hollywood majors, plus British television companies, control the distribution of films on terrestrial and digital television. Three television companies and the BBC produce and distribute most of British television material.

To take film as a particular example – companies like Fox, Warner, Columbia, UIP, Buena Vista (all American) dominate the distribution of the really big box office films in Britain. They control release patterns – which films are seen where and when. They provide all the advertising and promotion associated with those films, which is big business in its own right. More than this, the Americans also dominate cinema exhibition in Britain. Warner runs 17 multiplexes, Showcase runs 17, UCI runs 25, and then Virgin owns 20. One is talking about 800 cinema screens nationally. The company CINVEN owns both ABC and Odeon screens, or 128 cinemas with 640 screens. In 2000, these were being rebranded as Odeons, with small-screen closures and a continued move into multiplexes – a continued concentration of power.

The new media of satellite and cable are more in the distribution business than in production. Cable is now connected to 3,281 million homes. The market is dominated by the CWC/NTL group (pending merger approval). The only other major player is Telewest, which is itself merged with the payTV group FlexTech.

Activity (8): Distribution

By checking reference sources and film credits, MAKE A LIST OF THOSE COMPANIES THAT DISTRIBUTE FILMS via cinema and video release. SEE WHAT YOU CAN LEARN ABOUT THE FOLLOWING:

- the dominant distributors that control major film releases
- specialist distributors of particular kinds of film.

---

2 SOURCES OF FINANCE/COSTS

It is useful to have some idea of where the money comes from that pays for the media institutions and their products. This is because, as we saw with regard to advertising, it is at least partly true that he who pays the piper calls the tune. The amount of money available to make a television programme or film is going to affect what appears on screen. In other words, **the budget affects production values** – the look and apparent quality of the product.

The topic of budgets – the proportion of money spent on different items – is a considerable one on its own. (Table 4.3 gives you some idea of the amount spent on a drama production.) Not surprisingly, budgets are a crucial consideration in decisions about producing any media material. It is also worth remembering that budgets cover not only the cost of actual production, but also items such as the marketing and distribution of the magazine or film.

2.1 Television

ITV, or commercial television (and commercial radio), makes most of its money from selling advertising time. In 1999 this was worth £3 billion. Advertising rates vary enormously according to the time of the day and the size of the audience reached. The rates are measured in terms of TVRs or television ratings (see p. 239). All rates are negotiable, for all that the companies do have rate cards. But one could say that, for example, 30 seconds in peak time nationally, networked over the whole country, could cost £150,000 for that one play. Alternatively, a local slot of 30 seconds for one of the smaller companies could cost only £10,000. Television advertising is often measured in terms of the cost per thousand adults. Zenith Media – a media broker that does deals with the ITV companies on behalf of advertisers – expresses this as £7.65 per thousand for ITV, and £7.06 per thousand for Channel 4 (*Guardian*, 11 September 2000).

Commercial television also makes money from sales of publications such as *TVTimes*, from spin-off products such as records of theme music, books and toys. About 5 per cent of its income comes from these sources. Some ITV companies finance productions through co-production deals with foreign networks or with film majors.

BBC television also gets finance from co-productions, publications and spin-offs. Its main source of income, however, is from the licence fee (at the time of writing £109 a year), which is set by Parliament, but collected 'independently' by a special branch of the Post Office Services. This licence fee in theory makes the BBC more independent of commercial pressures. But it also needs to prove itself in the battle of the ratings, to prove that it is giving the public value for money, and so to help its case when asking for increases to this licence fee.

The total income of the BBC in 1999–2000 was £2,318 million, of which £82 million came from BBC Worldwide Ltd and a further £1.3 million from the new commercial arm, BBC Resources Ltd. Apart from the licence fee, additional income came from programme sales, spin-off products and its share of satellite channels such as UKGold. £1,244 million of its income was spent on the main terrestrial channels BBC1 and BBC2; £305 million was spent on the five national radio channels.

These sums may seem astronomical, but one should remember that quality drama costs £300,000 an hour upwards to produce. Other typical costs per hour are £200,000 for light entertainment, between £60,000 and £200,000 for documentary, and £50,000 for something like an afternoon quiz programme.

It is not hard to see that there are great pressures to make cheap television. Co-production is one answer for major drama and documentary series. But this produces other pressures – for example, to include American stars in drama material. The usual economy is to offer repeats (which are still not cheap because of the repeat fees that musicians and actors are entitled to), or to buy in foreign material. This is often American, and may cost £40–80,000 an hour, or even less.

Satellite television (BSkyB) obviously makes its money from subscriptions, as well as from advertising. It has about 10 million subscribers, half direct and half through cable. SkySport is an essential part of this package – two-thirds of satellite viewers subscribe to this. The rights to Premier League football (which cost £670 million in 1996) are a key part of the sport on offer.

Table 4.3 Example of a TV drama budget breakdown

	Cost in £
Artists	36,000
Copyright	8,000
Travel	8,000
Facilities	2,000
Production salaries	32,000
Studio	24,000
Film	16,000
Design	24,000
Sets	38,000
Recording	6,000
Materials, titles, script, miscellaneous	6,000

This gives a modest cost of £200,000 for about an hour of medium-budget drama. Quality drama costs could double these figures.

2.2   Newspapers and Magazines

The income of newspapers and magazines comes from their cover price and from advertising space. Comment on the potential influence of advertisers has already been made. The weekly gross income for the *Sun* would be something like £9.8 million or for *The Sunday Times* about £2.5 million.

The gross income figures include cover and advertising. The full-page costs are just that: what the advertiser pays added to what the reader pays. Rates for advertisements vary. Here are some examples of full-page advertising costs: £49,000 for a page in the *Sun*, £19,000 for a page in the *Guardian*, £20,000 for a page in the *Independent on Sunday*, £17,000 for a colour page in *Elle*, £16,000 for a colour page in *Cosmopolitan*, £10,000 for a page in *Sugar* or *More*.

2.3   Film

The income of a typical Hollywood feature (story) film would come from the box office returns, from spin-offs such as the soundtrack music or books of the film, from television/cable rights (which may be pre-sold before the film is released) and from video cassettes of the film.

The average film from a Hollywood major would now cost US$40 million (£24 million), plus about US$15 million (£9 million) in distribution costs. The

Table 4.4 Top 25 magazine titles and size of readership

	Title	Publisher	Frequency	Readership 000s	% coverage
1	What's on TV	IPC Magazines	weekly	4,513	9.7
2	Safeway Magazine	Redwood Publishing	monthly	4,256	9.1
3	Take a Break	H Bauer Publishing Ltd	weekly	4,196	9
4	Asda Magazine	Publicis Blueprint	monthly	4,032	8.7
5	AA Members' Magazine	Redwood Publishing	monthly	3,751	8.1
6	Radio Times	BBC Worldwide Publishing	weekly	3,649	7.8
7	FHM	Emap Metro Ltd	monthly	3,613	7.8
8	Cable Guide	Cable Guide Ltd	monthly	3,429	7.4
9	Reader's Digest	The Reader's Digest Association Ltd	monthly	3,391	7.3
10	Skyview TV Guide	Redwood Publishing	monthly	3,258	7
11	TVTimes	IPC Magazines	weekly	3,028	6.5
12	Sainsbury's Magazine	New Crane Publishing Ltd	monthly	2,790	6
13	Sky Customer Magazine	Redwood Publishing	monthly	2,771	6
14	Somerfield Magazine	The Brass Tacks Publishing Company Ltd	monthly	2,701	5.8
15	Woman's Own	IPC Magazines	weekly	2,478	5.3
16	Bella	H Bauer Publishing Ltd	weekly	2,255	4.8
17	Hello!	Hello! Ltd	weekly	2,230	4.8
18	TV Quick	H Bauer Publishing Ltd	weekly	2,159	4.6
19	Woman	IPC Magazines	weekly	2,066	4.4
20	Loaded	IPC Magazines	monthly	2,052	4.4
21	Saga Magazine	Saga Publishing	monthly	1,994	4.3
22	Auto Trader	Auto Trader Systems Ltd	weekly	1,923	4.1
23	Good Housekeeping	The National Magazine Company Ltd	monthly	1,861	4
24	Cosmopolitan	The National Magazine Company Ltd	monthly	1,861	4
25	National Geographic	Seymour International Ltd	monthly	1,812	3.9

Unweighted sample: 38,349; Estimated population 15+(000s) 46,150

Source: BRAD 2000 © National Readership Survey

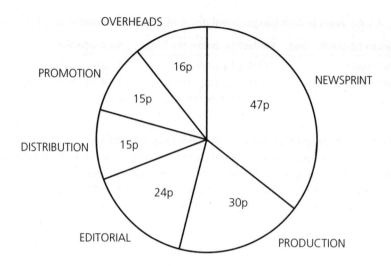

Fig. 4.2 Breakdown of cost elements for a typical quality Sunday newspaper

Each copy costs approximately £1.47 to produce, with an assumed cover price of £1.10. Of the £1.10 cover price, the wholesaler takes 16.5p, the retailer 36p, the publisher 57.5p. This means that there is a shortfall in costs of 37p to be made up by advertising on every copy, as well as profits to be achieved, also through advertising. This profit may be up to 50p per copy.

average budget for films wholly produced in the UK in 1999 was £2.24 million.

The effect on the British film industry is that there is no industry as such. There are no substantial sources of finance for films in Britain. The BFI *Film and TV Handbook* for 2001 gives an impressive figure of 100 UK films produced in 1999, with a value of £549.2 million. But close examination of what constitutes a UK film reveals that many are really co-productions or significantly financed by US money – and the profits go back to the USA.

The same caution has to be exercised when looking at the £123 million-worth of British cinema advertising revenue earned in 1999. It didn't all stay in Britain.

The most effective sources of income are Channel 4 Television–Film Four (spending about £17 million a year) and BSkyB, which will buy the rights to most British films (giving income from pre-sales). After these sources, one falls back on tiny amounts of support from organizations such as the Arts Council and the BFI. Otherwise a British film producer goes to the Americans. The most successful British film company is Working Title (*Four Weddings and a Funeral* and *Notting Hill*), which used to get backing from Polygram, but which now (typically) gets money from Studio-Canal (French television) and from Universal in the USA. It is Working Title that has made *Captain Corelli's*

Table 4.5 An average film budget breakdown per main cost elements

Production (above the line)	Production (below the line)	Post-production	Other
37.5% (£9 million) e.g. script, actors, producer and director	31.5% (£7.5 million) e.g. technical staff, locations, sound, film stock, sets, effects	10.5% (£2.5 million) e.g. editing, music, sound, opticals	20.75% (£5 million) e.g. insurance, contingency fees, general expenses

'Above the line' refers to known costs that can be fixed before production – e.g. director's fees.
'Below the line' refers to less predictable and controllable costs – e.g. those incurred during filming.
One might expect to spend about 20 weeks on production and post-production.
The total cost of £24 million could easily rise by 50 per cent to £36 million because of the costs of making/distributing prints and of marketing the film.

Mandolin, from the best-selling novel and has (again typically) done a deal with Miramax, the imaginative US distributor and backer.

2.4 Books

Here, much of the income comes from the cover price. A typical breakdown of expenditure would look like the example shown in Figure 4.3. Income also comes from co-editions with foreign publishers, serializations and dramatizations in other media, and a variety of other sources.

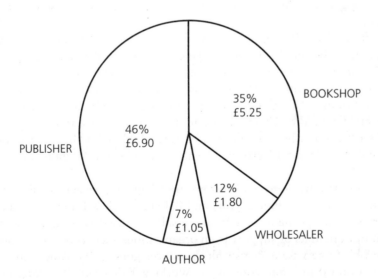

Fig. 4.3 Books: where the money goes

Breakdown of average book costs by % and at assumed price of £15.00

2.5   CDs

The income from CDs is once more all from sales (as it also is for vinyl and tape), though it is worth pointing out that a well-promoted band can also be earning from spin-offs such as posters and T-shirts. A typical breakdown of expenditure would look like the example shown in Table 4.6.

Note, however, that it should be understood that all of these examples are indeed treated as *product* to be merchandized, to a greater or lesser degree, and that there is often a crossover from one media to another. It is common for books to be marketed as a tie-in with a popular television drama series, for example, or for CDs of soundtrack music to be promoted with the release of a film. This reinforces a view that media institutions are in the business of producing goods for sale (see Marxist views, p. 48). However, such a view does not stop a debate about the quality of these goods, nor indeed a debate about something called Art.

Table 4.6 Breakdown of cost elements for a CD costing £13.99

	Costs in £
Arrangement and recording	0.75
Design and packaging	0.78
Manufacture	0.93
Advertising and promotion	0.67
Artist's royalties	1.66
Mechanical royalties	0.81
Dealer's profit	2.47
Dealer's discount	1.71
Overheads	1.29
VAT	2.41
Profit	0.51

Advertising and Media Finance

Is it a good thing that advertising helps subsidize the cost of media to the audience?

Is it a bad thing that most examples of media depend on advertising and sponsorship for their survival?

---

3   ASPECTS OF PRODUCTION

3.1   Routines

Whether we are talking about the production of news or of entertainment, the media organizations tend to create routine or habitual ways of making this material. American television, as typified by Universal Studios, has some formidable production routines, in which for most serials or series they must shoot three pages of script a day, in which everyone knows their place and their job – something like a mini production line. Even news, which has to cope with unexpected events, has routines that take it through its day (see Figure 4.4, for ITN's daily news schedule). These routines or habits are useful. They provide a firm framework for coping with the technology, the time constraints, and the numbers of people involved. But they can also create habits of mind in which things are done in a certain way because they have always been done in this way.

Routines are attractive to organizations because they make the work of production easier. Genre material (see Chapter 5) is a prime example of routine. A successful comedy series creates its own routine for making and

7.30	The duty Editors start work. They use early radio news and newspapers to draft a schedule (the agenda), which is also based on the previous day's stories (see the Look-Ahead Meeting). Sampling of agency material continues, as well as the daily electronic exchange (and purchase) of news during the morning, with other European news operators.
10.30	The Morning News Conference, with the duty editor, producers and other editors covering areas such as assignments and foreign news, in order to firm up the stories for the day.
11.30	The Early Bulletins Conference with the producer, chief sub-editor, copy taster, director, newscaster(s), in order to make final commitments to items.
12.30	Lunchtime News broadcast. Review of material and updates from regular sources, including reporting teams, continues.
3.00	A bulletin.
3.45	The Look-Ahead Meeting, in order to predict the next day's news, to be picked up first thing next morning. Reviews, updates and preparation of materials continues.
6.30	Evening news broadcast.
7.00	*News at Ten* Conference: discussion of main items and the presentation of the programme, also with the newscasters.
8.00	The ideal running order is completed.
9.30	A technical run-through.
10.00	*News at Ten* broadcast. Later, the night team takes over to update news and check the national dailies as the first editions come out.
5.30	Morning news broadcast.

Fig. 4.4 The daily routine for ITN news

striking sets, for assigning tasks to the crew, let alone for treatment of character. *Brookside* has created a kind of routine from its inception as a soap, with specially built houses as a real set and a regular pattern of work for all concerned.

3.2 Deadlines

All media production is always working to deadlines. In television, schedules are set up to create the material that is booked into the programme slots. These deadlines must be met or there is nothing on air. Newspapers have to be 'put to bed' by a certain time or they will not be printed in time to be put on trains or collected by vans and lorries to get to the shops in time for the morning customers. This awareness of deadlines is another reason for developing routines. The publicity machines of media organizations will be geared to the schedules that formalize the deadlines, and this publicity puts further pressure on the producers to create the material that has been promised. Magazines will have copy dates by which their material must be received and then knocked into shape for printing. The pressure to meet deadlines may affect what is put in and what is left out.

3.3 Slots

Print media have space slots, broadcast media have time slots. The material available must be cut or stretched to fill these spaces. Again, this could cause a kind of distortion of the message and its meaning. Television material is often geared to the 50-minute slot or multiples of this, because the remaining time in an hour is needed for programme previews and for advertisements, especially if the programme is to be sold abroad. Press material is cut to fill column centimetres, to fit around newsworthy photographs. Items are dropped from news programmes if they fall too far down the news editor's running order and there is some major event to be covered. Short articles may appear in newspapers mainly because they will fill an awkward space on a page. Indeed any subeditor needs a supply of these fillers to be sure that the page can be made up easily. The consequence of all this may be, for example, that the background to a news item is skimped on.

Again, when cost is also taken into consideration, one finds that night-time television fills its slots with old films or, possibly, cheap chat shows. This may not be the kind of television that the audience wants. It may or may not have much merit, but it fills the slot (and keeps costs down at a time when there are not enough of the paying audience viewing to justify high advertising rates). You never find blank sections in magazines because the editor feels there is nothing of value to put in!

3.4 Specialized Roles

All media production is characterized by the specialized ROLES of the production team members. To some extent this sense of specialization is reinforced by the protective nature of the unions to which technical staff in particular belong. Examples of such specialization include boom mike operators or lighting console operators in television. Given the complexity of the task of putting together magazines or television, it is not surprising that there is such specialization. But the fact is that it does have consequences for the media and their messages. One consequence is that **routine habits of production will be reinforced.**

However, these specialists still have to work together. **Media communication** is distinctive because, by and large, it **is produced collaboratively** and, as such, represents something of a consensus or a compromise view. The messages that we receive are not the creation of an individual. If there are value messages then it is the production team that actually creates them. But what they create also stands for and incorporates the values of the institution as a whole. **The team is the immediate source of the message, though they themselves are also part of the larger organization.**

3.5 New Technology

Media production is increasingly characterized by its use of new technology (see also Section 12 of this chapter, on media and new technology). Newspapers are composed electronically. They can be composed in one place and then printed hundreds of miles away after electronic versions of the made-up pages have been sent along wires. Television material is edited electronically, it can be passed around satellites, it can mix together live action and studio material. In such ways, new technology has transformed the process through which the communication is created and distributed to the audience.

Patterns of production now depend on this technology – most obviously in electronic news gathering and instant editing (minutes before the news goes on air if necessary). In some ways this new technology has opened up communication – choosing camera positions on digital sport screens, for instance. In other ways it has created a new tyranny because once the investment is made it has to be used. For instance, if hundreds of thousands of pounds are invested in equipment and staff in order to run O/B (outside broadcasting), then the pressure is on to produce O/B material regardless. What's more, the way any material is handled will tend to be the way that the workforce is used to.

3.6 Marketing Product

Part of the pattern of production in the media is a sense that one is creating product as much as communication, or a programme. The programme, newspaper, magazine is a commodity. It will only be put into production if it is seen as marketable. The irony is that a fair proportion of this marketing will take place through the media anyway. It is now common to see newspapers advertising on television in order to boost sales. Marketability affects initial decisions about whether or not to commission media material.

4 CONSEQUENCES

Having described the nature of the media institutions and the patterns of their production, it is reasonable to ask, 'So what?' What are the consequences of elements such as concentrated ownership and repetitive production patterns?

4.1   Mass Product

One obvious result is that the producers tend to try to create generally successful products for large audiences. Given the size of their investment, let alone habitual attitudes favouring mass production, it is likely that they will make every effort to get their money back. Film producers will prefer to appeal to a large and international audience, especially if they spend huge sums on making the movie. One exceptional example was Kevin Costner's *Waterworld* (1995), which is reckoned to have cost at least US$200,000,000. Equally you should remember that the term 'mass product' covers magazines such as *The Face* with a circulation of a few thousand. Such examples can still make money. This point is comparable with comment on 'narrowcasting' in the broadcast media. Channels such as KissFM or Rapture don't have huge audiences. A programme such as *Big Brother* (Channel 4, 2000) created huge cultural waves, was much discussed and was very popular with a younger audience. But its viewing figures were not that big by television standards – sometimes rather less than for the BBC documentary flagship programme *Panorama* (around 9 million). This reinforces the idea that the word 'mass' is both relative and rather misleading. Certainly this point calls into question the classic Marxist critique of the media, which said that mass media created mass product, a mass audience and mass culture. The situation is more complicated than that, when one has to make sense of media that produce material for audiences of a few thousand and a few million.

4.2   Targeted Product

Another consequence of the type of ownership that we have is that the **products of the various media are targeted on audiences,** indeed that audiences are themselves identified, even created (see Chapter 9). This means that films aren't made (by and large), unless the backers can recognize an audience or market for them. It means that the media makers are thinking like advertisers, trying to be specific about the type of person who is likely to want to buy their car or washing powder. It also means that media producers are less inclined to take risks, to produce material that may be excellent but that doesn't seem to fit any audience profile. They are generally happier with a film like *Scary Movie* for a youth/horror market than with *Among Giants* (British, with romance among the electricity pylons) for a not very clear market. What is clear is that the idea of targeting emphasizes the role of marketing. It also suggests that targeted audiences may not be waiting there to receive the book they had always wanted – so much as they are created by the marketers finding something that sells and then gives an IDENTITY to the audience – the readership of *Longitude*, for example, which spawned a succession of dramatizations in novel format about inventors and thinkers in the field of science. This book has also created its own spin-off versions in television documentary and drama.

4.3 Repetition of Product Types

It is important, if fairly obvious, to say that material based on **a popular formula is likely to be repeated.** *EastEnders* is soap opera based on the same essential elements that make the older *Coronation Street* a hit. Scratch recording (records mixed from new material and bits of other records) emerged from amateur street culture and was packaged into new kinds of dance music whose electronic formula and semi-rap lyrics are repeated again and again by record companies for profitable consumption by a larger youth audience – we are talking about various forms of hip-hop here. Jungle music has been at least partly snatched from its independent roots by companies, and packaged for profit. Hard garage, speed garage and the like are all variations on a theme. (In this case you should cross-refer with what is said about genre in Chapter 5.)

Institutions and Control of Product
Do the public get only the media product that institutions decide will sell?
Do the public as purchasers decide which products it is worth the institutions making?

4.4 Elimination of Unprofitable Audiences

This is a consequence of the profit motive and the high costs of some media production. What it means is that, **unless the audience can pay enough** (one way or another) **for a given example of product then it will be cut or not made.** The question is, what is enough? It is a notorious fact that 40 years ago a national daily newspaper called the *Daily Herald* went bust even with a circulation of over a million, because it was aimed at a relatively poor working-class audience and advertisers did not think it worth paying much to advertise in this paper. This meant that the cover price would have to go up. But that same audience would not have paid something like 60 pence in today's prices to buy the paper. That audience was what one might call economically insignificant. Similar audiences might be local communities who would like some of their own television. But television is expensive to operate. And so, in the absence of any special subsidies through one means or another, this relatively small audience receives no television product. This kind of local television was actually tried in Britain in a few towns as an experiment in the 1960s. But when it was seen that it would not make money, the plugs were pulled on such schemes. More recently, some local cable programmes have emerged as Britain has been rewired with fibre-optics in the 1990s. But the fact is that there are few programmes or channels on offer, and they have very small audiences.

If one relies on commercial funding for most of the media, we cannot realistically expect them to provide for every specialist audience and need. Equally, one should also look hard at what is called a reasonable profit. For instance, at the time of writing, CDs cost £12 to £14 each. There are many in the industry who are on record as saying that the price could easily be dropped to about £10 (as it is in the USA), and profits maintained. It can be argued that the profit motive can be taken too far, and that competition within a free market-place doesn't always happen – for various reasons.

So the way money is raised to pay for media and the way media industries are regulated in terms of how much money they may make are crucial in deciding who gets to see and to read what product.

4.5 Exclusion of Competition

The sheer scale of most media operations, the scale of investment, and the cost of technology as well as that of production and distribution, means that to a great extent competition is excluded. If we are talking about starting a national magazine or newspaper, let alone something like satellite television, then the investment and marketing costs are huge. Clearly it is enormously expensive to join the big-time club of media producers. These kinds of cost exclude most competition and the only people who can afford to join the club are those who are already in the game. It costs something like £400 million to set up a satellite television channel.

Even at a regional or local level, the costs of setting up a media operation of any kind, and running it, can be considerable. It is ironic that at the same time as the first community radio contracts were being issued (and it cost £300,000 to get London's Asian Sunrise Radio on the air) the more established independent local radio (ILR) stations were already going down the conglomerate road. For instance, London's LBC is owned by Crown Communications, which itself is valued at £59 million and, as such, is bigger than some regional television stations.

4.6 Polarization of Audiences

In fact, what has happened in the twentieth century, as media ownership has acquired the characteristics that I have described, is that audiences have polarized. Essentially, either **they are small**, specialist **and relatively wealthy, or else they are very large, mass audiences.** In the magazine trade for example, you either see fashion magazines with a relatively high cover price, such as *Vogue*, or else mass-circulation magazines such as *Woman's Own*. The same is true of national daily newspapers. There was room for a new upmarket paper like the *Independent*, or for expansion of the popular press tabloids. But the middle ground has shrunk, with papers like the *Express* losing readers.

4.7 Reduction of Choice

All of this adds up to a certain reduction of choice for the consumer. We should not exaggerate this, because we do have many specialist magazines, we do have more national daily newspapers than any other country, and we do have more and more programmes available to us as local radio expands and satellite television comes in. But, if you consider the type of material that is presented, then it is evident that the phrase 'more of the same' has a lot of truth in it.

The typical pattern of ownership and control, of funding for the media means that in cinema, for instance, we see, largely, what industry leaders decide we are going to see. Most towns have the same films showing at any one time. And because the big distributors operate a system of 'barring' the release of films to independent operators for a long time (sometimes forever), we may wait a long time to see them at a cinema near us. For the same general reason of control the smaller audiences for more unusual films – even fairly commercial ones – may not get a chance to see these films at a cinema, or on television or on video. Some films do not even leave the shelves of the studios, sometimes because a boardroom take-over means that the new studio executives don't want to release material created by their predecessors.

4.8 Independent Alternatives

One can take this degree of optimism further and say that, within a picture of increasing concentration of power and multinationalism, the media also reveal a counter-trend towards some degree of independence. The same technology that is used by corporations to extend global reach, enhance marketing and compete with more attractive product, also allows small organizations to produce on a small scale for specific audiences.

Micro-cinema is a phenomenon that has appeared via the Net, in which short films can be produced cheaply through relatively cheap technology (though not exactly at domestic level). This has spawned minor companies such as Atom Films. The Net is a distribution medium that is not yet in the control of the majors.

The legally binding terms of reference for television – 25 per cent plus of independent production – have created a host of small production companies since the early 1980s, companies such as Tiger Aspect and HatTrick. One has to be cautious in hailing a brave new world, because such companies still depend on the big organizations for distribution and access to an audience.

Government in Britain has also intervened in the case of radio to create a more open playing field, through its power to grant local and community radio licences. Near to where I live, there is a city community radio station in Bristol and a country local radio station, Kestrel Radio. Both of these are independent and do recognize local needs. This is in some contrast to larger regional and local stations (and indeed press) where, often, the material is something of a clone of national models.

Another example of specialized independence is in the restricted television licences granted to university media centres. These include Bath, York and Norwich. Manchester has Channel M, covering central and south Manchester, and partly supported by the *Manchester Evening News* newspaper. It is youth and entertainment oriented, with issues programmes. However, the question might be, independent as the channel is, does it really provide an alternative to the formats and dominant practices of mainstream television? Indeed, could it ever, given the fact that the young programme makers want to break into mainstream television?

Independence is a tricky term in that no one who seeks an audience can be free of some sort of market-place demands. But I think one might distinguish between television film production companies like Zenith or film production/distribution companies like New Line Cinema, which are just commercial producers on a smaller scale, and those media organizations that really do something in a different way for a different audience.

Again in my locality, there is an example of the Watershed Arts Centre, which acts as an exhibitor for many examples of independent media producers. Watershed presents, for instance, an autumn event of short independent films, perhaps funded and distributed through organizations – such as the Irish Film Production Board – that struggle to get a showing elsewhere. It also hosts an international animation festival, through its connection with the globally successful local company, Aardman Animations, which itself has backing from the US Dreamworks studio.

Independence is not always what it seems. The local newspaper where I live (*The Gazette*) talks local but is typically multinational in its origins. It uses names of local towns in its masthead. But it is actually owned by Newsquest, which is itself an arm of the US Gannet media corporation. Newsquest is the second biggest UK regional publisher.

Nationally one has the example of *The Voice*, a weekly newspaper aimed at the black community. The company owning this paper also produces magazines.

Activity (9): Ownership and Control

See what you can learn about patterns of ownership and market dominance in relation to types of product.

By checking reference book sources, and/or by checking examples displayed in a newsagents, MAKE A LIST OF WHICH COMPANY OWNS WHICH NEWSPAPERS AND MAGAZINES ON DISPLAY.

Library research – for example, through the reference book *Who Owns Whom* – would also help you establish if there are any more connections between the publishing companies you have identified.

So there are alternatives to the mainstream media. In finding small and specific audiences at a low budget these alternatives curiously mirror a trend towards narrowcasting in mainstream media – more channels for more particular audiences, though still within a commercial, genre-oriented model.

5 MEDIA POWER

A general consequence of the way that the media institutions operate, and of their huge financial base (and profits), is that they have a lot of power. McQuail (2000) interprets the phrase MEDIA POWER as 'a potential for the future or a statement of probability about effects, under given conditions'. In other words, having power is having the capacity to do something, but not necessarily doing it. So it is true that **we need to distinguish between what it is theorized that the media could do and what they actually do.** This also ties in with the fact that I lead up to effects in this book, because it is only then that one can see power in evidence. Equally, we have to be careful media analysts and researchers when weighing up the evidence. It is one thing to talk largely about the power of the media, as politicians love to do. It is quite another to define and measure that power, and to be sure it is there because you can see it working, affecting people and the world.

One also has to be cautious about defining that power only through the supposed influence of media texts. Texts are relatively easy to obtain and to examine. But the institutions that produce them operate within an economic system that also imparts power to those businesses. Power over distribution is especially important in this respect. The power of news agencies to access

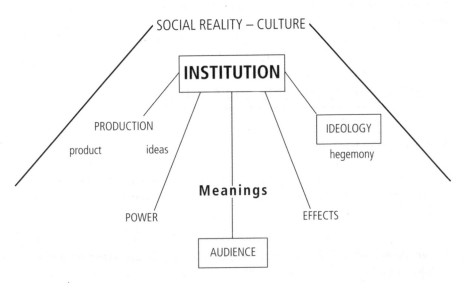

Fig. 4.5 Key concepts: institution

events, construct versions of them and distribute them to news producers is an example of where one might argue for power *behind* the text as much as in it.

5.1 Power of Monopoly

Relatively few institutions control much of the output in the major media industries. In general this means that the top five companies in each case control 50 to 90 per cent of circulation, of viewing figures, of sales in these industries, of market share. They have the power to exclude all but the richest competitors. They have the power to embark on yet more take-overs of other media industries. They have the power to resist attempts by others, including regulators, to control their operations.

Control of the media is not, strictly, a monopoly, but it has moved a long way towards that situation. This is partly because capitalist forces now operate a global market in which smaller companies are taken over or put out of business by competition. But, ironically, monopoly kills competition, which is supposed to produce choice. The near-monopoly situation means that relatively few media companies define what media material is available to us.

5.2 Power of Owners

Certainly we should be under no illusion about the reality of this power. Newspaper owners pressure their editors, themselves people of considerable authority within the industry, to produce newspapers in a mould they approve of. Conrad Black, who owns the *Daily Telegraph*, makes no bones about his power and will comment on things that he disagrees with, saying, 'What is the point in running a newspaper if you have absolutely no say?'

A contemporary European example of power and ownership is the aforementioned Silvio Berlusconi of Italy. He has considerable holdings in film, television and the press. He was able to use this to his advantage when conducting the political CAMPAIGN that led to his election as prime minister. In France, Robert Hersant owns *France-Soir* and the Figaro group of newspapers, among others, and has some interests in broadcasting. His newspapers have certainly represented political views that match his known affiliations with politicians.

5.3 Levers of Power

Marxist theory has been active in defining the meaning and applications of ideology within the media. For example, the phrase **ideological state apparatus** is used to describe social institutions such as education and the media, and to suggest that such institutions work, with the effect of reproducing an ideology centring on capitalism and its essential rightness.

Media power has also been seen in terms of two kinds of control.

- **Allocative control** is a general kind of control of the given operation in terms of allocation and use of resources, not least money. This is the kind of control that is about policy decisions. It is the control that owners and boards of management have perhaps to hire and fire executives, certainly to determine budgets, and ultimately to decide to do things like sell up or close down operations.

- **Operational control** works at the level of production itself. It is the kind of working control that editors and producers have. Producers in television have this kind of power when they commission re-writes of scripts, or decide that some part of a programme should be dropped. To some extent this type of control is diffused. For example, a camera operator shooting a news story or a documentary in the field won't have a producer or editor breathing down his or her neck, but, again, cannot stop the producer cutting the material once it gets back for editing.

5.4 Power over Product and Ideology: the Power of Ideas

So in general, media power is based on cash, legal power and management power. This power then becomes the power to shape the product.

The product then has the power to communicate ideology and its values. **The power to shape product helps frame our view of the world.** This is **power over the production of ideas.** Marxists would say that the media control cultural production. This argument suggests that they shape what our culture is, how we see it, what ideas inform it.

It may be suggested that these ideas then have the power to shape the views of the audience. However, at least this last stage of the power game (audience effects) is arguable. Much is believed about the power of the media over the values and attitudes of the audience. (Chapters 7 and 8 talk about this, and about the difficulty of proving some kind of cause and effect.)

5.5 The Power of Professionalism

One kind of power the makers of programmes and newspapers assume is that of being 'professionals'. This is a kind of expert power that is taken on partly because of the particular skills and technologies they have. But it is also elevated into something special and exclusive by these people being labelled 'professional'. If workers want to give themselves status, and suggest that they know about and do something no one else can do, then they like to call themselves 'professionals'. In the case of the media this has come to create something of a mystique. The word has been used, for example, to justify decisions made by news people about excluding information or about reporting stories in a certain way. In fact, this use of professionalism is very questionable. The quality of their work, their ability to make judgements, is not evidently any better than that of many other members of our society. So this word 'professionalism' describes an assumed power that others are asked to respect, but that needs to be disputed.

Margaret Gallagher (1988), talks about three different uses of the word 'professional', all of which add up to a notion of power and authoritativeness. These are:

- the idea of the 'expert'
- the idea of the 'rational bureaucrat' (like the expert civil servant)
- the idea of a special kind of worker whose business assumes 'moral values and norms' that place it and the worker apart from most other occupations.

News workers are inclined to invoke the third of these models, however unconsciously. Other media workers do this when they make decisions about including or excluding material on grounds of, for example, 'good or bad taste'. They claim, implicitly, a detachment from the material, which is actually a false claim, but it supports their professional status. They claim a right to make those decisions. They end up taking ideological positions, making value judgements on, for instance, whether or not to screen a certain scene shot for a film or a drama.

One could go further and say that **media professionalism is tied up with the values that inform the organization**. Professionalism becomes ideological. If the values are the same as those described for the dominant ideology, then professionalism is supporting this dominant view of the world.

Professionalism for media workers becomes a way of protecting themselves against criticism, especially when it is buttressed by various codes of practice. Journalists in particular support their position as being partly about defending the rights of the public and freedom of speech. I am not saying that this professionalism is simply a sham, but its precise validity and its consequences do bear examination.

5.6 Cultural Imperialism

The term CULTURAL IMPERIALISM refers to the way in which a culture can build empires abroad through the export of its media. The empires that are created are, it is suggested, built of ideas. When American comics, films, television programmes are sold abroad, **the country that buys them isn't just buying stories or entertainment, it is buying the ideas or messages in that material**. These messages are to do with US values, with American ideology. This is media power over culture. It is a power that extends beyond the original audience and culture.

In his introduction to *The Media Are American*, Jeremy Tunstall said, as long ago as 1977, that: 'each nation at the height of its political power also had the means and the will to beam its own image around the world as Number One nation' (referring to first Britain and then the USA). He argues that without what he calls Anglo-American media domination, 'many aspects of life in most of the world's countries would be different – consumption patterns, leisure, entertainment, music, the arts and literature'.

The most widely viewed pieces of media material in the world are two old American television series, *I Love Lucy* and *Bonanza*. They have appeared in every country with a television system, and have been much repeated. They contain ideas about family, gender, who has power in relationships. They represent American culture to these other countries. It is also the case that cheap American product can stifle the indigenous media –

if it wasn't there, then the media of those countries would have to develop their own product, containing their own beliefs and values, not to mention their own stories.

British culture is especially prone to colonization by US media because of the language match; and so it is that our language has changed in the last fifty years to absorb American phrases. Children's games have developed out of American comic-book heroes. Some of our visual language is that of American cinema or advertising. The commercial power of American institutions is in our market-place, with publishers such as Random House owning British names such as Jonathan Cape.

The question of the empire of ideas is another matter. It is proposed that the British acquire US values and attitudes from the US material. But this has never really been demonstrated, however plausible it may seem. It is another area where effects are assumed but not proven. Typically, the concern is there, if only in the respect that there is a 20 per cent agreed limit on the proportion of overseas programming on television.

One should realize that **the British also export their media and culture abroad,** and that we acquire other cultural influences. A particular example in the last 10 to 15 years has been the arrival of *Neighbours* and *Home and Away* on television, and of *Sugar* in the teenage magazine market-place, all from Australia. British teenagers have been 'colonized' by a seductive mixture of sun, sex, romance and gossip.

This negative view of the export of culture ties in with ideas about globalization (see p. 104). International control of media ownership and distribution, it is argued, undermines the culture of countries and of their regions. The internationalization of news by rich western media tends to impose a skewed view of the world to the South and to the developing world. Generally, this globalization of media is about economic as well as cultural wealth, and about ways in which successful western economies can make others dependent on them.

So, to counter a negative view of this imperialism one needs to ask if it isn't just a matter of cultural exchange. One needs to ask whether it really matters that Conrad Black, a Canadian, owns that conservative British newspaper, the *Daily Telegraph*. Does it matter that *Buffy the Vampire Slayer* is cult viewing for many young Brits? Does 'foreign' ownership actually change the culture of established media? Columbia Pictures was bought by a Japanese conglomerate (Matsushita) several years ago, now it has been bought by a Canadian distillery giant (Seagram), but Columbia product is no less American for all that. The British *Financial Times* prints a European and now a US edition. Brazilian soap operas sell in Mexico. I am not suggesting that the globalization of media, international take-overs and the promotion of material from English-speaking countries has no effect around the world, but I am suggesting that the effect lies not simply in ownership, nor is it only about US hegemony. Rather, the significance is about global capitalism, about the commodification of culture around the world. Probably what matters most, apart from audience preferences, are the economic conditions engineered (or not) by governments

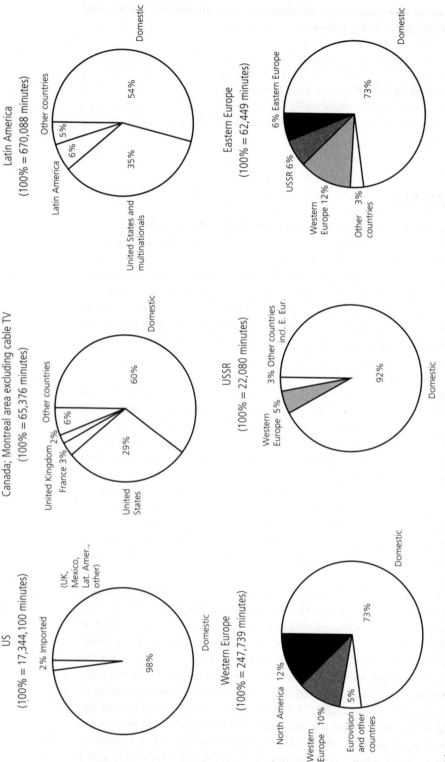

US
(100% = 17,344,100 minutes)

2% Imported

(UK, Mexico, Lat. Amer., other)

Domestic
98%

Canada; Montreal area excluding cable TV
(100% = 65,376 minutes)

Other countries
United Kingdom 2%
France 3%
6%

Domestic
60%

United States
29%

Latin America
(100% = 670,088 minutes)

Other countries
5%
Latin America 6%

Domestic
54%

United States and multinationals
35%

Western Europe
(100% = 247,739 minutes)

North America 12%
Western Europe 10%
Eurovision and other countries 5%

Domestic
73%

USSR
(100% = 22,080 minutes)

3% Other countries incl. E. Eur.
Western Europe 5%

Domestic
92%

Eastern Europe
(100% = 62,449 minutes)

6% Eastern Europe
USSR 6%
Western Europe 12%
Other 3% countries

Domestic
73%

Fig. 4.6 Total programme output for selected countries/continents, in terms of sources of programme material

Figure 4.6 shows, for certain areas of the world, how much programming is indigenous and how much is imported. To an extent the pie charts suggest that things are not too bad. But then one also notes that 40 per cent of programmes in the Montreal area of Canada are not Canadian; that 40 per cent of the programmes in Latin America come from outside.

to make possible the production of domestic and alternative media, and therefore of the values of that culture.

> **Institutions Shaping Culture**
> Is media power used to bring us global culture (Coca-Cola and Levi's)?
> Do the media use their power to support minority culture such as community radio and
>   local newspapers?

6 MEDIATION

The media inevitably transform everything they deal with. Literally, they come between us the audience and the original material they use. This is a truism – a self-evident truth. What is on the screen or on the page is not the real thing, but a version of it, a representation. I am not just talking about the way that events such as wars are packaged and presented for consumption in the news. The same is true of stories, for example. Sometimes this is very obvious – in tele-drama, for example. The story is actually changed from the book to suit the demands of television. But even in the case of, say, comedy, the finished version is not the same as the original script. It is a performance that has, among other things, been directed and edited.

So the media mediate everything they touch. The fact that there is a great deal of truth in a news article about, for example, some diplomatic negotiations, does not mean that it is the whole truth. Reading the article is not the same as being there. So the only real questions to discuss are to do with the degree of MEDIATION, how it happens and how it may affect our understanding of the meaning of a particular example.

Mediation is a process in which the meanings of our everyday lives are re-made in the media versions of life. And those media versions – of romance, for instance – are themselves changing and mediating one another – a hall of mirrors indeed! As Silverstone says, 'mediation involves the constant transformation of meanings ... as media texts and texts about media circulate' (1999).

The idea of mediation should remind us that all media material is actually a kind of **representation**. This means that it is a **construction**. It is not the real thing. It is not the original idea, the original experience, the original object. It is artificial. It is something constructed from sets of signs. The television image of the car, whether in a thriller or in a programme about a car show, is not the car itself. It is a representation of the car through a picture code. In the same way, a journalist's article about cars at the car show is just a representation of the cars in a written verbal code. This difference between real life and the artificial medium is vital. Especially when we are dealing with picture media, we are inclined to forget that the 'real'-looking picture is only a version of reality – something that has bias built into it. You should bear this in mind when reading the sections on representation and realism in Chapters 5 and 6 respectively.

It is also important to bear in mind that representations are about *how* the media present things, not just *what* they present – form as well as content. Representations are to do with ideas as much as with things. So, in my example, it would be ideas about cars that matter as much as the unreality of the car – ideas about masculinity, escape, personal space.

One question mediation raises is that of **intentionality**. From one view it could be said that mediation is unavoidable, it is an inevitable aspect of the process of manufacturing media product. Other views would take on the decision-making/choices aspect of constructing product. For example, Skeggs and Mundy in *The Media* (1992) refer to critiques offered by others when they say that 'every use of the media presupposes manipulation'. In that case we must ask ourselves who does the manipulating, how and why?

The media bring us an array of second-hand experiences. They stand between us and original experiences, many of which are necessarily outside our immediate sphere of experience. Metaphors such as 'window on the world' and 'mirror of reality' have been invoked as a kind of reassurance, but they are simply not true. We may appear to interact with a game show such as *Who Wants To Be A Millionaire?* but this is an illusion. We have no control over the performance that is the programme. It is a mediated, not an immediate, experience.

7 REGULATION

7.1 Definitions

Regulation of the media is about kinds of limitation on the operation of media institutions, a check on their power. REGULATION as a kind of control is usually discussed in terms of examples such as government issuing or withdrawing broadcasting licences.

But one may also talk about CONSTRAINTS on the media which would include factors that hold back what they want to do. These factors, like limited financial resources when making a film in Britain, are not the same thing as direct intervention in what goes on.

One may summarize four main constraints on media operations as being:

1 economic/market factors – what can be afforded, what will sell
2 the law – what is allowed
3 professional practices – what media workers have agreed it is OK or not OK to do
4 public responsibility – how media workers believe their responsibility to the public should affect what they do.

Regulation, especially that imposed by the law, opens up a third area of discussion: censorship (see Section 8 of this chapter). This especially is the area where regulation reflects principles and beliefs on the part of those doing the regulating. These beliefs are about what kind of media organizations are thought to be desirable, how they should operate and, most of all, what kind of material they should put out.

Broadly, regulation of the media can be described as voluntary or imposed, and internal or external. Voluntary internal regulation would include the codes of practice that broadcasting uses to guide its operations. Imposed external regulation would include the 'D notice system', through which the government tries to cut off reporting of items it considers to be 'contrary to the public interest' (with the implied threat that the Official Secrets Act might be used against those who report or publish in the face of such a notice). In a culture that believes in freedom of speech and the rights of the individual, it is perhaps not surprising to see that there are relatively few formal and external constraints on media operations.

However, there are those who argue that there are in fact too many examples of indirect regulation. One of these would be the threat to prosecute the former MI5 operative, David Shaylor, then living in France, for publishing (in 1999) what is described as confidential information on the Web. Shaylor argues that this information is not, and should not be, confidential, and is about his attempt to expose incompetent practices. It has been said that if Britain had a Freedom of Information Act and a Bill of Rights, then this kind of situation would be less likely to arise because the line of regulation would be more clearly drawn.

7.2 Self-regulation

In terms of output, the media are almost entirely self-regulating. That is to say, **the content and treatment of articles, programmes and advertisements is monitored and vetted by bodies set up by the industries themselves.**

There is:

- the **Advertising Standards Authority (ASA)** for advertising (but please remember that advertising is not a form or medium of communication, only a way of using media)
- the **Press Complaints Commission** for newspapers
- the **Broadcasting Complaints Commission** for all broadcasters (due, at the time of writing, to be merged with the Broadcasting Standards Council (BSC))
- the **governors of the BBC** for television and radio, operating through committees and a referral system
- the **British Board of Film Classification (BBFC)** for cinema
- the **Video Standards Council**, for video distributors
- the **Radio Authority**, for commercial radio.

There are also externally established bodies such as the ITC for commercial television, the BSC for film, video and television, the Radio Communication Agency for managing frequencies, Oftel for regulating the telecoms industries.

Government bodies that may involve themselves in things like take-overs or 'matters of public interest' are the Office of Fair Trading and its Monopolies and Mergers Commission, the Department of Trade and Industry and the Department of National Heritage.

These bodies set standards published in pamphlets, and interpreted or modified by them as they check complaints and check the product. Usually, examples the makers are doubtful about will be referred to such bodies. But it should be clear that these self-censoring organizations are not directly answerable to the government or to their consumers in any way. Their power to enforce decisions is very variable.

For example, the Press Complaints Commission attached to the Press Council is pretty toothless. It may hand down formal-sounding judgements about the propriety of certain articles, but it can do nothing much to bring the newspapers in question into line because it is, in fact, set up and paid for by them. Newspapers will now publish retractions and accounts of judgements by the Commission. But there is no sign that this stops the sensationalist, inventive and sometimes personally hurtful stories run by tabloids. The government has made noises but has not stepped in to act in the case of various issues that have arisen. This has a lot to do with our tradition of a 'free press'.

This Commission was set up in 1991 because of great concern about the ways in which the popular press does its job, especially in respect of invasion of privacy. But this concern didn't go away. There were subsequent enquiries and, in 1997, a code of practice was agreed. I leave you to judge whether or not this has done much good, by referring to my selected list that follows and to present journalistic practices.

- Inaccurate and misleading material should not be published.
- Apologies for errors should be published.
- There should be a fair 'right to reply'.
- There should be no intrusion into privacy, except when it is in the public interest.
- Reporters should not misrepresent who they are in order to obtain material.
- People connected with criminal cases shouldn't be paid for their stories – unless it is in the public interest.
- Journalists should not make 'pejorative or prejudicial reference' to people with respect to their sexual orientation, their gender, their religion, their ethnic background, their disability, their mental illness.

On the other hand the bodies for broadcasting and advertising are reasonably effective, not least because it is understood that government is much more prepared to intervene. An example of this occurred in June 2000 when the government minister, Chris Smith, said that he was prepared to bring in legislation if necessary to force the commercial companies (via the ITC) to reconsider the time of their ITN late-night news. There had been a furore about the move, five months earlier, from its long-standing 10 o'clock slot. What is interesting, even astonishing, here is that government was so prepared nakedly to interfere in scheduling, when it has no business trying to run the system at this level of detail, and when the ITC acts as a mechanism for monitoring and moderating the behaviour of the commercial contractors anyway. Ironically, the BBC has since moved its main news into this 10pm slot, prompting further outbursts from MPs and government. Again, it might be pointed out that the government does not run the BBC, even if it would like to!

In early 2001 there were government proposals to merge the functions of the ITC, the BSC and Oftel, since they overlap one another.

7.3   The Independent Television Commission

The ITC is a body set up by government, though theoretically independent of it, to regulate commercial television and radio (including ILR). It also operates a Cable and Satellite Division to regulate those media.

The ITC committees that vet programme schedules in advance, vet questionable programmes, vet most advertisements (including those going out nationally) are ultimately backed by a board of governors, half of whom are appointed by the government. The ITC no longer runs the transmitters as it used to, so it can't actually shut off programmes. But it could in theory shut down one of the contracting companies, like Meridian, if it summarily withdrew its contract or licence to broadcast. This power derives from the Act of Parliament that sets up the commercial system and that forces the commercial companies to pay for the ITC whether they like it or not. I have dealt with the ITC separately because it is not a body set up by the commercial television producers themselves. Equally, it may be said that it is not simply a government body, and so is partly an example of self-regulation.

It is particularly concerned with notions like IMPARTIALITY and with issues like the screening of violence. Its policy, through codes of practice, is very firm in many respects. No 18-rated film can be transmitted before 10pm. There must be at least three news programmes each day of the week. There must be an average of 10 hours a week of children's programmes. The range of conditions set, and the fact that the ITC awards the contracts to broadcast, adds up to a commercial environment in which a pretty strong public-service ethos is retained.

7.4   The Broadcasting Standards Council

This body became statutory under the Broadcasting Act 1990. Its members are government appointees. Its role is to 'consider' the portrayal of violence, sexual conduct, and matters of taste and decency in broadcast material of all kinds. It examines complaints, publishing its findings in a monthly bulletin. Although advisory only, these findings act as a form of pressure on the industry. The Council can order broadcasters at their own expense to publish findings either on air or in the press. Its independent role is unusual since, with the exception of the Broadcasting Complaints Commission, the broadcast media in Britain have been self-regulated. The Council may make reports to government on aspects of programmes falling within its remit.

The Council has published its own code of practice, which is very similar to codes produced by the ITC, covering areas such as advertisements, violence, sexuality, children's programmes. It is, for example, concerned that material should not cause people to become anxious about levels of violence or become desensitized to violence. Such views contain assumptions that I explore in the last chapter of this book. The Council, like other bodies of monitoring and control, finds it difficult to represent the range of views on, for example, swearing and sex. It asserts that swearing of a sexual derivation – e.g. 'fuck' – should not be heard before the notional watershed for child viewers of 9pm. It asserts, on the basis of surveys, that viewers don't approve of full-frontal male nudity. In so far as this is true, it does of course, when compared with the acceptance of female nudity, merely expose the working of ideology in our minds.

7.5 Editorial Control

In fact most of the real self-regulation takes place at editorial or programme level. The people who produce and make the programmes have a good idea of what is allowed and disallowed through, for example, codes of practice published by the broadcasting organizations. Nevertheless, it gives food for thought that, for instance, in spite of this, 20 to 30 per cent of the advertisements presented to the Broadcaster Advertising Clearance Centre are rejected for one reason or another. This does not necessarily mean that all those advertisements are offensive, any more than are the programmes we never get to see. You or I might actually approve of them. The fact is that you will never know or be able to judge.

Since media industries are dominantly self-regulated, editorial control of material is a very important constraint that defines what kinds of paper and programme we receive. In the case of the news arms of these industries, we are talking literally about editors. But magazines and books also operate through editors, and producers can have a similar constraining effect on programmes. News editors act as a kind of filter (backed up by their subeditors who do most of the donkey work of selecting and re-writing general news items to fit the space or slot). Producers can make decisions to change or leave out material. The BBC in particular uses a system of 'referral upwards', which means that if in doubt the producer asks a superior to check out material, perhaps in terms of its offending listeners' sense of good taste in the case of radio. In this way, the real constraint is the sense of values that permeates the institution; it is this sense of what will or will not be accepted by those in control at the top that shapes (and constrains) the decisions of those with direct responsibility for making programmes. In other words **institutional values act as a constraint**.

7.6 Legal Constraints

The most formal constraints on the operation of the media come through the laws that set up the relevant bodies in the cases of broadcasting and satellite transmission, and that cover specific issues such as libel, slander and official secrets. Remember that no one may broadcast anything without a licence from the government. So commercial broadcasting based on licences granted by the ITC is regulated by the terms of the Broadcasting Act 1990. By definition, pirate radio stations are those that operate without such a licence. The Broadcasting Act (and the broadly similar Royal Charter enabling the BBC to operate) is in fact pretty generalized in terms of what it says about programme material, using phrases such as 'not to give offence' or 'within the bounds of good taste'. The actual interpretation of these phrases brings us back to the voluntary bodies already described. There are no comparable acts setting up or describing what the press institutions may or may not do.

The other laws referred to below mean that the media organizations need legal departments to advise on what is or is not likely to give rise to a legal case. The goal posts tend to move according to judgements of the day. *Gay News* was successfully prosecuted by an MP invoking the old-fashioned notion of blasphemy as covered by the Obscene Publications Act for publishing a poem about Christ as a homosexual. But some other attempts to use this act have failed. The government fought a long battle in 1988/89 to stop Peter Wright's book, *Spycatcher*, being published anywhere in the world, because they claimed it breached the Official Secrets Act in what it revealed about Britain's spying activities in the 1960s in particular. They eventually lost their case against newspapers for publishing parts of the book. They won the case against British book publishers (or rather won an injunction forbidding publication), but they lost a famous case in Australia against other publishers.

More recently, the aforementioned civil servant, David Shaylor, published material in defiance of the Official Secrets Act because, he claims, it did not prejudice the security of the country, although it did reveal incompetence and a cover-up in MI5. He spent two years in hiding in France, from where the French refused to allow him to be extradited. He has now returned to Britain, has been arrested and the matter is in the hands of the courts.

Relevant acts may briefly be summarized as follows.

- The **Laws of Defamation of Character** (slander for the spoken word, libel for the written word); in particular, the **Defamation Act 1996**. This refers to material that, for example, damages a person's reputation. It is possible to defend an action by saying that the defamation was not intended. However, this will still make you liable for costs, plus an apology. The catch with this law is that it costs to sue, so in effect it only works for the rich.
- The **Official Secrets Act 1989** is usually operated through the D notice system, in which the Home Secretary's office puts such a notice on material it does not want to be published or broadcast (see above). Clearly the potential problem here is that government departments could wish to use the act to prevent publication of matters that are actually in the public interest.
- The **Young Persons Harmful Publications Act 1955** was directed towards comics and magazines in particular, and is intended to control the production of horrific or otherwise harmful material.

- The **Obscene Publications Act 1959**.
- The **Public Order Act 1986** is relevant in its sections that forbid the publication of material that might incite racial hatred and unrest.
- The **Prevention of Terrorism Act 1974** is generally geared towards control of information about, and coverage of events in, Northern Ireland.
- The **Contempt of Court Act 1981** forbids the publication of anything relating to a trial in progress that might prejudice its outcome.
- The **Video Recordings Act 1984** restricts what may be hired from video shops, and imposes categories on films available on video.

There are also particular provisions of other acts that may in various ways constrain the news operations of the media. For example, the **Criminal Justice Acts** forbid publication of evidence against people sent for trial from lower courts.

7.7　Financial Constraints

It is also worth remembering that there are practical constraints on what we see or do not see, what we read or do not read. Obviously, **the amount of money or the amount of time available to a programme will affect what it is like**. 'Market forces' are also a kind of constraint. That is to say, something that is popular and profitable is more likely to be produced than something that is not. For example, with the advent of deregulated broadcasting, and as more organizations have the freedom to make programmes, there are serious worries about who will pay for expensive television drama. Maybe we will be deprived of one-off plays by famous authors and will, if anything, see more popular fare such as Australian or American mini-series.

Activity (10): Regulation

Use this book (and any other sources that refer to regulation) to MAKE A LIST OF EXAMPLES OF TOPICS OR OF LANGUAGE WHICH YOU MIGHT NOT BE ALLOWED TO PUT IN A NEWSPAPER.

See what you can deduce about who would gain or lose from the fact that such material is not allowed.

8　CENSORSHIP

This section is brief because, for the most part, the relevant points have been covered under the heading of 'Regulation' above. Censorship is usually thought to be about **direct removal, part-removal or change of material that offends the censor**. A censoring body has the power to enforce its actions and decisions. **There is virtually no direct censorship of the media,** certainly not of a political kind. There are only the self-regulating bodies described above. However, one needs to consider one or two points here. First, one may argue that films are effectively censored, however it is via the industry itself. That is to say, no cinema chain or individual owner can legally screen a film (except in a private club) unless it has a BBFC classification. Also, the BBC and ITV companies take it on themselves to further cut some films shown on television. Second, even if regulation of the media, and of the broadcasting industries in particular, is through industry bodies, then there are those who would argue that it is censorship none the less. They would point to the lack of comparable interference in publishing. It is worth remembering that there have been some examples of specific external and direct censorship. From 1987 to 1995 there was the requirement (imposed by Act of Parliament) that broadcasters should not transmit soundtracks of utterances by members of the Irish Sinn Fein organization, and that they should not screen interviews with these people. The government decided that such reporting provided Sinn Fein with 'the oxygen of publicity', and that this was not in the public interest. This ban was an example of a contradiction in the dominant ideology because it ran counter to a belief in free speech and the public's 'right to know'.

So, whatever one may define as censorship in British media is exercised differently with different media. The BBFC effectively decides which age groups may watch which films. This control is quite powerful. It can stop communication before it reaches the audience. On the other hand, the Press Council has no such power. It can only express opinions about material after it has been published and in response to complaints. The ITC falls somewhere between these two models. It requires ITV companies to consult with it, and to let it see 'difficult' material. It has occasionally insisted on programmes not being screened. But usually any adverse judgements come after the screening.

One problem in making sense of censorship is its relative inconsistency. If we take the Official Secrets Act (see 'Legal Constraints', above) as an example, then there are two famous cases in the 1980s that had very different results. In both cases civil servants were actually taken to court for leaking information. So we are not dealing with censorship as such, but only with indirect censorship: how the results of the cases might affect what the media decide to put out another time. This is why it is easier and more accurate to talk about constraints rather than censorship. In 1984 Sarah Tisdall was sent to prison for leaking information that the Minister of Defence allegedly intended to deceive Parliament about the arrival of American Cruise missiles until it was too late. In 1985 Clive Ponting was acquitted in a court case in which the government wanted him to be put in prison for revealing that the same minister had also allegedly deceived Parliament about the circumstances of the sinking of an Argentinean battle cruiser during the Falklands war.

So there is some kind of censorship of media communication. But it does not, as the word suggests, operate via some centralized politically controlled body through which every single media item has to pass in order to be approved.

There is an organization – the **Campaign for Press and Broadcasting Freedom** – that is voluntary and supported by many journalists, and that works to oppose and expose kinds of censorship and control. Generally speaking, it is for a free press and against attempts by the powerful to limit access to and the publication of information those people feel is against their interests.

Institutions and their Regulation

Is regulation of the media so tight that it interferes with freedom of speech and the public's 'right to know'?

Are the media so loosely regulated that they 'get away with too much'?

---

9 MEDIA AND GOVERNMENT

It is worth looking briefly at the relationship between media and government, not least because, in general, the latter acts as a constraint on the former. These two institutions exert great power in our society, and are in a sense jealous of each other's power. Government seeks to curb the freedom of the media to say and do what they like in the name of the people they represent. But the media also claim to represent people, and would often like to be free of restraining power. The following summary of points of contact between these two institutions includes some of the factors discussed above.

- **The law**: through invoking laws like the Official Secrets Act to protect its information and operations, various arms of government (mainly the Secret Service operations) come up against the media and its belief in its right to say what it will.
- **Press conferences and press releases**: government departments (and ministers) are a major source of information for media news operations; to this extent they are in the hands of the government when it comes to getting newsworthy information via the relevant press officers.
- **Lobby briefing**: the two main political parties operate this system, which many of the media news people resent. In effect, the Chief Whips of the political parties have a list of acceptable journalists to whom they will give information (sometimes advance leaks) at such special briefings. Newspapers like the *Guardian* have taken to boycotting this system as far as possible. They feel that it is a misuse of government power over sources of information, which should be freely available to everyone equally.
- **Appointments**: it has already been said that the government has a kind of power in its ability to make senior appointments to the governing bodies of what are still the dominant broadcasting systems in this country.
- **Finance**: it has been pointed out that the BBC at least is indirectly beholden to government because its income from the licence fee depends on the agreement of Parliament to set it and increase it.

- **Direct control**: the government reserves certain powers, again in respect of broadcasting, to demand air time at the discretion of the Home Secretary.
- **Indirect control**: this is very difficult to prove, and usually only emerges when there is a public argument between media and government over reporting from Northern Ireland, for example. At such times it has been revealed that conversations take place between senior officials of the government and of the relevant broadcasting organization in which it is suggested that the programme concerned should not be broadcast. The ability of senior broadcasting officials to resist such pressure is itself a matter of concern, given the influence of politicians over appointments.
- **Media appearance**: another obvious point of contact is the appearance of politicians, including members of the government, on news and current affairs programmes. This is a good example of the mutual interests of these two powerful institutions. The broadcasters need the politicians as sources of information, as personalities to give their programmes credibility. The politicians need the appearances to give themselves credibility, in their own party as much as among the electorate. Broadcasters keep a list of such people whom they regard as sound 'performers' and who may be called upon to make interesting appearances in debates and interviews.
- **Party political broadcasts**: the political parties may demand these as of right. This is some measure of their power in the continuing tension between media and government. Traditionally the amount of air time, especially around elections, is something that is carved up between the Chief Whips of the Tories and the Labour Party, and senior broadcasters. This deal has been under strain in recent years as more parties of the centre have emerged and expressed discontent with their share in these arrangements. It illustrates how delicate is the power balance between media and government, and how far it has depended on a consensus between the two. Some people argue that this consensus depends too much on the people concerned sharing common social and educational backgrounds. In other words, it is a matter of class and power.

All these points of contact raise a number of issues. They are essentially about the degree of power politicians should have over the freedom of the media to say what they will, and the rights of the media to free speech, given the fact that what they 'say' and how they say it may influence the political views of the audience/electorate. There is concern over politicians' manipulation of their power over information through devices like the timing of press releases to coincide with news broadcasts. There is concern over the extent to which the media are representing political issues in terms of personalities rather than in terms of the real arguments involved.

The fact that we rely on the media by and large for what we do know about our governments and their operations reinforces the importance of the media in our societies. For example, there was a major report and enquiry in 1996 (the Scott Report) into the matter of the sale of arms to Iraq, which was forbidden. The enquiry took place as a result of media reporting and pressure following investigation of government complicity in enabling illegal sales to take place, and following a trial in which business people were acquitted of making illegal sales because it was clear that government had endorsed these (and because the trial judge over-rode government claims to the right to suppress relevant documents on grounds of national security). There is a heavy fog surrounding the question of who was right to sign what paper, and how far government and business were working within the law and the government's own rules. What is clear is that the British people would never have known about the matter if at least some of the media had not pursued their investigative functions in the face of political attempts at a form of PROPAGANDA.

Media and Government

Do you see the government as representatives of the people with a right to 'talk' to the people through media?

Do you see the government as interfering with free speech in the media and using media for its own ends?

---

10 PROPAGANDA

This word is thrown around inaccurately, not least where politics is concerned. People may talk loosely about government propaganda, when they don't like what they hear on, say, a party-political radio broadcast.

In fact **true propaganda, like true censorship, depends on centralized control of all sources of information about a topic.** So propaganda as such does not really exist in Britain.

Also, the term tends to be associated with advertising. To this extent it is defined as powerful and persuasive communication. But, again, it has to be said that advertising is not, in general, propaganda. You don't have to buy the car being advertised, and you can find out more about it if you really try.

One might have a case for arguing propaganda where it is not easy to find alternative views and information on a given subject. An example would be the government advertising campaign to persuade parents to have their children vaccinated against whooping cough. This campaign became a media issue, as it happens, because a few vaccinated children became ill, and then there was a public debate about the justification for the vaccination programme and the way in which the public had been 'persuaded' that it was necessary.

As one might expect, **the clearest examples of propaganda in this country have been seen in times of war.** In the last world war, Britain set up a Ministry of Information, not only to censor and filter information, but also positively to produce media material that persuaded the public of all sorts of things, most obviously of the importance of aspects of the war effort, such as 'digging for victory'. Because such persuasive and manipulative uses of the media were 'on our side', the word propaganda is not always associated with this kind of communication. Propaganda is so often thought to be what the other lot do. This is not true. Indeed it is part of recognizing the existence of ideology, of our particular way of looking at the world, that helps students of the media understand what is going on 'in their own back yard'.

This kind of news management still goes on – for example, in the 1999 war in Kosovo. In this case, our allied forces were represented by military press officers as fighting a clean war that targeted only Serbs. The Serbs fought their own propaganda war, representing themselves as victims. Neither position was true. There were certain incidents, as when allied planes mistakenly bombed a column of fleeing Albanians, that in the end could not be suppressed by the propaganda machine; the misrepresentation became too embarrassing. But, generally speaking, information about the progress of the war was controlled and was seen largely from 'our side'.

Previously, the Gulf War of 1992 had been even more managed by the military. It was easier to do this when the battleground was the deserts of the Middle East, not the 'home' territory of Europe. The allied press officers literally controlled where the journalists went and what they were told. The illusion of this being a clean techno-war was largely maintained until it was all over.

One may regard this as an example of propaganda, defined as the invisible control of news information in order to persuade the public/audience of a particular view of the war. The interesting question is how far the government was the sole source of this propaganda, and how far some media organizations (the *Sun*) were happy to ignore some issues and uncomfortable facts, and to report the war in a particular kind of patriotic light.

Anything approaching a definition of propaganda that comes through news media is a matter for concern because we rely on the integrity of news organizations for objective information about what is happening 'out there'. Even tabloid newspapers are regarded by many as offering 'truth' at least in respect of hard news stories. McQuail, in *Media Performance* (1992), talks about 'the near impossibility of identifying it [propaganda] in news output in any certain or systematic way'. He refers to the fact that it may not be the CHANNEL from which the propaganda comes, but rather the source the channel uses, e.g. the people who gave the press conference. It is true that is not easy to notice or prove a sustained campaign of deliberate misinformation from some concealed source. At the same time, when associating the idea of propaganda with bias, he does point to particular presentational devices and uses of language, which signal that something is going on. It is these devices which the media student needs to be aware of, and to interpret. He refers to 'flattering language; non-attributed sources; suspicious juxtaposition of items'. So I would argue that if textual analysis throws up signs that someone wants us to read a text in a particular way, then this suggests that something like propaganda is happening. It is then another matter to determine the source and the real intentions of that source. (See also the information on news bias, Section 1.12 of Chapter 7.)

11 FUNCTIONS OF THE MEDIA

11.1 General

The word 'functions' covers **what people think the media are there to do, what they actually do and what their purpose seems to be.** It is, for example, the function of a careers service to give advice to people. The media themselves have their own view of what their functions are. Generally, of course, these are seen by them in a positive light. For example, the various television acts that establish commercial broadcasting refer to requirements to provide a news information service, to maintain proportions of British material, to observe impartiality, and so on. But how things work out in practice may seem rather different. So what are the functions of the media?

For a start, that rather depends on differing critical beliefs about the media, since their functions are not written down explicitly. It also depends on views of what they intend to do, and what they actually do – for audiences, for society, for cultural groups. A commercial, market-forces view might say that the media only function to satisfy our needs. But it isn't that simple. If one argues that the media function to provide information, then what is done with this information might look rather different from the points of view of a newspaper owner or a shipyard worker, from the points of view of a Conservative MP or a Labour councillor.

The list below summarizes ideas about media functions. The type of function is followed by opposing views of what that function may mean in practice. These opposing or negative views are described as DYSFUNCTIONS. This should give you some ideas for discussion about how the media institutions may be judged in terms of what they do with their communication.

This points up the fact that one is also talking about what are called **media debates** (see the key questions I have highlighted in each chapter). In effect, a debate is a discussion about a key question relating to some aspect of the media. Examples of such questions connected with the function sections that follow might be:

- Should the media inform as well as entertain us?
- Do the media reflect our culture or do they shape it?
- Do the media give us a fair range of views across the political spectrum?

The media themselves often act as a forum for discussion of these questions. They raise debates and provide a platform, they report such debates carried on by other bodies (Parliament, for instance). In fact one could say that one of their functions is (or should be?) to raise debates about themselves.

11.2 Entertainment Functions

The media provide entertainment and diversion for their audience.

- Such entertainment functions to provide healthy amusement and pleasure for the audience.

- Such entertainment functions to divert audience attention from serious social issues and inequalities.

11.3 Information Functions

The media provide necessary information about the world for the audience.

- Such information functions to help us form a view of the world in geographical, social and political terms.
- Such information functions to structure a particular view of the world and to pacify the audience.

11.4 Cultural Functions

The media provide material that reflects our culture and becomes part of it.

- This material maintains and transmits our culture; it provides continuity for that culture.
- This material develops mass culture at the expense of the diversity of SUBCULTURES.
- This material can maintain the status quo in cultural terms, but may also discourage change and growth.

11.5 Social Functions

The media provide examples of our society, of social interaction, of social groups.

- These examples socialize us into beliefs and relationships that help us operate successfully as members of society.
- These examples socialize us into beliefs and relationships that naturalize one view of society, and stop us obtaining and acting on any alternative views.
- These examples serve a kind of function called **correlation**, relating one event to another for us, putting together events and a sense of what society is and what it means.

11.6 Political Functions

The media provide evidence of political events, issues and activities.

- This evidence enables us to understand the operation of politics in our society and to work more constructively in that political process.
- This evidence gives us the illusion of participating in the political process, but actually endorses the authority of those who continue to run our lives unquestioned.
- The media are capable of mobilizing public opinion; that is to say they can raise issues that the public may not have thought of, and they can suggest a way of looking at those issues. In this way, the media are also capable of shaping opinions about political events and issues.
- In wartime in particular (e.g. the NATO conflict with Serbia) the media

serve a political function of propaganda, not least because the government then controls sources of information.

Media product may be an expression of functions as perceived by the media themselves. For example, if a media organization sees its main function as to entertain the audience at all costs, then it is likely to try and produce a lot of fun material that will appeal to a lot of people. This seems fine in principle, but in practice it may produce a lot of 'rubbish'. (Discuss what *you* think is garbage, and what is not!)

The people who license British television organizations believe that the media should carry out an information function, that they should function to please minorities as well as the majority. So they write this into contracts.

Activity (11): Media Functions

Using my list of functions in Section 11 above, MAKE A NOTE IN EACH CASE OF AN EXAMPLE THAT ILLUSTRATES THE POINT MADE; TRY TO THINK OF EXAMPLES ACROSS THE WHOLE RANGE OF MEDIA.

In this case you should reach some conclusions about whether or not you think the list is valid.

12 MEDIA AND NEW TECHNOLOGY

Institutions of the media have been transformed since the 1980s by the advent of new technology. In particular this has related to applications of computing power. It has affected how material is made, how it gets to the audience and has even created new media. It has affected aspects of media operations, such as financial management, that are not evident to the audience. Given that one could write another book about the subject, I want to look only at a few aspects of this change, which is of course still going on.

One of the most interesting things about new technology is that it calls into question exactly what we mean by medium or media. It also finds new uses for old technology. It builds bridges between media and related technologies. It brings about changes in media use and social interactions.

Not all new technologies are necessarily successful. The huge-screen IMAX cinema is actually a development of old technology. It's great as an exhibition piece, but it has no chance of infiltrating regular cinema and television – analogue or digital.

On the other hand, DVDs have become the new format on which to publish many versions of sound and image. In terms of media, they cross over from the multiplying use of what we still call 'the computer' to a more general use that will replace the video as a play medium. And it is typical of the exploding forms and uses of new technology that, at the same time, recordable CD-Roms are also coming in to replace the linear format of the video tape. Digital television (DTV) is planned to be an industry standard in a few years. It offers producers the chance to edit and play with the product more flexibly. It offers more channels to the distributors. It offers more material and interactivity to the audience/user.

And it is this area of technology as carrier, as changing the sourcing, manipulation, storage and distribution of information, that is showing some of the most dramatic changes. WAP phones and their successors may not appear to be in the mainstream of Media Studies, as defined in terms of the great entertainment media. But they do provide access to the Net, and the Net now includes entertainment functions. As I write this (early 2001), WAP sets are, frankly, oversold. They are very limited in terms of what they can reliably access at the moment. But there is now an interesting potential overlap between such phones, computers and handheld 'organizers'. New devices like the iPaq are beginning to bring these functions together. New portable devices will reliably access BBC 24 or CNN, wherever you are. They may be able to instruct the downloading of music to a larger machine at home. They will, typically, blur the lines between media and its technology as a social tool (phone talk), as information source (checking rail times), as entertainment (games machine), as functional tool (e-shopping).

New media have created new institutions, expanded old ones and created new product to sell to the audience. CDs have virtually killed off vinyl and have involved the production of a whole new technology (and market) selling the equipment to play them on. Now CD-Roms have arrived as computing power becomes the norm at home, and with the effect of displacing the book as source of information. They themselves are being replaced by DVDs, which can contain an entire movie. Computer games machines have become a separate new division of entertainment. McQuail (2000) argues that there are four main categories of new media:

1 interpersonal communication media – e.g. e-mail
2 interactive play media – e.g. computer games
3 information search media – e.g. internet search engines
4 participatory media – e.g. internet chat rooms.

He also says that new media may be distinguished from old in the following respects, so far as users are concerned:

* interactivity – with the source
* social presence – sense of contact with others when using the medium
* autonomy – sense of control over the medium
* playfulness – enjoyment through using the medium as opposed to from it
* privacy – in the experience of using the medium.

The Net is becoming pre-eminent among new media, and yet it does not fit with conventional models for the media because it is not a product, nor is it owned by a media institution in a 'conventional' way (see the section on distribution, below).

New technology is changing the whole 'look' of institutions and what we understand them to be. The BBC is proposing that it should be allowed to open up new digital television and radio channels for more 'special' audiences. This is logical, given the trend towards narrowcasting and targeting audiences. The commercial broadcasters (Nickelodeon) are already protesting about proposals for two daytime channels for young children. The BBC is looking for four new television channels and five new radio channels, including some for black and Asian audiences. They argue that by making more broadcasting more attractive to particular audiences on digital only (at a cost of £300 million) then they will help the government make the overall switch to digital it is keen on.

Media production increasingly depends on applications of new technology. This book is written and composed via computers. It can be 'typeset' in one country and printed in another. Lighting in television studios is controlled via computers. News is gathered via cable and satellite links. Film rushes can be replayed instantly from slave video cameras linked to the film cameras. We now have non-linear (digital) editing (in computers) of film sequences, including advertisements. Increasingly, feature films are being edited in this way, in segments, before being translated back to celluloid. Some people argue that film as product and film distribution will go entirely digital. In 1998 an experimental film called *The Last Broadcast* was shot on digital cameras and distributed to five cinemas across the USA via satellite and in the form of compressed computer files. The British director Mike Figgis has made *Time Code 2000*, also shot on digital, which shows four views of a drama in real time, all on screen at the same time.

New forms of **distribution** are changing the way that we access media material around the world. **The Net** is an unusual example of a system that can access text, pictures, pop music, even short films, literally on a global basis and at very little cost. It is raising costly questions for existing media owners about copyright and control of product. It is unusual because it is not institutionalized. No one owns it. It exists in a cyberspace spun out of existing cables and satellite links, and focused on the computer memories of servers and the functions of millions of machines around the world. It enables individuals to become authors in at least a small way, to publish materials on their own web sites. Equally it allows existing publishers to extend their domain and offer access to their products as e-books, to be downloaded and paid for electronically. It changes the idea of audience, if you think of an audience in terms of being in one place and/or consuming at one time. It changes ideas about production and distribution with, for example, e-shopping.

Live Planet is an entertainment portal on the Net, supported by Larry Ellison of Oracle computers, and by Matt Damon and Ben Affleck, two Hollywood actors. It involves a webcam strapped to a runner crossing the States, with people trying to find and catch him.

Another example of new distribution is darkerthanblue.com, a company supported by Chrysalis Entertainment (which owns Galaxy Radio), designed to promote and distribute jazz and blues music.

It tends to be assumed that the Net is all about freedom and individual enterprise. But one must be cautious. Big media companies now have huge, slick web sites and a lot of business on the Net. They are replicating their success with other media. For example, UN&M owns a division named Xilerate. This division includes web sites for parents, for the lads (Megastar), for music, for business, for investment, and more.

If you look at the news chapter of this book (Chapter 7), you will see that I have referred to the information wars conducted over the Net between NATO and Serbian sides in the 1999 Kosovo war. The Net is not a force in itself. There are various struggles to make dominant use of it, if not to control it. Capitalist e-commerce forces have emerged in the last five years. Right-wing Christian pressure groups have web sites. Equally, resistance to the Burmese military autocracy is also conducted via e-mail and web sites.

'Video on demand' via telephone or cable lines is another kind of distribution that is taking off. Successful area experiments have been carried out in the States. The BBC is now looking for ways of making this happen, and for making a lot of money from its huge back catalogue of programmes. This is a variation on payTV, in which you choose what you want to watch and when. In 2000, urban experiments were taking place in British cities via companies such as YesTV and VideoNetworks.

Satellites are put up by giant telecommunications companies in conjunction with military authorities or governments. The channels on the satellites are owned by developing organizations where, typically, even that public corporation, the BBC, goes into commercial co-ownership with FlexTech (an American company) to run a suite of channels called UKTV (e.g. UKGold, which uses the BBC's huge back catalogue of television material).

Satellite digital (and cable feed) channels are exploding in number. NewsCorp's Star Channel is coming to Britain on SkyDigital. It will compete with existing Asian channels such as Zee TV. In the Far East, Star broadcasts to 53 countries on 28 channels, in seven languages. It is part of the Murdoch global empire. The effect of British Asian channels, plus Star's news and entertainment in Hindi, is a double-edged one. It is recognizing the needs of an ethnic minority, as well as commercial interests. But the increase in such narrowcasting, tailoring media to specific audiences, does, ironically, work against the idea that national media can generate a national identity, with the same shared sense of culture and perspective. A lot depends on how far audiences exercise their rights to choice, and acquire a range of perspectives on the world.

The expansion of means of distribution has enormous implications for culture and for the commissioning of product. In 1988 the government said in a white paper, 'as delivery systems proliferate, national frontiers begin to blur or disappear. There will be increasing demand from an international market for programme material.' It is new technology that provides the delivery systems. Co-productions are becoming more and more common internationally (e.g. *Life in the Big Freezer*, 1999). The danger is that if new technology opens up international markets, then it is those markets and those audiences the media producers may feel they have to please – the kind of problem that has already mortally wounded the British film industry, which is continually defining itself by reference to Hollywood.

Media product is transformed by new technology in ways that steal up on us and that we take for granted unless we can remember a time when things were not done in a certain way. For example, films such as *Toy Story 2* (1999) and *The Matrix* (1999) involved kinds of computer animation and computer matteing that were not possible at the beginning of that decade. Such films create a new version of reality for the next generation of viewers, where the impossible becomes routine. It is generally agreed that it is only a matter of time before the authenticity of the computer-generated image converges with that of the reproduced image. And even reproduced images are now being captured ever more frequently by electronic 'movie' or still cameras. Such computing control of visuals has changed everything we watch. This is fairly obvious in some television title sequences. It is not so obvious in the way that photographs are routinely touched up in magazines, most obviously to bring us idealized images of people, rather than the 'real' people themselves.

Everywhere we turn to look at media products, new technology has changed what we see. Advertisements are full of images that mix the real world with computer-generated images. The news is full of computer-generated graphics. The weather moves across our screens in simulated images. Newspaper and magazine pages mix text and image in a layout that is courtesy of the computer.

Convergence is possibly the most important concept of all if one is trying to make sense of new technology and media. Not only are the institutions converging in the sense that they all take stakes in one anothers' industries, but also the technology is converging so that the idea of separate forms of communication is becoming less and less true. In particular, one can see that words, pictures and music are now all available on CD-Roms. And CD-Roms can be played via computers, which themselves can be linked to screens and audio systems. The next generation of DVDs are becoming common-place. It is not hard to imagine a time when video tape and even film as celluloid in cinemas will become redundant. Similarly, electronic still cameras are standard in many industrial applications (e.g. magazine and newspaper image processing). They are now moving seriously into the domestic market as quality becomes cheaper, and more people have the computers on which to store and process their electronic images. The conventional camera is on its way out.

The convergence of institutions means a magnification of power over product and ideas within the product. The convergence of technology for reproducing texts could mean that a lot more is available more easily to a lot more people. However, the fact that all forms of communication are encoded in the digital language of machines also makes it easier to manipulate them, to change 'what is said'. Whatever happens with the control of information, ideas and entertainment, clearly existing trends towards a visual culture, towards more and more kinds of entertainment, will continue.

Issues of access, choice and copyright are also raised by new technology, which offers, potentially, a huge diversity for the consumer, but headaches in terms of protecting property and collecting money for the 'new media'. Lorimer discusses this in *Mass Communications* (1994) where he points out that the development of cable television has been hampered to a degree by the self-interest of the established broadcast technologies. Similarly, there has been a reluctance to develop technologies such as DAT audio into the domestic markets because it would be so easy for consumers to make perfect pirate copies. In spite of an agreement to assign a percentage of the income from selling tapes and equipment to royalties, there has been no rush to release popular material on to DAT format.

A more urgent crisis for the music corporations has been the release on to the Net of powerful 'compression' programmes that allow rapid downloading of music tracks. These may be sourced by individuals or by companies like Napster, which make use of the programmes tied to music store files. The MP4 programme is now 'loose' on the Net. It can compress a movie to 1 per cent of its 'size'. There is an interesting question of whether individual trade in such film copies will prompt film companies to use the law to try to shut down such duplication and distribution. In spite of winning battles in courts, the music companies still have not stopped the haemorrhage of product. The whole business sets up interesting issues of 'people power' and of 'audience access' versus 'property rights' and 'creative ownership'.

In some cases media giants are actually joining with the 'independents'. Bertelsmann has done a deal with Napster (2000) that contradicts the attempts of Sony to get Napster closed down. Ericsson has done a deal with digital distributor DX3 (EMI-backed) and a cable company, to try a system that will link the Net with home stereo systems and allow the downloading of music to play directly into the home hi-fi.

Jason Toynbee (in his 2001 MeCCSA conference paper) comments on how the Net and providers like Napster have changed the distribution of music. They have 'spoilt' the hitherto cosy arrangement between producers and recording companies in which they get money for publishing as well as for recording music. He describes Napster as 'entrepreneurship meets idealism'. Meanwhile, new copyright laws are being enacted to try and wrest back control of the growing electronic leak of music from the Net to home computers.

New Technology and Media
Does new technology 'improve' media, bringing us benefits such as digital television?
Does new technology only serve to increase the power of the media to make us spend
more money and more time on more entertainment?

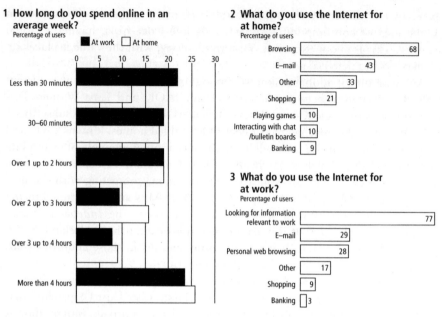

Fig. 4.7 Internet usage

Source: Datamonitor

13 GLOBALIZATION

Global domination of media industries by a few multinational companies is a consequence of the continuing pattern of mergers and take-overs around the world. Such concentration of ownership has consequences itself – for product and distribution – loosely to be described in terms of 'less difference, but more of the same to more people'. So the term globalization also refers to the standardization of product (see the section on genre in Chapter 5) to sell successfully to an international market. Action movies have been popular with Hollywood because they are light on language, deal in simple plots and themes, and can be sold through star image and visual action.

It does seem that certain media products are more easily globalized than others: news (CNN), music (MTV), movies, television serials (BBCWorld). This has something to with the universality of their narrative appeal and with their comprehensibility (Can they be dubbed? How much does spoken language matter?).

If the production of media material or texts has gone global, then this leads to another point of critical concern – media or cultural imperialism. American texts will transmit American values and ideology to consumers around the world. Indigenous product, as in the example of British film, will be wiped out or changed in its nature. There is a loss of a sense of national identity in the receiving countries. This global culture lacks connection with the lived experience of those in receiving countries. In particular there is the promotion of the idea of consumption – some goods like Coca-Cola, having a global identity. This is about exporting western ideology, with the value it places on ownership and material goods.

An example of globalization stemming from mergers is in the current US$183-billion deal between America Online (AOL) and Time Warner. This also indicates the significance of new media. AOL has 26 million subscribers. Time Warner cable reaches 20 per cent of US cabled homes. It owns CNN and Home Box Office movie channel. Then there is another example of expanding global ownership which it has been argued (*Guardian*, 11 September 2000) proves that newspapers are still a healthy medium, competing with the new media that are supposed to be replacing them. INM is an international media group run by entrepreneur Tony O'Reilly. It owns the *Independent* and *Independent on Sunday*. It is a leading newspaper publisher in Ireland, South Africa and New Zealand. It has large radio stations in those countries (plus Portugal). It has a turnover of £1 billion a year.

However, one does need to counteract this apparently gloomy picture of global monopolies with some qualifications. First, it isn't just US product that sells around the world: British television sells in Europe; Indian film is distributed in Britain; Brazilian soap operas are distributed around South America. So there are national media businesses that are surviving, and there are kinds of cultural exchange. It cuts both ways. There are some concerns about the importation of western popular music into various countries in Africa. On the other hand, the same process of globalization, especially as backed by technology that provides wider access, is bringing African music to the West in a way that didn't happen 15 years ago. One also needs to consider models of cause and effect. The imperialism theory implicitly assumes that media simply do things to people, whereas it may be that receiving cultures actually do things with foreign material: adapt it and mentally accommodate it in ways that work against a thesis of cultural subjugation. Globalization should include uses of the Net to mobilize international opinion regarding autocratic rule in Burma by a military junta.

It also needs to be said that, as an idea, globalization is about more than the media. International travel and package holidays are relevant. So is international aid – for example, to build dams that change the ecology and economy of a whole nation. The idea is also one that operates in terms of economic power and difference. Poor people in poor countries can't afford western goods, including things like television sets, which could bring a new set of meanings into their homes. Within other countries there may be a sharp differentiation between have-nots and a minority that can afford to buy into the global culture (see also Section 5.6 above).

Chris Barker (1999) sees globalization as a 'time–space compression of the world'. We can e-mail instantly to the other side of the planet. We can be familiar with faraway places through satellite television. The rise of multinationals is the 'restructuring of capitalism on a global scale'. That is to say, what the media industries did with the economies of countries in the last century, they will do to the world in this century. They can do this because telecommunications have developed to the point where there are 24-hour financial transactions around the planet. US companies employ European secretarial services online so that those companies can work through the US night and have reports prepared for the morning.

One may also argue that the concept of globalization includes such phenomena as the global marketing of films dubbed in various languages, as well as the international marketing of sport, such as cricket, American football or the Olympics.

REVIEW

You should have learned the following things about the media as a source of communication and as institutions, through this chapter.

1 DOMINANT CHARACTERISTICS
- The media are mainly characterized by the following aspects: monopoly, size, vertical integration, conglomeration, diversification, as multinationals, control and domination of production/finance/product/distribution, particular values.

2 SOURCES OF FINANCE/COSTS
- The media have access to enormous sums of money through their means of finance. These means are dominated by selling advertising space, by the sales of their main product and through the sales of associated products.

3 ASPECTS OF PRODUCTION
- There are distinctive patterns to the way in which media material is produced. These may be summarized in terms of routines, deadlines, slots, specialized production roles, use of new technology and heavy marketing of the product.

4 CONSEQUENCES
- There are major consequences to the way that media institutions are set up, run and financed. These may be summarized in terms of mass product, targeted product, repetition of product, elimination of unprofitable audiences, exclusion of competition, polarization of audiences and reduction of choice for the consumer. However, there are some alternatives to the dominant patterns of ownership and distribution.

5 MEDIA POWER
- The points already made lead us to conclude that the media have a great deal of power over what we read and see. The nature of this power may be discussed in terms of ownership, monopoly, levers of power, power over product and ideology, the power of professionalism, cultural imperialism.

6 MEDIATION
- The media inevitably change the material they draw on and shape it in certain ways. They construct this material and the meanings in it. They offer us representations, but not real life or real events.

7 REGULATION

- There are certain constraints on the ways that the media operate and so on the product we receive. These may be summarized in terms of: self-regulation through certain industry bodies such as those for the press, advertising or film; regulation of broadcasting – through the Broadcasting Standards Council or through the Independent Television Commission; editorial control over the production team; and legal and financial constraints.

8 CENSORSHIP

- The term censorship has been used to describe interference with production and the cutting of material by, for example, the BBFC or by the government using the Official Secrets Act.

9 MEDIA AND GOVERNMENT

- There is a power relationship between media and government. The government exerts power over the media in various direct and indirect ways. The media need the government as a source of information, the government needs the media as a means of communication.

10 PROPAGANDA

- This implies total control and deliberate use of media towards some end, which does not happen in this country.
- Some talk of the influence of government and advertising on the media, as being something like propaganda.
- There has been propaganda in times of war; this may be discussed in relation to government management of news.

11 FUNCTIONS OF THE MEDIA

- These may be summarized in terms of entertainment, information, culture, social and political functions.

12 MEDIA AND NEW TECHNOLOGY

- The arrival of new technology, symbolized by computing power, has changed institutions, production, distribution, product.
- The convergence factor, based on a common digital language, is bringing media and institutions together.
- Access to this new technology raises problems of media access and of pirated products.

13 GLOBALIZATION

- Refers to the way in which media ownership and media operations now work across the globe. This brings wider cultural influence: cultural imperialism. It changes the way in which we understand the world. Using new technology 'shrinks the planet' by making more material more quickly available from ever greater distances.

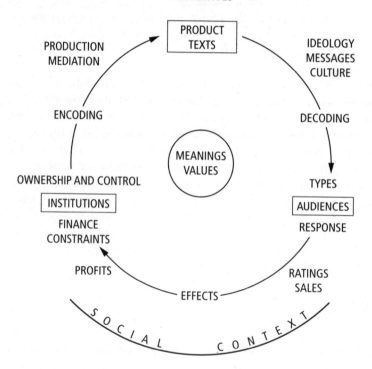

REPRESENTATION
INFORMATION AND PERSUASION
GENRES REALISM
NARRATIVES

PRODUCTION
MEDIATION

PRODUCT
TEXTS

IDEOLOGY
MESSAGES
CULTURE

ENCODING

DECODING

MEANINGS
VALUES

OWNERSHIP AND CONTROL

TYPES

INSTITUTIONS

AUDIENCES

FINANCE
CONSTRAINTS

RESPONSE

PROFITS

RATINGS
SALES

EFFECTS

SOCIAL   CONTEXT

5

Media Product 1: Texts

Genres, Representations, Stars

Having dealt with the source of the message we will now deal with the means by which it is carried. And just as the source was linked to the messages, we must relate the media material to the messages or meanings, which are the subject of Chapter 8. The point of what is said, and the means through which it is said are inevitably joined together.

This chapter is about ideas that help make sense of the product. It looks at genres, stereotypes and versions of realism. It does not describe programmes or newspapers in detail, or how they are made. That may be interesting, and you may wish to do some follow-up reading (consult the reading list at the end of this book), but what is most interesting is the 'SO WHAT?' question. We see many films or magazines coming out of the media institutions described and commented upon in the previous chapter but, SO WHAT? So those many films, magazines and other examples of product show some significant patterns when we look at them overall. These patterns are significant because they suggest that meanings may be carried to the audience and how. Once more those meanings matter, the messages matter, if they shape our view of the world.

1 REPETITION

The first thing to notice is the sheer repetition of the production line material. **Much of the content and treatment of the output of the various media industries is basically the same.** This is most obvious in such examples as film sequels, television series, follow-ups and cover versions of records. Sometimes this is inevitable where there is competition for the same audience, which likes the same things. For example, it is hardly surprising that every newspaper has sports coverage and repeats sporting stories. The popularity of sports can be seen in the number of people who go to sporting events. There is also evidence that television coverage relates to active involvement in sports, as with the expansion of snooker halls in the early 1980s.

The repetition of new single releases across various radio channels, or the repetition of certain styles of music across channels, must also signify something. It certainly reinforces impact.

'Impact' means that, to put it at its simplest, **if something is repeated often enough it will tend to be believed and remembered.** This is a basic principle on which advertising works. Some of the most successful product adverts have used the same slogan for years – for example, 'A Mars a day ...'. Repetition includes types of treatment. Such **repetition of treatment causes it to be accepted as the 'right' way to handle the material,** the way in which one expects the material to be handled. Music videos have been through various phases, from the original convention that the group mimed to the song, through various treatments such as 'telling the story of the song', or using as many new electronic effects as one could cram in.

The sheer repetition of electronic drum sound and of sampled records in popular dance music has created acceptance of this treatment, and a willingness on the part of the audience to buy more of the same. It has become the norm. Equally, there is enough variation on a theme to show that there is a kind of dynamic interaction between media and audience: musicians and studio producers experiment – the audience reacts; the audience buys and supports kinds of music in clubs – the producers react.

The repetition of electronic special effects in films, especially science fiction, has created a similar acceptance and audience demand. Viewers expect to see convincing laser battles, just as viewers of television news expect to see authentic footage of wars in other parts of the world. Indeed they expect to see what is happening – drama and action – with brief packaged explanations, rather than, say, photographs accompanied by longer background explanations.

There is nothing 'natural' about the way in which material is handled. We expect to see things done in certain ways as the result of years of repetition, which creates an understanding between the creators and the audience. If we are going to unpack the meanings in media material, then we must expose the idea of 'natural' for the con job that it is. We must get to the heart of the con (which we are all happy to join in!), by noticing the repetition and asking how and why it takes place.

The main reason why we have repetition of content and treatment is because it sells. All media operators want to make money, to attract audiences, to improve their ratings, to improve their readership figures – whatever is appropriate to the given media. The repetition may help acceptance of the content or form of the communication. But **it still has to be based on something that is attractive to the audience.** There is no way we can be persuaded to buy something that we really do not like or want. There is no way that we can be sold something that we really do not believe in. There is more about persuasion and effects in the final chapter of this book, but for the time being you should accept that there is no evidence to support any kind of CONSPIRACY THEORY about the media – that the gnomes of press and television invent items and ideas that they force upon us through some kind of fiendish plot. The truth is more insidious and of no less concern – that they pick up on things that are already there.

So **the causes of the kinds of repetition that we can identify have to do with** pragmatic and commercial motives rather than intentional and ideological ones (though this doesn't mean that ideology and hegemony are not at work in the background). They are connected with the production routines that we have already considered. It is easier to do things the way they have always been done than to change one's routines. Why change what you are doing or the way you do it if it is making you good money, so the argument might go.

What is being repeated, remember, is any one of three elements:

1 the categories of media product (e.g. type of programme)
2 the content of that product (e.g. type of character)
3 the treatment of that content (e.g. the device of reprising sections of film with freeze frames at the end of a television film in order to give the actors credits and more screen time).

The consequence of this repetition is that it reinforces these three elements in the minds of the reader or viewer. But, more than this, it reinforces the covert messages embedded in the material. This is where ideology comes in. And this is why it matters. For instance, television has produced hundreds of hours of police thrillers. Many of these have male heroes who are mostly action men, with little sign of the personal anxieties and problems that dog most of us mortals. These examples give us the not-very-covert message about what it is to be a good cop and good guy. Do your duty and to hell with the effect on your relationships. Having said that, it is encouraging that some programmes that break this mould – *Prime Suspect*, for example – have in fact been very successful. *Prime Suspect* shows us that women can also be good cops, and still deal with personal problems.

Mention of such a type of programme brings us neatly to a major concept and way of categorizing material in the media genres. So let's look at what genres are and why they matter.

2 GENRES

2.1 Definition

A GENRE is a type or category of media product, like a spy thriller. It has certain distinctive main features. These features have come to be well understood and recognized through being repeated over a period of time. Sometimes there are variations on the genre, which may be (rather awkwardly) called a subgenre – the Bond spy thrillers or the space-odyssey type of science fiction film. The term is generally associated with fiction material, though news could also count as a genre of television.

In some ways it is easiest to define genres by their generic titles – science fiction, cop thriller, western, quiz show – but this lands us in a chicken-and-egg situation. Why do we dredge up such a title in the first place? To say that genre is, for example, thrillers or that spy thrillers are a genre, takes us round in a circle and does not sort out what genre is.

The term does not necessarily cover all sorts of repetitive material. In particular, **it should not be confused with modes of realism or of style.** Documentary or melodrama, for instance, are ways of handling the material and, as such, cut across any genre. They may have certain repeated elements of their own – use of natural lighting or exaggerated confrontations – but they don't have any clear pattern of expected subject matter or of character. In other words, we could have a melodramatic cop thriller or indeed melodrama in any other genre. But not all cop thrillers are melodramatic. In the same way, other modes – such as comedy and romance – may have certain recognizable repeated traits, but they are not as predictable as genres. Any story, genre or not, may be treated as a comedy. But comedy in general is not sufficiently predictable to be seen as a genre.

Genres have a history. They develop their form, their formula and the range of their subject matter. British television soap opera started with a middle-class model – *The Grove Family* – but rapidly moved into a version of working class-ness. It has now combined with other genres to bring its kind of realism to, for example, the police story. At the same time genres are historically located. *The Grove Family* was a kind of archetypal nuclear family for the 1950s. Its attitudes were those of its time; its viewers would be shocked by the teenage excesses of *Hollyoaks*. Genres may also be located in historical events – the western is an obvious example. They end up mythologizing those events and real personalities – stories about the Mafia, for instance.

But within this extensive framework it is particular characteristics of genres,

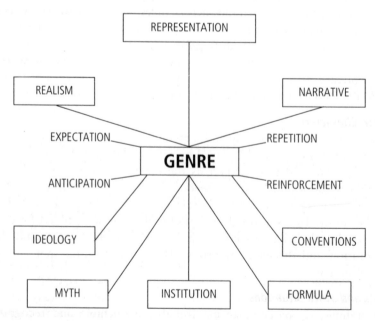

Fig. 5.2 Key concepts: genre

such as predictability and repeated elements, that make them distinctive and that help define them. We will now look at these.

2.2   Key Elements

All genres have a portfolio of key elements from which they are composed. Not all examples of a genre will have all the elements all the time. There may be permutations of these. It is these elements that make up the **formula** of a given genre. They add up to what we unconsciously expect to see, and enjoy seeing or reading. The way that the elements are put together is itself formulaic. As with other topics in this book, I hope to make conscious what you really knew all along, and to make some sense of it. You should also realize that any genre is more than the sum of its parts. So in what follows I will describe the parts separately, but you should understand that whatever the genre means to you comes as a result of your taking in all the elements together.

■ *Protagonists*

All genres have recognizable protagonists or lead characters. These may be heroes and/or villains. Sometimes these lead males and females are so predictable that they have the same qualities across a number of genres (see the section on archetypes, on p. 33). Such males would be courageous and good looking, and likely to rescue a lady in distress at some point. By the same token, the lead female is likely to be very good looking, and play second fiddle to the male hero. A popular film such as *The Matrix* exemplifies this tendency, though it is more extreme in action comics (*Doc Savage*) or cheap American television material (*Star Trek*). It is also true that many of these male protagonists are loners, whether one is talking about, say, the western or about the private eye movie. Sometimes actors invest such a character with some individuality – usually because they are seen to be fallible – but in many ways one would be hard put to truly distinguish one genre hero from another simply in terms of character and behaviour. The same could be said of quiz show hosts, who are also part of a formula and a genre. They are a kind of protagonist who isn't much different from one show to another.

■ *Stock Characters*

Another part of the scenario includes recognizable though minor characters, who sometimes are repeatedly played by actors who specialize in such a part. Walter Brennan used to be expert as the old timer in westerns, dispensing homespun wisdom and hitting a beetle with tobacco spit at 50 paces. The robot servant is a stock character in science fiction, all the way from Robbie the Robot in the 1950s, through to C3PO in the *Star Wars* films of the 1980s and 1990s. Lovely Leila (or whoever) is a stock character in many quiz shows, as decoration and dispenser of prizes. The reporter-on-the-spot is a stock character in news.

■ *Plots and Stock Situations*

The storylines, or parts of them, are also predictable and recognizable. Gangster films are almost invariably about the rise and fall of the gangster

James
LEE BURKE

THE NEON RAIN

"His is a name to watch"
Los Angeles Times

(a)

AGATHA
CHRISTIE
The Mirror
Crack'd from Side to Side
HAS THERE EVER BEEN A MURDER WITH A MORE INTRIGUING MOTIVE?

(b)

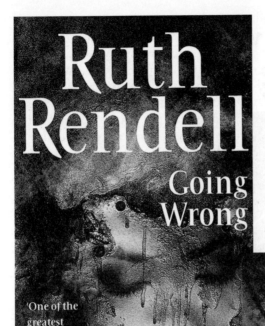

(c)

Fig. 5.3 Iconography of the thriller

The icons on these book covers provide an instant point of contact for the target audience. Of course there is more to the cover designs and their meanings than just the image of a dagger, for example. Equally there are similarities between the covers which place them firmly within the genre. These are all points which you can tease out.

(d)

hero, and will include a final shoot-out scene in which morality triumphs and the anti-hero gangster dies in a hail of bullets. Soaps are just as predictable, however complicated the storylines become over weeks of viewing. There is bound to be a scene in which someone turns up from the past of the hero/heroine and has some kind of confrontation. Romantic stories often include a plotline in which the heroine cannot get the boy because of some awful obstruction to their love, perhaps simply the fact that he does not notice that she is there. But it will all come right in the end; or it will turn out that he is a bad lot anyway and she is better off without him. Further examples of stock situations within plots are plentiful – for instance, the scene in police thrillers where a suspect is given a grilling.

■ Icons

This element is crucial to genre because, above all, it is the aspect of the genre we immediately recognize and lock into. There are three main types of ICON: objects, backgrounds and sometimes stars. The icon is a key SYMBOL of the genre – see the icon and you know immediately what territory you are in. All the other elements of the genre are likely to be assumed once you have recognized the icon and interpreted it. Icons such as the laser/ray gun of science fiction, are potent symbols. They stand for the main ideas and themes of the genre. A starry background with planets stands for adventure and exploration. The titles sequence of independent British television news (ITN) has used the icon of Big Ben in one form or another for years. It stands for integrity and authority – ideas the programme continues to project in the way it presents its material. (See also Section 2.4, on iconography.)

■ Backgrounds and Decor

These elements are also typical, distinctive and recognizable for a given genre. Their importance varies from example to example. The interiors of a current soap such as *Neighbours* are pretty anodyne. But the pub interior of *EastEnders* is distinctive and a part of the character of the series. A shot of rain-slicked city streets at night with high-rise buildings is likely to lock one into either the private eye or the cop thriller. If such backgrounds become very distinctive, then they become icons. Some interiors are most recognizable in terms of their decor (the furnishings and their style). The glossy tinsel-and-flashing-lights decor of many quiz shows is distinctively part of their genre. So are the control room, consoles and screens of sci-fi interiors.

■ Themes

The themes or ideas that run through and come out of the stories are very much part of genre. Some are relatively common to genres, some are more special. These themes also tie in with the value messages that are projected. For example, all genre NARRATIVE says something about conflict between good and evil, between alternative views of right and wrong. But the theme of deceit and betrayal is more special to private eye stories, where the hero is often double-crossed by a female.

These generic themes often emerge as oppositions: opposing sets of ideas that have to be worked through until one set prevails – usually that of the dominant ideology. In the private eye film one has, for example:

- honesty vs corruption
- truth vs ignorance
- loyalty vs deceit
- self-sufficiency vs dependency
- persistence vs surrender
- integrity vs temptation.

2.3   The Formula

So all these elements add up to something called the formula. They are, if you like, headings for the kinds of item one would expect to see in all genres. When you look at particular genres then of course, as with the examples above, it is particular items that you describe for that genre.

For example, in *Television Soaps* (1992) Richard Kilborn starts off talking about the characteristics and the formula of soaps in terms of the 'never ending story'. He also points to the complexity of variations on the formula of any genre when he says that although the audience has a considerable 'fund of knowledge as to what soaps are and how they work', their main concern is usually with 'the individual model rather than with abstract questions of design'. However, media students ought to be concerned with the design and what we can learn from it.

So in the case of soaps we can list other likely elements of their formula, such as matriarchal figures, family-centred drama, conflict through misunderstanding, emotional crises, locations that act as a focus for the community, a range of generations in the characters, episodic structure with cliff-hanger endings, parallel multi-stranded narratives.

Mary Ellen Brown (1993) describes this genre in these terms:

- a serial form that resists narrative closure
- use of multiple characters and plots
- use of time that parallels actual time (with the implication that the action carries on even when we are not watching)
- abrupt segmentation (jumps) between parts of the narrative structure
- emphasis on dialogue, problem-solving and intimate conversation
- male characters who are 'sensitive' men
- female characters who have power outside the home
- set in homes, or places that function as home.

The audience's knowledge of the formula helps them know what is going on and gives them the pleasure of feeling they are on familiar ground. And if it gives them a blueprint for making sense of the drama, it also gives the production company a blueprint for making the drama, one which it can feel confident it shares with that audience.

It is good to recognize the existence of a formula, but genre study is not just about enumerating elements. It goes on to be about why that formula matters in terms of the meanings it inscribes into the text, and the meanings the audience decodes from the text.

Genre and Formula

Does the fact that many media products work to a formula make them boring?

Is this formula half the fun in reading and viewing?

2.4   Iconography

Iconography is about the study of icons in genre, the study of their meanings and of their contribution to the genre.

Icons within a genre text may be seen as part of the formula. These are **highly recognizable elements of the genre that immediately identify it** and unlock associations with:

- the other elements of the formula
- the prevailing values of that genre.

Iconography is mostly discussed in relation to film genres. I suggest that this is partly an accident of the history of criticism. It is possible to argue for some icons in other media. Is Bob Marley not an icon for reggae music? Are not Daleks still icons for a British television science fiction audience? If there is a media distinction in respect of the presence of icons, then it may be more to do with the relatively slow output of cinema (compared with broadcasting). Film genres and their icons have developed over a period of years, and have the reinforcement of being distributed globally, across the cultural boundaries that often hem in understanding of television, for example.

For films, their stars, or key objects, or familiar backgrounds, are the elements that usually have the power of iconography. Schwarzenegger is still an icon of the action movie. Space-suited figures and a starry background are icons of the science fiction movie.

But one also has to recognize that the power of icons may fade with time. Though the buttes of Monument Valley may have been iconographic to the western at one time, the fading popularity of the genre has diminished familiarity with the backgrounds of the west. At least one may argue that the Colt-45 still has image power. I leave you to reflect on what other film elements may now have this iconographic power.

Iconography's importance is not so much about the fact that it helps categorize a genre, it is more to do with the symbolic power of icons. The Magnum police special stood for masculine strength and indisputable justice in the *Dirty Harry* films of 20 years ago. The light sabre of the *Star Wars* film cycle stands for a blend of noble traditional combat and cutting-edge technology.

You also need to recognize that icons can work in stock situations that are themselves quite iconic. There is the Mafia gangster murder in the restaurant, invoking an iconic combination of clothes, guns, the background and a whole chunk of story that everyone 'knows'.

2.5 Recognition and Attraction

So genres have this quality of being very recognizable for what they are, sometimes from just one or two shots or pictures. Indeed **the story makers depend on this recognition for instant communication with the audience.** The great thing about genre material, from their point of view, is that no time is spent setting up a character or explaining a situation. If it is familiar then the audience knows the kind of person or scene that it is dealing with. In fact the story makers can trade in recognition in order to tease the audience, by doing something it does not expect.

So the attraction of genre material is, among other things, the **mixture of familiarity and the unexpected.** The audience will run the video of *Scream 3* partly because they already have had the pleasure of being frightened out of their socks, and partly because they expect something a bit different, without knowing what exactly.

2.6 Anticipation, Expectation and Prediction

All media material gives some kind of pleasure to the reader or viewer. This is why the audience buys the product. The nature of that pleasure is another matter. Obviously, the kind of enjoyment we get from reading a newspaper is not the same as that from reading a novel. Within genres specifically, there is a range of pleasure to be gained – not just some sort of gut excitement at seeing Bruce Willis take on the villain in a *Die Hard* film, which provides the excuse for violent special effects in that kind of movie. There is also a kind of pleasure gained from being able to anticipate what will happen next. This is most obvious in the mystery thriller genre, where one of the main points is to second-guess the identity of the criminal – *The X Files*, for example. There is pleasure to be gained from predicting what will happen. People discuss soaps such *Brookside* in terms of the motivation and likely behaviour of the characters: 'I reckon she's going to run off with him' and so on. There is the pleasure of expectation realized. The reader's trembling hand turns the page of the comic, expecting to see the hero get out of a tight corner, probably through another display of martial arts.

2.7 Seriality

This notion refers to the way in which media material, especially genres, repeat and re-work story elements. Berger (1992) discusses and explains the ideas of Umberto Eco on this subject. He describes a four-part typology as follows.

1 **The Retake** – where a new story is built around characters from a previous successful narrative. An example would be *Star Wars*.

Table 5.1 Television genres and television viewing: interests in types of programme

	Total interested[1] %	Very interested %	Quite interested %	Not that interested %	Not at all interested %
National and international news	85	48	36	10	4
Local and regional news	85	41	44	10	4
Films – recent releases	81	42	40	11	6
Nature and wildlife programmes	76	44	32	12	10
Adventure or police series	70	25	44	17	12
Plays and drama series	68	21	47	16	14
Situation comedy shows	66	18	48	19	13
Soap operas	61	32	30	18	19
Crime reconstructions	59	21	38	19	19
Sports programmes	56	33	23	19	24
Holiday and travel programmes	56	18	38	22	20
Health and medical programmes	55	16	39	23	20
Quiz and panel game shows	54	22	32	22	22
Older or classic cinema films	53	22	32	20	25
Hobbies and leisure programmes	53	12	40	28	17
Current affairs programmes	52	13	39	21	24
Chat shows	52	12	40	24	22
Variety shows	50	16	34	25	22
Alternative comedy shows	48	15	33	22	27
Films suitable only for adults	42	12	30	24	32
Programmes from/about European countries	42	7	35	25	30
Consumer affairs	42	7	35	26	30
Science programmes	39	12	27	23	35
Women's programmes	38	11	26	21	38
Education programmes for adults	37	11	27	28	31
Pop or rock music	36	14	22	18	43
Arts programmes	23	7	16	31	43
Programmes about politics	22	5	17	26	49
Programmes for older children	22	5	17	19	55
Church services	21	6	15	19	57
Business and financial programmes	19	4	15	26	52

Contd.

	Total interested[1] %	Very interested %	Quite interested %	Not that interested %	Not at all interested %
Programmes about religion	18	3	15	22	57
Programmes for the under-5s	17	5	11	14	66

Base: All TV viewers. Notes: 1. Sum of 'very' and 'quite' interested (may not sum exactly due to rounding). 'Don't knows' excluded.

Table 5.1 gives a different angle on the idea of genre and popularity. It shows that people say that they are most interested in news, even though it is soaps that consistently make the top rating of what people actually watch. Similarly one could reflect on the fact that although sport has a dominant position in programming (not to mention the content of newspapers), still one-fifth of interviewees said that they weren't interested in it.

2 **The Remake** – where a known story is retold with variations in an 'up-to-date' version. An example would be *Dracula* or *Wyatt Earp*.
3 **The Series** – where a new story or set of stories is made around one central character. Detective series in all media are a good example of this – say, *Inspector Morse* on British television.
4 **The Saga** – where the story is built around the development of a family over a period of time. Many soaps are examples of this, for instance *The Archers* on radio, or *Neighbours* on television.

This is a useful description that draws attention to key features of genres, such as conventions, repetition and the formula.

2.8 Repetition and Reinforcement

This topic is worth returning to (see Section 1, above). The whole of genre depends upon it. **The building blocks of genre, its elements, as well as the messages that genres communicate, all depend on being repeated, so that they continue to be known and understood by the audience.** To some extent, a genre can become self-perpetuating once its key elements are established. The more the stories use the same elements, the more the audience accepts that this is what the genre is all about. But genre is not static, it is always adding variations to its elements and its formula. The whole invention of *Star Trek*, and its transfer from television to film is a good example. But **the meanings, or messages, are also repeated and reinforced: they become 'natural';** they are believed the more they are 'said'. The dominance of white ethnic groups across the entire range of genre material in the multiracial US and UK clearly carries a message about 'white rules, OK'.

2.9 Formula, Code and Conventions

When we recognize and make sense of genre material we take all the elements together. **This combination of elements special to a genre represents a kind of**

formula. This formula may vary slightly from genre piece to genre piece, but essentially it is there all the time, composed from the elements that have been described.

Each **genre also represents a kind of special code, shared by** its makers and its audience. In terms of semiotics, or the study of signs and their meanings, we are dealing with a secondary code (see Section 9.3 in Chapter 3). For example, a film musical is based on all the primary codes of speech, non-verbal communication, music, and so on. We have to know these in the first place in order to make any sense of it at all. But there are special qualities to the musical that overlay a secondary code on the primary one. For instance, it is a part of the code that people may break into song at improbable times.

So **there are various sets of rules for what should be in a code and how these elements should be used and combined.** For example, there is a general rule for chat shows on television (as with light entertainment programmes) that hosts and guests should make their entrance down a staircase. Such rules are called conventions. Most programmes, whether they are genre or not, reveal some conventions in the way that they open. You should try an evening's viewing devoted to the beginnings of programmes and see how many rules of the game you can spot.

The idea of convention is double-edged in the sense that it can draw attention to what is similar when comparing texts, or it can highlight what is different. This is just as important because what keeps a genre fresh and popular is the ability of its producers to invent variation and difference, without losing the security (for the audience) of a degree of sameness or repetition.

The very existence of conventions allows the media producer to assume knowledge on the part of the audience, and to play with it. If the audience guesses that the body is going to fall out of the cupboard, then don't let this happen: anticipation and anti-climax. And, having lulled the audience, let the body fall out as the curtains are drawn: shock and the unexpected.

The same principle of using audience knowledge works with so-called **hybrid genres.** In such cases the audience is intrigued and pleasured by the grafting of one genre on to another. The television series *The Sopranos* fuses the soap and the Mafia movie, so that sentiment and home problems collide with scenes of violence and crime. This series, with its mixture of humour and personal grief might also be described as postmodern. For example, an episode shown in the UK in 2001 showed two Mafia members using butchers' tools to dismember a body. The black comedy of juxtaposition between their matter-of-fact conversation and the gory task, all held in a medium front shot, is very much of the style and form of what is called 'postmodernist form'. Here indeed, qualities such as irony, and matters of form, emerge as more important than plotting and the usual structural features. So, the handheld camera and formless narrative of *The Blair Witch Project* (2000) falls into the same category. The film's ability to engage the audience in a realist experience was more important than the formal plotting devices of classic modernism. Yet the film was still located in its horror genre because of the conventional use of elements like fearful reaction shots, heavy breathing and implied terrors just off-camera.

2.10 Genres and Histories

Genres – especially film genres – have a historical dimension that affects what they are supposed to be about. Sometimes it is 'history as origins' – genres like the western and the gangster movie are actually rooted in real events and real people. This is most obvious with biographical-type stories – films about Billy the Kid, for example. But genres also have their own histories; they develop over many years and build up their own background, which is familiar to fans of the genre. Tim Burton's *Mars Attacks* (1999) depended for its effect on audience knowledge of science fiction 'history' and of comics in particular.

In terms of actual history and genre history, there is also the phenomenon of **genre cycles**. In this case one recognizes phases in the development of a genre that have a lot to do with the events and the attitudes of society in a certain period of time. For example, there were a lot of sci-fi/horror films around in the 1950s – like *Them*, which was based on the idea of giant mutated ants – which were tied to contemporary fears about science and the effects of atomic radiation in particular. There were the Hammer horror films of the 1960s, which involved many busty female victims. These represented both a certain relaxation of cinema CENSORSHIP about showing cleavage and underwear, but also historically tied in with a conservative view of women's 'rightful' place as victims.

Genres can also 'eat themselves' by making stories explicitly about their own histories. A contemporary example is *Shadow of the Vampire* (2001), which is based on the making of the classic horror film *Nosferatu*.

So genres may be based on actual history. They will certainly re-write that history and make myths out of real events and people. They have their own history of development, but their history is also tied in with social change and shifting values, which can be read into the films of certain periods.

2.11 Genre, Industry and Audience

Figure 5.4 makes it clear that there is indeed a tight relationship between the media industries that manufacture genre products and the audience that consumes them. Genres are good for industries because they are generally good for profits. They are good for profits because, by definition, the audience pays for them consistently, and sometimes very well. The audience is attracted to genre material and pays for it because it takes pleasure and satisfaction from the material. The producers are also happy to make genre material because, being familiar, everyone knows how to handle it, and because they may literally be able to re-use sets and props. In television, the soap genre is of special economic importance because a successful soap provides a secure base on which to build an evening's programming, and a secure base on which to build a company's fortunes (*Brookside*).

The crucial entry point in the circle of profit and pleasure is the nature of this pleasure. I would suggest that there is something here that does not seem to be about pleasure at all, on the surface. This ties in with the messages the audience obtains from genre material (indeed all media product), whether consciously or unconsciously; and perhaps the important dimension is to do with confirmation of beliefs. **Genres tend to confirm what we believe and what we want to believe.**

This links with ideology once more. It ties in with a suggestion of Feuer (1987) that we can categorize genres in three ways.

1 The **ideological** refers to the idea that genres are distinctive in the way that they incorporate values of the dominant ideology; indeed that perhaps some genres incorporate values more or less specific to themselves. For example, most police detective stories endorse the position of the police person and the law.
2 **Ritual** is about the way in which genres distinctively cycle around between industry and audience. The 'fashion' for serial killer movies is a particular example of this.
3 **Aesthetic** is about textual characteristics – aspects of form.

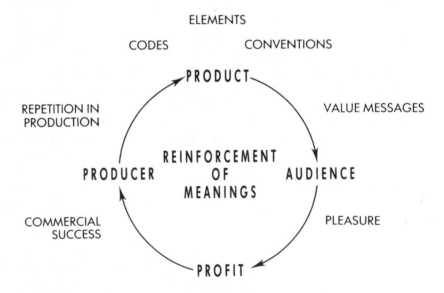

Fig. 5.4 Genre: a model describing key elements

The circle of pleasure and profit maintains the conventions and meanings of the genre.

2.12 Genre and Myth, Genre and Culture

These beliefs are part of our culture. They may be special to our culture. For instance, soaps deal with the idea of true love. Sometimes they send the belief message that true love is more important than material goods, and perhaps more important than marriage (infidelity is a popular theme). Many other cultures would reject both of these ideas out of hand. They would not even put them up for discussion in their own genres.

You should also realize that other cultures do have their own genres, which have exactly the same main elements as have been described. The Japanese enjoy Samurai stories – historical adventure dramas. We would find it a little difficult to make sense of them because we don't know the conventions. We would certainly not appreciate the full importance of their messages about respect, ritual and loyalty.

All media material is inevitably a product of the times and the culture that makes it. It is arguable that **genres have a special place** in this respect. This may be for two reasons. One is that they carry their messages in the protective wrapping of an established popular form of entertainment. The other is that they are based on core topics, which if not universal, at least don't age quickly. The crimes of thrillers, the family turmoil of soaps, the science of science fiction are likely to be with us for the foreseeable future. The war film, for example, may be 'used' to say things about real wars that concern people at a given period of time. *Saving Private Ryan* (1999) was a version of World War II for the American market. *Warriors* (2000) was for the Brits – about moral dilemmas in the Bosnian war for the British UN peacekeepers.

But, of course, genre is not only based on real events, or on factual events of history (see Section 2.10, above), **it may be based on versions of that history, or even on nothing more than myth and legend.** (A MYTH is a story that has no basis in fact, but that nevertheless represents some kind of truth for its culture.) The story of Billy the Kid has been re-written many times through the western in comics, novels and films. In general, those versions have become myth, because people wanted to believe that he was a genius with a gun, that he helped the poor, and so on. The truth is very dull and rather unpleasant, but many Americans want to believe in the individualist as hero, in the rightness of winning the west. In the same way, the Dracula horror story has been re-made many times in various media. The Bram Stoker novel is the genesis of this story, but this is almost irrelevant to the fact that audiences want to deal with their fears of death. They are fascinated by the idea of being immortal, yet feel one should be punished for becoming immortal like God. Hence the creation of the Dracula figure. As a piece of myth, it works through themes and anxieties within our culture.

There is also an interesting point about the association of genres with popular and therefore supposedly lowbrow culture. There is an opposed assumption (a dichotomy) that original, unpredictable non-genre material is somehow more highbrow, culturally superior, simply better. This valuing of that which is special and unique is rather peculiar to a western tradition. It is allied to the example of the status of the novel, created by the lone artist, and not in a genre. There is no absolute logic to this position. In India for example, endless re-tellings of the stories of the gods, whether in film or in puppet theatre, are not devalued in the minds of people simply because they are a genre.

2.13 Intertextuality

The notion of INTERTEXTUALITY is not peculiar to genres, but it is strongly exemplified by them. What it refers to is the way in which we understand one text by reference to others. The links between texts operate in many ways, the most basic of which will be the visual and verbal languages they share. On one broad level you could say that all comics are understood by reference to one another, even to all other texts. We understand the world with reference to everything that we have experienced. But intertextuality really makes sense when one gets down to specifics. For example, one understands a romantic kissing scene with reference to all other such scenes.

Other links are those to do with borrowed techniques or with allusions in one text to another. For example, in 2001 a series of advertisements on television for Lloyds Bank made light-hearted allusion to fairy stories, and also used the technique of having a voice-over story-teller.

Genres are understood intertextually, both through examples of the same genre and through other genres. So, in a particular sense, one understands aliens in science fiction by cross-referring one alien story with another, through our knowledge of other stories. In a more general sense, one understands aliens with reference to enemies in war films or creatures in horror films, for example.

So it seems that intertextual referencing works on three levels: the super-general; the general; and the specific. In the first case there is a kind of referencing that works even across genres – the racist image of a Latin villain in a western works in the context of other such villains in cop or spy thrillers. Second, referencing happens within the genre – one kind of robot in science fiction resonates off all robots in science fiction. Third, there is the explicit reference exemplified in the film *Scream 3* (2000) in which scenes and characters are intended to be understood by the audience as coming from other particular horror movies. This film is also an example of how intertextuality has become a key feature of postmodern media material, in which matters of form and reference are at least as important as structure and narrative direction.

Another way of recognizing intertextuality is in parodies. We understand the jokes through our knowledge of other genre texts. Parody reinforces the very existence of a genre because if we did not 'know' about the genre and its features it would not be possible for the author to make fun of them, knowing that the audience understands what is being referred to. As Lorimer (1994) says, 'intertextual connections are part of the taken-for-granted knowledge, understandings and competences used by consumers of popular culture'.

> **Genres and Ideology**
> Do you agree that genre stories tend to promote the ideas of 'those in authority'?
> Do genres sometimes push ideas that go against authority or conventional ways of
>   thinking about people and society?

2.14 Case Examples and Value Messages

I would like to round off this section by having a quick look at some specific
genres in various media. In particular, it is worth having a look at the
dominant characteristics and value messages present within each genre.
Remember that all fiction material now travels freely between film and
television media. All films are shot with the television aspect ratio (screen
proportions) in mind.

■ Film and Television Crime Thrillers

Television helps keep this genre alive through its appetite for more and more
material, so that new variations appear every year – *Lock, Stock* on British
television or *The Sopranos* from US television.

The ability to create action sequences and to go into real or simulated
locations gives a particular edge to this genre, which is also fed by
documentaries about police work and through crime-solving programmes such
as *Crimewatch*. It has a sense of being contemporary and immediate. Crime is
a topic in daily newspapers. However, it is worth pointing out that the sense of
realism in crime genre material may be that of the hall of mirrors. We get our
ideas about 'real' crime from the media, for the most part. Authentic accents or
locations don't make the material substantially true.

The genre concentrates not merely on the cop hero as crime solver, but on
the nature of the crime and on retribution for the criminal. The cop thriller
genre legitimizes the depiction of criminal acts, which has its own fascination.
It also must deal in fundamental value messages about right and wrong.

Indeed, the particular interest of such genre material is that it raises
questions about when the law is effective and when it is an ass; about when
police are fair and when they lapse into criminality themselves; about who
should be punished for what, and how. It raises questions about the nature of
punishment itself. It has been argued that the genre is popular because it raises
questions that people are anxious about – the extent of crime and what is being
done about it. Others argue that the genre actually creates anxieties. Certainly
it represents crime in a way that does not fit reality. For example, it is not the
apparently vulnerable who are most likely to be victims of crime – it is young
males. Others again would argue that crime stories are ways of
accommodating and resolving lawlessness in the minds of society. If one
believes that the genre overall deals with the crime it depicts, then it is telling
the audience that crime is managed by authority and can be dealt with.

This of course is a notably ideological position. In this sense, beneath the action and the human drama, cop thrillers are very political stories. This genre explores morality and issues of social control. Although many crime stories endorse the need for a certain kind of law and order that works for the status quo, again it is fair to say that some question this. Genres can be challenging under the cloak of conventional elements.

■ Magazine Romantic Stories

One should distinguish between these stories and romance as a mode of treatment of stories in general. These stories do contain repetitive elements as described above, whereas romance in general may appear in almost any other kind of story in any other medium in any other genre.

Such romantic fiction centres on a heroine, with strong supporting roles of female rival and best friend, and the male romantic object. It has well-defined plots and stock situations involving romantic encounters, romantic conflicts, and obstructions to romance. Its iconography is least well defined. So far as it is distinctive, it relies a great deal on the exchange of looks, the embrace and the kiss. The backgrounds are often historical (poor girl in love with rich man) or exotic (she met him on holiday in a foreign place). There is also a strong vein of background realism (girl next door falls in love with home town boy). Again, backgrounds are not strong in iconographic terms, once more weakening this as a distinctive genre.

The dominant themes or messages are about the value of romantic love, often tied to the value of marriage as a means of sealing that love (and ending the story!). It is significant that romantic stories for young females rarely engage with life after marriage or with serious issues of personal relationships – all that matters is love itself. Associated messages are about the importance of being the centre of the loved one's attention, about being misunderstood by parents and/or friends, about being recognized as an attractive and loving person.

■ Television Quiz Shows

Because genres are dominantly fiction, this may seem at first an unusual example. But, in fact, it works if one looks at quiz shows in detail. Indeed it shows the power of packaging media material, and the convenience of typing it for producers and audience.

Quiz shows are a kind of story. If we concentrate on the subgenre of game shows, then the compere is a kind of narrator who takes us through a familiar story of competition and success. The participants are the heroes and heroines. The obligatory female is one stock character, the studio audience is another. The icons are the well-known compere and the sets with flashing lights, display boards and the like. An example of a stock situation is when the competitor has to make a decision as to whether or not they will go on to the next stage of the game, take the money on offer, or whatever.

These stories also have value messages attached to them. Remember that these are the whole point of examining and describing the characteristics of this genre. These messages are about it being OK to compete and to aspire to material goods. They are about turning the consumption of goods into fun.

And there are other messages that have to do with stereotyping (see Section 3.1, below). The treatment of the female 'hostesses' as objects is a fairly obvious example. Less obvious examples come through the treatment of the participants by the compere. Usually they are talked to in such a way that they are firmly subjugated within the television system. It is as if that system does not want the participants to get above themselves: they must stay within the rules laid down by the programme. I have even heard remarks made about the national dress of ethnic minority participants. These remarks clearly conveyed messages about what was to be seen as 'normal' and 'dominant' in our culture. They diminished the participants. They were essentially racist.

■ Television News

This is another overtly non-fictional genre that looks more fictional the more closely one inspects it.

Again, we have an omniscient narrator, who might also double as hero, steering us through the events of the day, coping with news coming in through the earpiece, bringing the drama to a successful close with the final summary and amusing tailpiece. Stock characters in this drama are the reporters, star subjects of world events, the experts and the eyewitnesses. The main plot of the news has its highs and lows of drama like any story. The individual stories are themselves dramatized to a greater or lesser degree, having qualities of conflict and suspended endings so that we watch the next episode to see who will 'win'. Stock situations exist because the news has its conventions of content and treatment like any genre. These conventions add up to the same thing as NEWS VALUES. For example, what is valued, as a rule, is disaster, major political decisions, deaths of the famous, royal activities … you can add to this list for yourself.

The **dominant meanings** of this genre are first to do with the authority and integrity of the news organization itself. This is essential if it is to be believed and trusted: hence the conventions of treatment such as face to camera, actuality film footage, conventional-looking newsreaders and reporters. But, second, these meanings are to do with the kind of world that we live in. These messages very much support what is called the **dominant ideology** – that is, the view of the world held by those people in our culture who actually run things. The truth or importance of these messages is another matter. What gives cause for concern is the way they are obscured by being naturalized. As viewers we should be able to decode the communication completely so that we can decide whether or not to accept such messages. On one level we should be able to stop and decide whether or not we really want valuable news screen time occupied with the activities of a wealthy middle-aged lady called the Queen. Maybe she isn't that important. On another level, we might ask ourselves whether messages about the importance of increasing industrial output, of having continued economic growth, are also valid. They may fit one view of the world, of a certain kind of capitalism, but there is nothing intrinsically good or right about perpetually producing more goods. It might be good to have a situation in which no one gets more of anything, but in which our culture improves the quality of what it has got. These comments are not meant to represent any one view as 'right', nor are they meant to suggest that all news is biased or completely lacking in alternative views on issues and events, but they are meant to question the notion of being right, which is at the heart of news messages about our way of life.

■ *Film Noir*

This brief case example is interesting for two reasons. First, because it has never really made it on to the small screen successfully, though there have been examples, such as *Hazell*, a private eye series, back in the 1970s. Second, it clearly raises questions about how far genre is about form or content.

The original film noir goes back to the 1940s and films like *The Big Sleep* (1947). Typically it is about a private eye investigating murder and a web of deceit, at the centre of which is not just the criminal but also the femme fatale – the seductive, attractive, deceitful and usually destructive woman. In this respect we have a genre formula – protagonist (the private eye), antagonist (the corrupt villain), stock characters (the femme fatale), typical plot situations (private eye gets slugged or drugged in one scene), typical backgrounds (rain on the city streets), and so on. A later example would be *Chinatown* (1973).

But then what is also distinctive about the genre is its style – high-key lighting that creates harsh contrasts between strongly lit faces and dark menacing backgrounds. Also its camera work – disturbing angles, distorting wide-angle lenses. Such devices for creating a sense of disturbance and fear combine with tortuous plots, nasty kinds of suffering and murder, and ambiguous morality to create a notable mood of cynicism and fear. This style, these preoccupations, came to be applied to any number of crime stories – genres such as murder mystery, cop thriller, even spy stories. John Dahl is a contemporary director who has used such content and style in a number of his movies. *The Last Seduction* (1994) has the femme fatale as the lead and dominant character, who screws the males in all senses of the word. There are scenes using lighting and camera in a 'typical' manner. But then this isn't true of the whole film. And if the story is about crime, it isn't about a private eye obsessively trying to unfold a mystery. Michael Mann's *The Keep* (1983) is actually a kind of horror story, set in an old castle towards the end of the last war. But it is stuffed to the point of melodrama with film noir stylistic devices.

In a sense it is typical of genre that, contradictorily, it starts off being all about a category, but in the end categorizations fail because genres also mix with one another as they explore the limits of their themes, their content and their form.

3 REPRESENTATIONS

Just as the material that rolls off the production line is dominated by genres, so too **there are dominant representations of people in the product**. In fact, many of these representations appear in genres, though not exclusively. For example, newspapers represent groups of people in certain ways. Advertising – which is

Activity (12): Genre

To investigate the relationship between genre and audience, take an episode of one soap opera and LIST ALL THE ELEMENTS OF PLOT, CHARACTER AND THEME THAT YOU CONSIDER WOULD APPEAL TO A FEMALE AUDIENCE IN PARTICULAR.

- Identify those elements you think are typical of this kind of programme.
- Discuss your results with someone of different gender to you, to evaluate how valid your findings and judgements seem to be.

a way of using various media – certainly does this. Even pop music may give us such representations through videos and, possibly, lyrics.

So, once more, look at the media as a whole if you can. Because the ways in which women or students or working people are represented are put together across the media and understood by us through all the media. If you think this sounds like more repetition and reinforcement, then you are right.

What is represented is certain views of these social groups. It is these views that, unconsciously, we learn to accept as normal – to the exclusion of alternative views. Too often such views are negative. In his book *Hiding in the Light* (1988), Dick Hebdige points to the ways in which young people are represented in terms of 'confrontations, of consumption and of life style'. So often they exist in media texts only when they are a problem.

In the soap *EastEnders*, one has the example of one of the young male leads who is clearly a problem. He has stolen goods, bunked off school and got a girl pregnant. The girl herself is also about 'a problem' – the teenage mum. This is not to say that such representations are disconnected from social reality, but it is the case that young people in such series are rarely shown as 'not a problem' – rather like 'good news', which doesn't make conventionally attractive news material. The pages of young women's magazines are full of problems. The accumulative message is, 'you're young, so you've got a problem' or 'you are a problem'.

Another touchstone of the collective representation of the young is in television sitcoms. The film *Kevin and Perry Go Large* (2000) is a spin-off from Harry Enfield's television parody of the difficult, inarticulate teenager. The Asian comedy team behind *Goodness, Gracious Me* has a pair of inarticulate, awkward Asian hip-hoppers. Ali G of Channel 4's *Da Ali G Show* parodies hip-hop youth culture, managing simultaneously to ask interviewees piercing questions and yet making his assumed character look stupid. These kinds of representations operate in a collective way across the media. The accumulative effect of representations is like death by a thousand cuts.

It is arguable that representations also create groups that may not actually exist, in our complex societal relationships. So I might suggest that the very idea of and definition of different youth subcultures – of the teenager – is one that has, to a fair extent, been created by the media. It is convenient to media

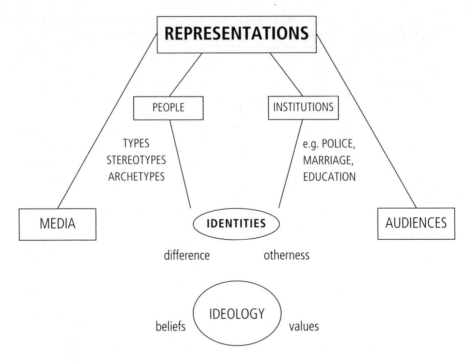

Fig. 5.5 Concept diagram: representations

producers to generate a recognizable group called 'youth' and then divide it down, because that enables them to target material at the groups. Indeed, the very process of creating a group in people's minds becomes the same as disempowering that group, attracting negative baggage.

3.1 Representation by Type

You may think that this section is really just about stereotypes, but people can be represented in certain ways through certain devices without becoming actual stereotypes. Also, the term representation needs to be explained through other concepts (see Section 4, below).

I would suggest that when it comes to putting people into categories, there are actually three levels at which this happens. At each level the representation becomes simpler, cruder, more generalized, more clichéd, more worrying in terms of the value messages underlying what we see or read.

■ *Types*

At the most general level we can talk about something called a type. We recognize a category of character in a story, such as the shopkeeper type, but for various reasons this character does not emerge as a stereotype. One reason may simply be that the character is not drawn in very strongly; it may also be that it lacks a clear set of characteristics reinforced by years of repetition, which mark immediate stereotypes such as the fanatical German officer in a war comic. Again, it may be that, while the character is a recognizable type in a story (the eccentric old lady who solves crimes over her knitting), the fact is that it is actually drawn in some depth.

■ Stereotypes

The true stereotype is a simplified representation of human appearance, character and beliefs. It has become established through years of representation in the media, as well as through assumptions in everyday conversation. It is a distortion of the original type because it exaggerates as well as simplifies. It has qualities of being instantly recognizable, usually through key details of appearance. It has attached to it implicit judgements about that character (covert value messages).

Stereotypes are not only attached to disempowered groups – the disabled, the housewife. There are stereotypes of 'upper class' or 'the flashy rich bastard', but what happens in both cases is that the group stereotyped is diminished by the representation, and the creator or consumer of the representation feels different and more powerful themselves.

Stereotypes are much like icons of genre in that they are recognizable and they do carry along ideas. Stereotypes are not necessarily bad in themselves – it depends on how they are used and what value judgements they unlock. For example, a 'safety in the home' advertisement including a comfortable granny in a rocking chair, which is used to make children aware of the dangers from electric sockets in the home, could be said to be OK. It represents the granny as kind and careful; it is being used for a socially approvable purpose. Whether all older females wish to be seen in this way is another matter, of course ...

■ Archetypes

The most intense examples of types are also very deeply embedded in our culture. They are the arch-heroes, heroines and villains who epitomize the deepest beliefs, values and, perhaps, prejudices of a culture. Superman is an archetype, just as all those heroes from mythology are archetypes. Archetypal characters in genres really belong to all of them, and are not entirely special to any one. For instance, the power-hungry villain who wants to destroy the world might turn up in spy thrillers, science fiction or horror stories. Qualities of courage or beauty, goodness or evil, are drawn most firmly and simply in these archetypes. They are the stuff of comics (*Judge Dredd*), of cheap television (*Buffy the Vampire Slayer*) of low-budget film (the *Nightmare on Elm Street* cycle). They may be enjoyable in the story, whatever the medium, but they also take us into realms of fantasy.

3.2   Representations and their Construction

We have said that groups of people are represented in certain ways through the media. This representation also helps create the idea that people are defined as belonging to certain groups. So it seems that **the media organize our understanding of categories of people and about why certain people should belong to certain categories.** These categories become part of our thinking

Fig. 5.6 A stereotype: with analysis of key features

Fig. 5.7 From *Police, Camera, Action* and *The Bill*: representations of the police

The two images of the police from one fiction and one factual programme both contribute to the total of all such representations (not to mention to representations of law and order). In one still, a real policeman is attending an incident on the motorway, involving a burning lorry. In the other, a fake policeman is questioning a boy in the street. You couldn't tell for certain that one image is from a fiction and one from a documentary – something to discuss in the first place. But then one also has to consider how the police are represented overall, in terms of what they do, what they are like – in the end, how we are to regard them. These policemen are out on the street, involved in drama, dealing with people, on active duty. The police I know actually have quite a lot of dull repetitive work to do. But this is hardly represented in the media. You can take it from there in terms of adding to what you believe is said through the media about police work and the law.

process. We use them to judge people in the real world as well as in the media. Such categories are called perceptual sets. So representations of people in the media help build and maintain these perceptual sets, which we use in everyday life.

Types are a construction within the mind. They are composed from certain elements. In exactly the same way as genre, the elements become familiar the more they are used – repetition and reinforcement. In the first place, these elements are those of **physical appearance**: hair, clothes, distinguishing features. In fact, some people think that this is all that representation is about, and so completely miss the point about meaning and value messages. **Typing takes place by age, by race, by occupation, by gender.** Let us consider the elderly oriental male. This wise cliché will of course have features such as a wispy beard and moustache, long grey braided hair, a gown to wear, and an inscrutable gaze. He has a long pedigree, all the way from the *Fu Manchu* films of the 1930s, to the *Rupert Bear* comic stories in the 1950s, through to the computer-generated character in the *Blair Witch* computer game for the new millennium. But this type, like others, is also constructed from certain behaviours, actions and relationships. These other elements of construction may appear in our example as dignified restrained behaviour, acting according to a sense of honour, perhaps using magic or so called oriental wiles, and lacking relationships other than that of master to pupil.

Another example might be the mad scientist, who also has a long history – the films about *Frankenstein* in the 1930s, *Dr Strangelove* in the 1960s, *Back to the Future* in the 1980s, and so on. This character is likely to be a lone male, eccentric, sometimes pathological, probably with wild hair, untidy clothes and behavioural tics. Such a representation does no favours to the public and career images of scientists and of science. Elaborations on the character include being obsessional, not being able to form relationships, lacking a sense of social graces and conventions. In many ways the mad scientist is represented as a case of arrested development.

Representations are also constructed through the medium used: the written or visual language that tells the story. If we consider television or film, then it is, for example, obvious that close-ups of physical attributes are used to draw attention to them, and so they cue us into the type that is being built up. This refers to how the type is constructed as much as to what it is constructed of. In the case of our oriental, a typical close-up would be a reaction shot, drawing attention to the character's impassive expression and reflectiveness when faced with a problem.

3.3   Representation, Meaning and Ideology

What is represented through these types is far more than a view of categories of people or of what they are supposed to look like. We are also seeing a representation of attitudes towards that type. Because they are constructed with certain characteristics and treated in a certain way in the story, **we are told implicitly what we should think of them.** We are being told what the type should mean to us. **We are being given a set of value judgements** because we are decoding value messages behind the surface representation. In the case of our mad scientist, the representation links to ideology because it connects with a fear of the power of knowledge. Science can produce a kind of power over our material and psychological world. It can bring changes to the world as we know it. We fear change. It can threaten our belief structures, not least those incorporated within our religions. So scientists have to be 'kept in their place' by being shown as not knowing everything, or being ridiculous, evil or even wrong.

All types carry meanings of one sort or another, which may be critical of or demeaning towards the category of person so created and represented. One favourite type of comedy has been that focusing on the mother-in-law – unattractive, strident, demanding, in battle with the relevant son- or daughter-in-law. Individual examples representing this type may vary in treatment. Only some may be thought stark enough to be considered downright stereotypical. But if we take all the examples together, then what is represented is more than the appearance and behaviour of this female, it is also what this behaviour means. It may mean, for instance, something about male fears of strong-minded females, especially those who cannot be dealt with slickly in terms of their overt sexuality.

3.4   Absence Means Something Too

With regard to people and types, it is worth realizing that meanings about groups of people are created by omission. In one study of American magazine fiction it was pointed out that, while ethnic minorities formed 40 per cent of the total population, they only appeared in fiction as 10 per cent of the characters. In this country, minority ethnic groups form about 5 per cent of the total population, but even this small percentage may be significant by its absence. We can point to the fact that, for instance, Asian minorities are relatively absent from sitcoms. If one misses out groups within the population then one is saying things about their lack of importance, as well as about the relative importance of those who *are* represented.

If one looks at tables (see, for example, Table 5.2) describing the presence and absence of non-white presenters in certain television programmes (Philo, 1999) then the patterns of results speak for themselves. There is something odd about television where, even in a selected research period, no non-white people present the weather or quiz shows.

Another category of person notable for their absence is that of the disabled. Of course, this covers a wide range of disablement, including those who become disabled through accident not birth, through illness or through age. More than 10 per cent of the British population is disabled to some degree and in some respect. Much quoted research by Negrine (1992) suggests that only 1.5 per cent of characters portrayed on television are disabled. The difference between the two sets of figures certainly suggests that this category of people is rendered less significant by being relatively invisible.

Table 5.2 a and b The representation of race in terms of TV presenters

a) Programme categories containing white presenters only

Type	Programmes	Presenters	Non-white	White
Light entertainment	11	13	–	13
Quiz shows	20	20	–	20
Game shows	14	14	–	14
Comedy/satire	5	7	–	7
Chat shows	5	6	–	6
Music	5	5	–	5
Weather	115	115	–	115
Business news	9	14	–	14
Current affairs	18	19	–	19
Documentary/features	8	11	–	11
Garden & home	5	11	–	11
Health	5	5	–	5
Travel & holiday	1	1	–	1
Consumer	6	11	–	11
Access	3	3	–	3

b) Programme categories containing non-white presenters

Type	Programmes	Presenters	Non-white	White	Non-white male	Non-white female
News	146	173	24	149	4	20
Audience participation	8	8	1	7	1	–
Cookery	11	11	1	10	1	–
Religion	7	7	2	5	–	2
Science	1	2	1	1	–	1
Sport	22	36	2	34	1	1
Lifestyle	17	83	8	75	8	–
National history	7	9	1	8	–	1
Children's TV	59	93	12	81	5	7
Education	58	77	15	62	10	5

Source: Philo, 1999

Representations and their Ideas

Do representations of people promote false ideas about social groups?
Do they just use general views and opinions to make a 'good story'?

4 REPRESENTATION AND CULTURE

When the media represent groups of people, they also say things about their culture or subculture. The media tell us a great deal about US culture and the American way of life. They tell us about British cultures and subcultures – youth, the Scots, northerners. Whether what they tell us is the truth is another matter. What is true is that a certain view of these cultures is represented.

What these views are partly depends on what the audience chooses to view and read. On the one hand, if you took in documentary and current affairs material in broadcasting, as well as the quality press, then you could have a fairly wide-ranging view of the USA. On the other hand, if you only view American television thriller series, read the tabloids and popular magazines, then you will have another view, which could be described as limited. This view puts white American males up front, emphasizes violence, shows far more of the city than of the countryside, is mainly concerned with issues of law and order, and so on.

So **not only are the media selective in the views of culture they show, we the audience are selective too in what we choose to take from the media.** Having recognized this, it is still fair to comment on the ways in which the media do indeed define our views of culture and of cultural groups in particular. For instance, Britain, like most countries, tends to have one consensus view of our 'main' culture, with views of separate regions measured in some contrast to this. That is to say, all our national media are based in, and reflect a consensus view out of, London and the south. This may be comparable to a centralized Parisian view of France contrasted with views of the Bretons or of the southern French. In the USA, New York and Los Angeles may define the centre, as compared with the south or the midwest.

British northerners (or Bretons or midwesterners) are rightly recognized as a subcultural division. What may not be right is the way that they are represented. Our northerner, as perceived through television comedy, magazine articles or radio drama, frequently comes across as plain-speaking, living in a relatively poor urban environment and much occupied with sports such as football and rugby. You can elaborate on this view of the northern type. It is symbolized by fictional media characters such as the elderly heroes of the television drama series, *Last of the Summer Wine*. We see and hear little or nothing about young people in the north or about fine arts in the north, nor even about economic success in the north.

We can extend this kind of analysis of cultural definition to all kinds of groups and areas. We may ask ourselves what view is given us of Muslim culture in Britain or of rural life. Then we may ask where our views, our images, come from. And then we may question their validity.

4.1 Identity, Difference, Otherness

Representations help create an identity for the group being represented. They often assume that an identity already exists. They trade off previous representations to reinforce an existing identity. What is often of concern is that the identity (or representation or stereotype), may be a negative one. It works against the interests of the group being represented, but for the interests of a larger group. This larger group is assumed to exist, perhaps in opposition to the group identified. For example, the group described as 'travellers' has an identity that partly trades off other representations such as 'hippie', and previous models such as 'gypsy'. The identity comprises features such as rootlessness, lawlessness, fecklessness. These negative features work against the interests of such people wishing to lead an independent, alternative lifestyle. They assume by contrast that the majority of citizens are responsible and law abiding, and more approvable as people.

Identity is about how we come to see and to value ourselves, partly as a result of taking in media representations. It is also about how others come to see us: 'we' are one thing, 'they' are another. The media can picture us to ourselves as we are seen by others. We acquire ideas about how we may be seen as different.

This is a classic model in which the differences of the group singled out are emphasized by contrast with the main culture. These differences may be to do with looks, religious practices, social behaviour, morality. **The identity is one of being different.** In some cases, as much as having difference imposed on them, some subcultural groups may wish to assert difference in order to maintain their distinction from the dominant culture. Rastafarians are both represented through oft-repeated surface features such as dreadlocks and the smoking of ganja, and they may assert such features along with others, such as the value placed on family life.

The idea of 'difference' contains the implications of 'normal' and 'standard' – a benchmark. If a group is identified as a group then it is also identified as being different from other groups, a minority as opposed to a majority.

Representations are negative when they emphasize that the given group is composed of 'others'. They are not like 'us'. This is what racism is about: accentuating difference but ignoring similarity. It is the same thing for class or for age, for criminals and prisons.

The combination of difference and otherness, incorporated within an identity, acts as a way of pushing the group so created to the margins, to the edge of what is acceptable. For example, there are variations on the threatening older woman theme – 'hag', 'witch', 'mother-in-law', 'old bag'. I suggest that to give older women such identities in stories is a way of disempowering them and of diminishing a threat to males. The 'problem' for others is that such women may be other than compliant, prepared for marriage, evidently young and attractive, looking for a partner – in other words they are not easily represented as young women are in pop videos, magazines or any number of media examples.

4.2   Common Sense and Naturalization

The beliefs represented about groups and institutions are given the force of being 'naturalized'. They are endorsed by a discourse of common sense. So everyone 'knows' that it is common knowledge that old women aren't sexy. Views about what is OK or not OK are endorsed as common sense. Opposing views are therefore made difficult, to the point of impossible, to conceive of.

Representations feed back into these beliefs, to confirm or oppose them. This circularity creates dominant meanings, which in turn reinforce the dominant aspects of ideology.

The NATURALIZATION of the beliefs behind representations is also part of ideology. It makes natural and common sense that which is neither of those things. Some will argue that being gay is unnatural. This is far from true: the study of many species reveals frequent examples of same-sex bonding. Some have tried to argue against immigrants and immigration on grounds of 'common sense'. But there is no common agreement on the sense of such racist views. There isn't even any material sense to them, given the declining numbers in European populations and workforces.

It can be said that 'common sense' and 'naturalization' of views are themselves manifestations of ideology – hegemony or the invisible exercise of power at work – ways of stopping people from seeing that representations are actually against their interests.

4.3   Institutions and Groups

Institutions such as the police or family are represented to us in various ways. This happens in genres especially, but also in other material. These representations are reinforced across the media – intertextuality at work again. They are usually mixed up with the representation of people by type. For example, one is likely to talk about how the media portray old age if one talks about how they portray old people and, maybe, how they represent the institutions of old people's homes.

Again, if one teases out the full range of meanings in a genre text, perhaps through structural analysis, then one may also end up talking about the meanings given by representation. For example, in soaps, one kind of structure is provided by the different families and the pattern of relationships within the family. Often, one family may be opposed to another, or members of a family will be in patterns of bonding and conflict. But in talking about what that structure is and why it matters in terms of making sense of the story, then one is like to say something about how families are represented – as a shifting pattern of enmities and alliances. One is getting to the same meanings in media study by different routes of analysis.

Genres in particular offer us formulaic and fairly predictable versions of people, institutions and aspects of our culture. Genres include material such as news. In this case the representation is largely not fictionalized, and is closer to life than, say, an escapist action movie. Yet even here it is worth noticing that, whatever the medium, news is a re-presentation of events, of people, of views. It is still a version of the world.

The word representation can be instructive if it demands that we ask questions such as the following.

- How is this topic being represented?
- Through what particular devices?
- Why is it being represented in this way?
- In whose interests is this representation?
- What is really being said about the topic being represented?

In discussing representation, McQuail (1992) refers to the example of crime reporting with reference to various pieces of research over the last 30 years. He says that 'the media consistently underplay petty, non-violent and white-collar offences, and emphasize interpersonal, violent, high-status and sexual crime'. So it is that we acquire a notion of categories of crime, as well as of categories of criminal.

■ Representations of the Disabled

If one takes people with disabilities as an example, then it is clear that representations that show them as 'unable', as a 'problem', as 'other', are not in their interests. The fact that they are lumped together (like black people or Asian people) further concentrates on the common denominator of impairment (not wholly capable), and ignores the enormous differences between kinds of disability and their causes. One stands in a different relationship to the world if one is partially deaf or if one suffers from cystic fibrosis. The disabled are diminished by being lumped into a mass. They are marginalized by representations that concentrate on the impairment and that ignore all the other capacities of that person. This 'ignoring' may include the failure of the rest of the world to provide enough hearing loops or lifts, for example. Disability is represented to the disabled, not just to the rest of us. It may not be how they see themselves – as, at worst, not fully human. In many images, the wheelchair is an icon of a 'condition'. It represents a lack of ability to participate in work or play or sex. Actually the wheelchair is an aid and a convenience for someone with certain kinds of difficulty: it is just a fact of life, not a stigma.

The representation of disablement intersects with others – with gender, for example. The female disabled can end up as being shown as a special class of victim. The male is often shown as being deprived of rightful active characteristics, but struggling against this to overcome adversity, to become active in some other way. The Tom Cruise character in *Born on the Fourth of July* (1990) is a classic example of this.

It is instructive to compare the news media representation of the blind Education Minister, David Blunkett, with the fictional representation of the deceased cellist Jacqueline Du Pre, in *Hilary and Jackie* (1998). Blunkett's disability is largely ignored. There is little comment on his guide dog or on his mobility. He is a man doing a job, not a blind person. He is a powerful politician. But in the film the heroine is shown in a descent from a state of grace – perhaps being punished for seducing her sister's husband – and certainly more and more as a non-person, as a classic victim. Her representation is dominated by her disability in more ways than are explained by the fact that it did in the end kill her. It is the kind of false perception described elsewhere as 'the halo effect': concentration on one feature by the perceiver so as to be blind to the other characteristics of the person perceived.

It has been suggested that negative representations of the disabled have something to do with fear. We fear impairment, we fear the unknown, we fear the less than perfect – thank you, advertising! – and so we try to diminish that which we fear. If representations reduce the disabled to 'victims' or to 'children' then they become more manageable in our heads. As Jessica Evans suggests (1998) representations of disablement, especially in adverts, conveniently ignore social issues about how we don't integrate the disabled with the rest of society. They often show disablement as a 'pathology' – the problem of a condition that has to be cured.

On the positive side, one can refer to examples such as the reporting of the Paralympics (2000), which did celebrate achievement, which did show athletes competing and succeeding within the terms of disability, not in spite of it. Another positive example is the character David in *Four Weddings and a Funeral*, who is played by a deaf actor. His part is integral to the story. He is neither patronized nor marginalized.

This is in effect an alternative representation, an alternative pattern to the way things are dominantly handled. Alternative does not have to mean opposite. To substitute a domineering female boss for a male equivalent in some drama does nothing to empower the representation of women. Rather, one looks for that representation of a woman in an economically powerful role that takes it for granted that she handles the responsibility, happens to be female and in no way drags in conventional features such as drawing attention to body image.

Activity (13): Representations

Use a set of newspapers for one day (for example, from a library) to carry out the following activity.

MAKE A LIST OF WHICH SOCIAL GROUPS ARE REPRESENTED IN THE NEWSPAPERS. It is up to you to choose your categories, such as age, gender, class, occupation, ethnic background.

Having made your list, then make another list of those social groups that are not represented.

From these lists, you can draw conclusions about who is on the news agenda, and which groups are excluded.

5 PRESENTERS, PERSONALITIES, STARS

5.1   The Importance of Personalities

The media rely on 'star characters' as a means of contact with the audience for much of their product. These characters achieve both larger-than-life qualities and also a comfortable familiarity, so that for the television audience they are integrated into their circle of friends. People go to see an actor from a radio soap series such as *The Archers* open a fête: they go to see the character from the drama, not the actor. People write in to agony aunts as if they were an intimate friend. Readers write to the editor of comic books such as *Superman*, discussing the life and history of the hero as if he were a real person, not a figure of fantasy. Of course this says a great deal about the audience, and its needs and perceptions. But the media collaborate in this familiar relationship. They do it of course because it makes for good ratings and sales. People are interested in people. What the audience is encouraged to forget is that they are not dealing with real people, only a symbolic version of a person represented through forms of communication. And even if I now continue to refer to the real person behind the newspaper article or in front of the camera, then still the character that we perceive is different from this real person. It is constructed through the medium.

Such **characters are constructed like representations** (and may draw on types). For example, the comedian Jim Davidson fronts various television shows: his persona is that of the 'cheeky London chap', always there with a quick comment. Such a character has a long tradition in British comedy. He has brought his persona to hosting television chows. Equally, some hosts – Oprah Winfrey or Mark Lamarr – are 'made' through their hosting. They build a successful persona: television makes them a star. The personality cult is strongest in television, with thousands of hours a year to fill, and with its point of intimacy in the home. It is a medium that encourages an emphasis on character because of this point of reception and because its visual images represent a simulation of life experience and interactions. But even other media can trade on personality. Newspapers have their columnists – the vituperative Julie Burchill, say. Radio has its voices – one of the most famous has been Alistair Cooke, with decades of his *Letter from America*.

5.2   Stars

'Stars' are actors or actresses who achieve enormous status because of the attractive persona they project. It is significant that the word usually refers to film and not to television. The international scope of the film market and the previous dominance of the film industry (which, after all, invented the star system) have contributed to this. Another crucial difference is that film is known to be something made, an edited, fixed story that is not happening as we watch it. But television is quite often live and very often deludes the audience into thinking it is live even when it is actually pre-edited or just a

(a)

(b)

Fig. 5.8 A Channel 5 newsreader (a) and Ma Slater from *EastEnders* (b)

'Personalities' are manufactured in the first place because of their sheer repetition – their exposure to the audience. In this case it follows that genre material is most likely to generate personalities, like this character from *EastEnders* (b) or the newsreader from Channel 5 (a). These people have a persona, composed of various qualities that also come to stand for the programmes with which they are associated. Is there something about the newsreader's persona as standing for the style-with-news authority of Channel 5? Is there something about Ma Slater that stands for the matriarchal qualities in soap operas?

repeat. Again, the viewing conditions are different: cinema-going is a more exotic activity than sitting in one's living room. Even now cinema stories often operate on a scale, within backgrounds, that the small screen can neither afford nor do justice to. So it is that film stars also lend themselves more readily to achieving the archetypal and mythic persona.

Robert de Niro has that quality that makes him bankable – the tough, don't-mess-with-me and even slightly out of control character that he has built through films such as *Mean Streets*, *Taxi Driver* and *Cape Fear*. Even as the sax-playing Jimmy Doyle in *New York, New York*, or as the gangster who needs a shrink in *Analyse This*, or in the comedy *Meet the Parents*, he retains that larger-than-life image. He is masculine, self-sufficient, has near-cocky self-assurance and a quick wit, which makes him admired and always watchable. Even in comedy or as a sympathetic character, there is something dangerous, unpredictable and yet attractive about his persona.

Julia Roberts is equally and archetypally a female persona, definitely sexy, but also vulnerable, feisty and with a sense of humour. She redeemed a shallow part in *Pretty Woman* by retaining a degree of dignity and determination – see also *Notting Hill*. These qualities – a female star to admire for a new decade – took central stage in *Erin Brockovich*. Here, as a mother of three she pulled her life back from disaster, won a lawsuit against a huge corporation, and netted the love and support of a biker-turned-househusband. This is not to argue that these films are profound, but the star persona transcends ordinary films.

What you need to do in dealing with the 'SO WHAT?' question is to consider first how the persona of stars is made up and, second, how it appeals through the medium. Because whatever it is that makes up these screen personalities (and even a journalist as personality or television star) is something that appeals to the values of the audience and that gives them pleasure. These are powerful points of contact. These bring in the punters. These make the films successful. Whatever value messages the star character communicates, these are the more significant because they are seen by so many people and appear to be so attractive to those people. And the messages communicated through the film as a whole are also likely to be worth examining because they are being reinforced by repetition to audiences in various countries.

The **star persona** is a set of characteristics projected by the star through the roles that they play. It is, if you like, the collection of dominant personality traits that we the audience read into the star's performance. It is arguable that some of the most successful stars can be 'read' positively in slightly different ways by different audiences, particularly different genders. For example, much has been written about Madonna, who can be read as sexually attractive by men, and as strong and sexy by women.

The **star as cultural myth** has much to do with how far the persona is in tune with the desires and beliefs of a culture at a particular time. Clint Eastwood has achieved mythic status partly because he has been so successful for so long in the entertainment world: famous for being famous.

Stars have commercial value. They can sell pictures and programmes. If you want to do a deal to make a picture then you need a package. Part of that package must be the star. The star's appeal to the audience can help sell the package and make the deal. And even once the picture is in production, **the star becomes a marketing tool**. There is a correlation between rise to fame and market value in the career of Ewan McGregor, who was catapulted by the indie hit *Trainspotting* to international billing in *Star Wars: the Phantom Menace*. The star image appears on posters, the star appears on television programmes or at film festivals. Stars boost profits. Even a successful television anchor as star can secure a good contract because their appeal makes for good ratings.

So stars are very important to media product, both in terms of commercial profit for the institution, and in terms of attraction for the audience. They are also important to media study because whatever it is that appeals says a lot about ourselves, our beliefs and values.

5.3   Presenters and Personalities

The same argument applies to the presenters and personalities of television. They are crucial in our understanding of most programmes. They, like stars in film, attract us to the programmes. They also carry meanings within the persona that they project, and bring us to the programme as a whole, with all the other messages and meanings this may hold.

Many programmes rely on the **presenter as a point of contact**: chat shows, quiz shows, news, documentaries, current affairs, magazine and consumer advice shows. The presenter becomes another person in the living room. The personality creates the atmosphere for the show: jolly, serious, knowledgeable, or whatever. She or he becomes **the narrator of the storyline** that is unfolded through the programme. The presenter often explains things to us, introduces people to us. Most of all the presenter has the privilege of talking to the camera. The director (or the editor) makes sure that they do. They are given the screen time to establish their personality and their relationship with the audience. Other people are denied this privilege. There is no justification for this convention, but it is very powerful. News reporters or even chat show hosts hate it if the subject addresses the camera and so the audience. This upsets the mythology of their special relationship with us, the audience. The power of the look, of face-to-face address is considerable. The viewer is directly engaged by the eyes, which is very different from simply watching a vox pop in the street or a conversation in the studio.

So you should look at what the presenter does for the programme, and how they shape its 'story'. You should consequently consider the power they have to shape the meaning we take from that programme, especially as their position is endorsed by addressing the camera (often helped by the invisible autocue). I also suggest that you evaluate the significance of all this by working out what happens when the rules are broken. Why does it matter when the vision mixer makes a mistake and cuts to a side view of the presenter addressing us?

Part of the answer lies in the fact that presenters contribute to the 'seamless robes' of television. **They are there to keep things running smoothly, to make sure that we are not aware of the technology that makes it all possible.** It could be said that they are there to stop us asking questions about what we are being told. Even the presenters of quality documentaries are part of this mythology of the effortless power of television. They too can become elevated by the medium. The historian guides us through places, documents, reconstructions, as if a god, and much like the newsreader.

Television also relies on the personality of the characters who front its drama. This is especially so in the case of the soaps, *Roseanne* or *EastEnders*. It is arguable whether these well-known people should be regarded as stars or personalities. If there is any distinction to be made it is in respect of awe and intimacy. The stars of film are unattainable and untouchable.

Often their parts are not representative of our everyday experience, but many of television's fiction stars have roles within our life experience. They are not heroic. They make publicity appearances as they try both to trade off their popularity and yet also enhance it by being seen. These television stars are, by and large, much like the presenters – even though they do not talk to us, they create an intimate and familiar relationship between the programme and the audience.

The significance of presenters and stars in the media is partly that they provide a crucial bond between the medium and the audience. They are a commercial element within the product. They pull in the audience. They perform certain functions according to certain rules, which affect how television programmes in particular are understood.

Personalities and Television

Are personalities on television essential to how television programmes work for the enjoyment and understanding of the audience?

Could the programmes function without many of these people?

REVIEW

You should have learned the following things from this chapter about media texts – genres, representations and stars.

1 REPETITION

- The main elements of media product and the way that these are treated are often repeated. This kind of content and treatment has been made 'natural' for the audience by years of exposure to it. These elements are nevertheless often attractive and sell well. The main consequence is that the messages and meanings in the product are also repeated. They have ideological significance even if they are not intentional.

2 GENRES

2.1 A lot of media product, especially story fiction, falls under this heading.

2.2 Genres are built from combinations of key elements: protagonists, stock characters, plots and stock situations, icons, backgrounds and decor, themes.

2.3 These elements add up to a formula shared by producers and by audiences.

2.4 Iconography refers to the study of those elements that are extremely typical of a genre, and therefore immediately recognizable and immediately connected with all the other elements and themes of a genre.

2.5 Genre material is quickly recognizable through previous exposure, and is attractive to the audience.

2.6 Genres work on the audience and give pleasure because they are predictable.

2.7 Genres display seriality in repeated story types.

2.8 The content, treatment and messages of genres are reinforced through being repeated.

2.9 Genres not only work to a formula, they also have their own codes and conventions governing what we expect to see and read, and how it will be handled.

2.10 Genres have a history that may be partly about real events on which their stories are based, but also about the growth of genre conventions. It is about genre cycles, or groups of films in the life of a genre.

2.11 Genres give pleasure to the audience and so sell well. This means that they are also profitable to media industries and so tend to be repeated, with variations on the formula.

2.12 Genres create elements of myth in their stories. This is attractive because it represents certain basic beliefs and aspirations in our culture.

2.13 Genres exemplify intertextuality, in which one example is understood by reference to all others.

2.14 We may look at examples of genre, such as crime films, to see what the formulae are and what meanings, beliefs and values are carried along with the formulae.

3 REPRESENTATIONS

- The media construct various representations of social groups by building images of and value messages about them.

3.1 These types may be characterized in terms of types, stereotypes and archetypes.

3.2 These types are constructed from repeated elements such as appearance and behaviour.

3.3 These elements carry meanings about character, relationship, and about how we are meant to view and value the types. These values may be described as ideological.

3.4 What is not represented is as important as what is shown.

4 REPRESENTATION AND CULTURE

- These representations of people say a lot about our culture and our beliefs. They may represent our values, they may reinforce them.

4.1 They create an identity for the group represented. In a negative way, this often includes the idea that the group is somehow 'different', is made up of 'others', is not the same nor as 'normal' as the main body of society with which the group is implicitly contrasted.

4.2 These ideas about difference and otherness are naturalized, or made to seem common-sensically true.

4.3 Institutions can be represented as much as groups of people. So one can represent the police as well as police men and women. Representations of the disabled typify the construction of negative views.

5   PRESENTERS, PERSONALITIES, STARS

5.1 Personalities act as a point of contact between media material and the audience. They are used to interpret that material for us. They are also 'constructed' like fictional characters in order to be attractive to the audience.

5.2 Stars are also attractive personalities. The term is usually used with relation to film. Stars have a persona and an appeal that is part of the film product that is sold to us.

5.3 Presenters appear in television in particular. They often act as a kind of narrator to a given type of programme, telling us what it means, perhaps preventing us from making up our own minds freely.

Fig. 6.1 Two images of war

These two images of war and conflict illustrate the idea that realism is a matter of conventions –
that the 'dividing lines' of reality between one television programme and another are not clear.
One of these images is from drama, the other from news. Which is which, and why do you think
this?

6

Media Product 2: Texts

Realism and Narrative

1 REALISM: FACTS AND FICTIONS

Realism is an important dimension of most media texts. We may see it as a feature of the text; it also helps define the relationship between the audience and the text – how we will approach the autobiography as opposed to the novel, for instance.

We judge a great deal of media product in terms of whether or not it is realistic. This is especially true of story-type product. So it is very common to hear people react to a film with phrases such as 'It wasn't very realistic, was it?' Even the lyrics of popular music can be judged in this way: 'It was just like something that happened to me; it was so truthful.' And we expect newspapers to be about things that have really happened. It may be suggested that some media products are more believable than others, and so we may be more likely to take them more seriously, and to take on their ideas more readily.

But the first problem that this idea raises is, simply, what do we mean by realism? There is a whole set of words we use in various ways to define realism, without thinking about it. It is these words we will now look at.

1.1 Definitions

- **Believable or credible:** what we see or read is something that we believe could have happened. It may resemble the world as we know it. (But remember that there is a lot that we believe to be true, but that we have not really checked out for ourselves. We get it from the media. So how violent are the streets of New York?!)
- **Plausible:** what we view or read is at least possible within its own terms of reference. Someone could have acted in the way they did in a given story, or the development of the storyline is possible in principle. There is some consistency in the material, even when we know it is basically fiction. So, for example, we may find it implausible to be told that the murder has been committed by the long-lost twin brother of the accused hero.
- **Probable:** has much to do with ideas of cause and effect. We tend to think in terms of whether or not it is probable that one event would follow from

another, or whether it is probable that a character would have taken a particular course of action.

- **Actual/actuality**: the material seems to have an immediate kind of physical reality about it as if it is really happening before us, or even as if we are really there. Often documentary material has the quality of actuality.
- **Verisimilitude**: this word, like 'actuality', suggests that something is true to life. But we also tend to use it when we feel, for example, that people's behaviour has an authentic quality, that it is like life (as we believe it to be).
- **Truthful**: this is an important word because material doesn't have to be entirely believable in a literal way to seem truthful. A story can say something truthful about human behaviour and motivation, even when it is improbable in terms of its situation and background. Many plays, not least Shakespeare's, are fairly improbable in terms of storylines, and certainly in terms of how real their settings are, but they might say something important about the beliefs and values of the characters, which the audience agrees with. These beliefs and values then become the 'truth' that we are talking about.
- **Naturalistic/naturalism**: this describes an impression that the material is of everyday experience, set in places that are ordinary. Television docu-dramas have specialized in creating this impression by using devices such as real locations and ordinary people as actors.

■ Some Criteria for Realism

So when we say that something has the quality of realism we could be talking about a number of elements:

- how accurately the background is depicted
- how believable the behaviour of people seems to be
- how probable the storyline is (if we are talking about fiction)
- how true the points made by the material seem to be.

In all this the complication is that realism is all relative. It is relative to our experience. So if we have experienced or even read about something that then appears in a magazine, we may find it more believable than does someone who has not had that experience. It is also relative to the mode of realism.

1.2   Modes of Realism

These refer to the **categories of realism** that we learn and have in our heads when we are making judgements based on ideas such as realism, truth, believability. We change the basis of our judgements according to the mode of realism that we think we are dealing with. We do not expect a computer game to be all that realistic; we do not expect it to look as real as film material, nor the situations to be as plausible as those we read about in a newspaper. We do expect a television documentary to be realistic; we expect it to be more real and believable than a romantic novel, for example.

One can take this idea of relativity in realism, depending on the sets of conventions used, and make a general description for film and television of modes categorized as follows, from the least to the most realistic:

fantasy → fiction → docu-drama → drama-doc → documentary.

Of course, documentary itself also comes in various types (see Section 1.7, below). And you might think about how/where you would fit in news material or live broadcasting to these modes of realism.

1.3   Conventions

We are back to these hidden rules. The fact is that **all these different modes of realism have different rules**. A change in the rules changes what is expected. The particular medium, or mode within the medium, has particular expectations. These expectations are aroused as soon as we start reading, viewing, listening. We expect an autobiography to be different from a novel, a situation comedy to be different from a current affairs programme, and so on. We have prior knowledge about the newspaper medium, we do not expect it to make up stories. We will have read reviews or publicity material about a film and so will know if it is fiction, and even what kind of fiction. *Castaway* the film (2001) is not the same in terms of realism as the BBC television series *Castaway* (2000). The film is an entirely made-up story that has an actor (Tom Hanks) working through what it would be like to be marooned on a desert island. But the television series is about a group of real people put on a real Hebridean island (albeit in a rather unreal situation). Ironically, we now have a television drama, *2,000 Acres of Sky* (2000), which is definitely fiction, but which is about life on a remote Hebridean island (set in real locations).

In the case of television, programme title sequences are crucial in letting us know what set of conventions our brains should switch into before the main part of the programme starts.

The rules we are talking about come across in many different ways. For example, in situation comedy, canned laughter is acceptable. In documentary, long shots of someone talking to the camera and being heard are acceptable. In radio journalism, recordings of someone talking through a poor telephone link line are acceptable. In film fiction, sudden bursts of romantic music are acceptable … you can easily extend these examples. But generally we don't mix these sets or rules. So once we have locked into a particular set of rules for a particular kind of realism, then we have set up particular standards for and expectations of the quality of realism in the product.

1.4   Realism, Narrative, Ideology, Genre

John Fiske says in *Television Culture* (1987) that 'realism does not just reproduce reality, it makes sense of it'. He is drawing attention to the fact that if one aspect of realism is about content – what looks and sounds real – another aspect is about form – how things are put over. This matter of form also refers back to the last section about conventions.

Realism has a lot to do with narrative – how one tells the story, or rather how one uses the medium or form in order to cause people to construct a story

Table 6.1 Realism — film and television — dominant conventions

Fiction	Documentary
Controlled lighting	Natural lighting
Re-recorded sound	Natural (live) sound
Multiple camera set-ups	Single camera set-up
Actors for characters	Real people
Music	Music infrequently
'Invisible narrative'	Narrator V/O, narrator to camera
Mobile camera	Fixed camera, usually
Studio sets and locations	Actual locations
Editing pace	Shots held/lack of editing pace
Unfolding drama on screen	Interviews on screen
	Captions on screen

in their heads. There is a 'typical' way of telling a story in our culture in various media, without arguing too much about the shuffling around of various cards in the deck of conventions. This usual way of making a narrative can, I suggest, be called mainstream narrative, or a classic realist text (see Section 2.7, below). The two phrases lead one to the same thing, albeit from slightly different perspectives.

One could go further and argue that the conventions of narrative are to an extent exactly the same as the conventions of realism – they are two aspects of the same devices of form. The point here is that mainstream narrative in any form strives to divert attention from itself. Story-tellers don't want you to realize that they are telling the story, and that it is really just a collection of devices for making up the story, then it is a short jump to the idea of realism. It seems real because there is apparently nothing between you the reader and viewer, and the stuff of the story – you are there, you are in the story, it is happening before your eyes. This 'trickery' abounds in every example of the media. For instance, because we are supposed to be watching a news interview as if it is really happening, the producer puts in 'noddies' of the interviewer apparently asking the questions – though these were not shot at the time, and are not needed for any practical purpose. We could just as well hear the questions as voice-over. But we are put in the classic third-person narrative position that seems so realistic to us, by being made able to apparently see the interviewer as well as the interviewee.

Realism is tied in with ideology – that is to say stories have meanings about beliefs and values in particular. These beliefs and values are the stuff of ideology. There are dominant values in the generality of popular texts (the dominant ideology). Realism helps make them dominant because the idea of what is real is tied in with the idea of what is true; what we believe to be true, we tend to believe. Many media critics have also argued that realism helps make dominant discourse dominant. So if you get sucked into a romantic story on television, or an adventure novel because it all seems very believable at the time, then you are also absorbing dominant discourses about masculinity or femininity. It is likely that you will be absorbing and reinforcing covert values about what it means to be male and female. The novel will be about physical prowess and risk for the male, and about relationships for the female.

Fiske points out that there is an argument here for saying that 'all popular culture inevitably serves the interests of the dominant ideology', that it 'provides the common ground between producers and audience-seen-as-consumers', that popular media material positions 'the viewer as a subject of and in the dominant ideology so effectively that any radicalism of the content is necessarily defused by the conventionality of the form'. So if a sitcom such as *Men Behaving Badly* raises questions about masculinity in the content of its stories, it completely undermines serious questioning by the way (form) that it makes a joke of everything and carries you along through conventional story-telling.

Modes and conventions of realism are linked to genres. Degrees of naturalism and authenticity attach themselves to soaps, but horror stories do not assume naturalism, indeed they allow for a degree of fantasy and we adjust our expectations accordingly.

1.5   Sources of Realism

It is important to remind ourselves that all our views about what is real or truthful depend on a number of kinds of experience.

- **Cultural experience**: we draw on the years of learning throughout our lives about what our culture sees as real. For example, we have learned a language of visual imagery and so believe that a larger object concealing a smaller one in a picture is closer to us than the smaller one. But this is just a convention of the code of visual communication. It is just another one of these sets of rules. Another culture that has not learned the rules this way would say 'What a silly picture [painting, photograph or film] – the creator has put one thing in the way of another' or 'The bigger object must be more important than the smaller one.' And of course all the sets of rules for the various modes of realism are learned through our upbringing in our culture.
- **Real life**: that is to say we may judge what is or is not real on the basis of what we have seen, done, felt. In particular, we may judge realism in terms of probability from our life's experience. From life we know something about cause and effect, about likely human behaviour. So then from that experience we can judge whether or not what happens in the media is probable.

Fig. 6.2a Still from Middlemarch © 1994 BBC Education

This and the following figure represent two qualities of realism. Fig. 6.2a is about authenticity, with attention to historical detail and accuracy. One feels that one is 'really there', even though we know that the story is actually taken from a book.

- **The media themselves** are also woven into our reality: if we have seen part of a documentary about American Indians, and then watch a television drama set among American Indians in New Mexico, we will judge the

Fig. 6.2b Still from *EastEnders*

This picture is more about naturalism. We are persuaded that these are ordinary people in the natural surroundings of a kitchen. Soap locations are generally those of everyday life. We are also persuaded of this naturalistic realism, perhaps, because soap characters are often 'working class' and because soap stories are on television so frequently that they become part of the patterns of our real lives. What do you think?

realism of that drama partly in the light of the other piece of media material. The point is that we may never have been to New Mexico in our lives, so we will base our judgement on this second-hand media experience that someone else has created.

- The **credibility of the source** also matters: it is possible to argue that while there is less output of documentary on television, its credibility and reference to reality 'out there' weighs more in the balance than the majority of fictional material. That average of 20 hours a week on terrestrial channels, that 2 hours a year that the average documentary maker produces, has a particular 'weight'.

1.6 Realism and Programming

Realism affects how we relate to media material, especially fictions. It is important to understand it because it affects the credibility of messages in the material. And for both those reasons the media producers find it important to maintain and promote the various modes of realism and their rules. It is convenient to package material into kinds of realism just as it is pre-packaged into genres. The producers want the audience to feel comfortable with their product, to know where they stand. They want the relatively realist modes such as documentary, or media such as newspapers to have credibility.

It is especially important in the case of television that viewers are able to distinguish one programme from another in the endless stream of material. If you pick up books from shelves labelled fiction or travel, then you have a pretty good idea about their kinds of realism before you start. But television is like an endless procession of open books in different modes, without the shelf labels. This is where the title sequences and programme previews come in, as well as the cues in the programmes themselves.

It is perhaps no accident that some of the most hot-tempered public debates about the media revolve around television in particular. The arguments, while sometimes seeming to be about programme content, are actually as much about programme treatment. In other words, the debates about bias in news on television are also debates about how items are handled, about the fact that it is generally believed that people believe what they see on the news. Similarly, the debates about certain dramas are often about how conventions of realism are used. *Our Friends in the North* is a British series based on real political events, including corruption. Drama documentary productions such as this example are, by definition, a blurring of the lines between fact and fiction. The argument about this drama had a particular edge because it looked pretty real and because parts of the storyline had some connection with known events in real life.

A strong example of the relationship between realism and product, especially genre product, is that of television soaps. Everyone 'knows' that these fall generally within the mode of fiction. But within this broad category there is still a scale. They are in a different part of the scale, we tend to assume, from a horror movie, On this scale we expect soaps, especially British soaps, to have locations or characters from life. Kilborn (1992) says that they 'seek to create the illusion of a reality', they have 'a sense of lived experience'. This quality of realism is in the authentic detail of sets or of dress. It is in the extended time span that is a luxury of soaps running over months and years, the possibility of matching real time. It is in the ideological dimensions of realism, where soaps tend to reflect attitudes and values, even their shifts over a period of time. The very longevity of some soaps makes them part of our life's experience. This in itself causes them to become part of our reality. I suggest that we accept a rather different kind of realism in soaps produced by other cultures (e.g. the USA or Australia) simply because they are from other cultures, and we can't have the same kind of life reference.

The problem in distinguishing between drama and documentary (and in defining this in programming) is exemplified in the work of the director Dominic Savage. His film (or television programme?) *Nice Girl* (BBC2, May 2000) is based on real stories about teenage pregnancies, but uses actors and an improvised script. Significantly, it was co-financed by BBC Drama and BBC Documentary.

1.7   Documentary

It is dangerous to assume that documentary in cinema and television has some kind of privileged position in relation to reality and to realism. It is just another kind of mode or of programme, with a particular use of conventions. I am not saying that documentaries may not have a closer connection than fiction films with some conception of 'the real' in our heads. But it is important to realize that when one brings in ideas about meaning, ideology and the truth, then documentaries can be just as partial as fiction.

A documentary film such as *The Thin Blue Line* by Errol Brown, about a claimed miscarriage of justice, mixes interviews with real people and graphic presentation of facts with the dramatic reconstruction of events. It proposes that the subject at the centre of the film has been wrongly imprisoned for murder. It was held to have played a part in that person's eventual acquittal. It isn't trying to be objective or balanced.

Similarly, Michael Moore's *Roger and Me* uses devices such as handheld camera, the reporter going 'live' into situations, and a narrative collage of interviews with real people – all around the subject of General Motors' closure of its plant in Flint, Michigan. But again there is no doubt that, through editing and comment on the soundtrack, Moore is gunning for whoever is responsible for the closure. The film isn't just a report on the situation.

Television, the medium in which documentary has found its 'home', and has developed for the last 50 years, gives good evidence of how one can say that documentary is just another way of telling stories. The last few years in particular, have seen the arrival of various 'takes' on the form of documentary. Docu-soaps use authentic footage of real people living and working in real places. But they edit this footage into dramatic narrative, creating heroes and villains, and conflicts to be resolved. There has been the interesting example of *Big Brother* (2000), a kind of docu-game-show, in which a group of contestants volunteer to live together in a manufactured house and garden, from which they are voted out by the others and by viewers. The documentary element is there in the 24-hour real-time multiple-camera surveillance of what goes in the house between those real people. Some of these cameras are webcams that viewers can access via the Net, and watch this real life drama in real time. But the interference of the production team in what is going on, the edited version of the programme, denies this the kind of observational detachment of, say, a classic wildlife documentary.

Television is traducing the old safe boundaries of documentary conventions and exposing their realism for the relative thing that it is.

1.8   News and Fiction

The truth of the matter is that **there is no absolute reality or truth in the media.** We may like to think there is, we may find it convenient to have sets of rules to define relative kinds of reality and truth. But look at the facts. A newspaper such as the *Independent* reads as somehow more realistic than the *Mirror*. The former has more hard news stories and a less dramatized style than the latter.

And yet one cannot say that because the *Mirror* may prefer a majority of human interest items (perhaps a film star's divorce) to an item about what is happening in the House of Lords, that the divorce item is not actually true nor real. Similarly, television news, while not being simply untruthful, has qualities of drama in the way that it selects some exciting stories or makes excitement out of something like a kidnap story. And it certainly is not simply The Truth. If it could achieve this, then we could make do with one news programme only. So the lines between one kind of realism and another may be more blurred than we think.

1.9 Packaging and Categories

We are socialized into believing that the divisions are sharper than they are through the various ways of packaging the product. It is packaged through generic labels (thriller or soap); or through treatment (fiction or documentary); or through audience targeting (for women or for sports fans); or through structuring (a page of adverts followed by a feature article or a soap followed by a quiz followed by a sitcom). All these various ways of packaging media product aim to get the product and the audience together to achieve maximum sales, maximum ratings or readership, maximum profits.

From one point of view this makes the process of communication as smooth, as seamless, as effective as possible. What it also does is to project the messages very effectively. So once more we will have to return to the issue of what these messages are, whether or not they are intentional or covert. To this

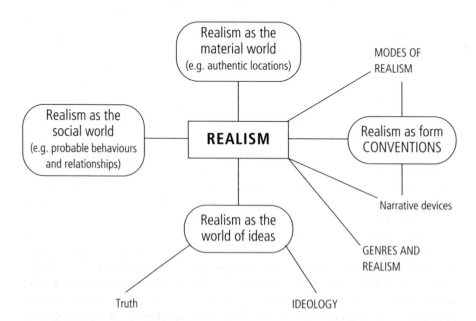

Fig. 6.3 Key concepts: realism

extent the product is not just the book, the record, the programme, it is also the meaning. If there is a production line, a process by which material is produced repetitiously, efficiently, in quantity, then it is also a meanings production line. **It is a production line of values, it is a reinforcement of values.**

Realism on Television

Is the line between truth and fiction on television (e.g. docu-soaps) now too blurred for people to easily sort out what is true and what is false?

Does realism just go on changing its conventions and we adapt to these changes?

---

2 NARRATIVE

The media tell stories. These stories are not just fiction, they are about factual material as well. Newspapers talk about 'the story' when they refer to a piece of news. Preferably we should use the word 'narrative'. **The media are full of kinds of narrative,** if only because all these media have to unfold their material in sequence. Just as a radio drama will introduce characters and situations at the beginning, a magazine article introduces its subject and theme at the beginning. Just as the drama goes on to unfold a story with themes to bring out, the article unfolds its information and the points it wants to make. **There is narrative whether one is talking about fact or fiction.**

Narratives refer to one another – they are intertextual. We understand one narrative because we have experience of reading many other narratives.

Even if one is just talking about fiction narratives, it is worth remembering how many there are in the media. Magazines and even Sunday newspapers carry short stories. Comics are full of stories. Many popular songs are based on a story. Video games are stories that you take part in.

I have already talked about the presenter as a kind of narrator for television product, but let's remember that the narrative is organized before anything appears on screen. Narrative is by definition a kind of artifice. It involves selection and construction of material. It implies the discarding of alternative constructions. Its 'sense' relies on conventions shared between producer and audience. The narrative of a television documentary is organized through a script, through directors' and editors' decisions. The 'storyline' for a newspaper is arranged by the subs and the editor deciding what goes on what page. So the idea of narrative draws attention to the way in which material is organized for consumption by the audience. It can make the material and its ideas more digestible. **At the heart of narrative is meaning** – what the story is about. How we understand what the story is about depends on how we decode the narrative. This is what we are going to look at now.

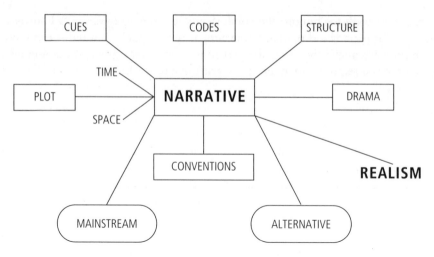

Fig. 6.4 Key concepts: narrative

2.1   Narrative, Space and Time

One crucial thing narrative does is to shape the material in terms of space and time. That is to say, **it defines where things take place, when they take place, how quickly they take place.** Even when television is broadcast live it can still pull off this narrative manipulation. In terms of space and place, you can be watching a sports programme being unfolded from a studio in London. The narrator is based there. But this narrator/presenter can project us to other places where sporting events are taking place. We can be sent to Las Vegas to watch a boxing match. At this boxing match the narrative may be shifted in time. For instance, we have the replays of crucial points of the action. These have the effect of distorting real time and events. Often the replays are used between rounds, so that we lose a sense of the stop-go action, and are given an illusion of continuous activity in the ring. The replay is also a distortion because it is a flashback. Fiction on screen is very prone to use this device, to compress or lengthen screen time. Sergio Leone, director of spaghetti westerns, developed a trick of spinning out real time on screen when there was a moment of tension between characters. He used very long-held reaction shots around faces before there was an explosion of real action, in order to heighten tension by making the viewer wait for it.

2.2   Narrative Modes

We can recognize at least two modes of narrative that need to be structured:

1 **narrative of events** – things that happen and the order in which they happen
2 **narrative of drama** – which is more to do with character and relationships.

In this case, the narrative structure is marked by things like dramatic tension and crisis in relationships. If the hero shoots the enemy agent, dives into the lake and triggers the remote control device that will destroy the ... whatever it is, then this is one kind of order of events. If the heroine has a tense argument with the hero and decides that he was never her type and that she is going to leave, then nothing has happened in terms of events, but a lot has happened dramatically – there has been conflict, a change of relationship, and the story is about to change direction.

Activity (14): Narrative

Take any lead story from a newspaper, and from it WRITE OUT THE BARE FACTS OF WHAT HAS HAPPENED TO WHOM, IN WHAT ORDER. This is your plot.

Then take your plot summary and WRITE IT UP AGAIN INTO A MORE DRAMATIC STORY FORM, but still keep it short. This is like writing the treatment for a film. So now you have drama.

From doing this you should learn the following:

- the differences and overlaps between plot and drama
- the fact that news stories do have a narrative, like many examples of media text
- the idea that, in terms of realism, there isn't such a big jump from the factuality of news stories to the fictionality of other kinds of story.

2.3   Narrative Structures

Most narratives are structured on the basis of an opening and a closure. In principle one does not have to do this – you can just cut into the storyline. But in fact often there are devices used that say 'this is the beginning', 'this is the end'. A newspaper article is opened by its headline and closed by some verbal exit line and by a graphic marker such as a horizontal line. Television programmes are opened by titles and closed by credits. This kind of structuring is designed to help us make sense of the material. Television especially need this, so that we know where one programme begins and another ends. It needs it especially because it also has a larger kind of structure that runs over the whole day. It opens with breakfast time and closes with the late film and announcer's finale – or whatever.

This sense of structure extends through the whole piece of media material. It organizes the order of its 'telling'. It organizes the understanding of the audience. The BBC's *Top of the Pops*, showcasing current chart hits and hopefuls, has a very rigid structure. It requires alternation between the presenters and the bands on stage. There are three ritual run-downs on the charts. There is always a number (with video) to play out at the end. The very music it plays also has structure. One example would be:

chorus–verse–chorus–middle eight–verse–chorus. Magazines and newspapers have a pretty regular overall narrative structure. This is what helps to sell them to the readers – the comfort of finding items in their familiar places: the poster pull-out in the middle, the sport always at the back, and so on. Yet again, the individual articles will have their own structure. For longer newspaper articles, the paragraphs and subheads mark this out, as information about the event is added, and the angle is pursued.

There are various structures that shape fiction. One kind of circular structure shows the dramatic event (a murder?), which is the impetus to the story at the beginning. Then the main part of the narrative is a flashback that shows events leading up to the murder. By the end we have reached once more the point in time where the murder took place. Then the murderer is discovered. In the most conventional narrative one is introduced to the protagonists (heroes and villains/lead characters); and to the background; then to a problem or some sort of conflict that has to be sorted out; then taken through a set of events in which the structure is about 'will it or won't it get sorted'; finally, just when everything seems impossible, there is a grand finale in which everyone gets their just desserts.

You should try analysing the structure of various examples of narrative to see how they are organized. Remember that the particular point is to hold your attention, to arouse your emotions, to give you this sort of pleasure in viewing or reading, ultimately so that you come back to buy more.

Don't forget the narrative of non-fiction forms. News is prone to create drama. We accept that fiction generates high spots of dramatic tension. We are used to experiencing what we call 'cliff-hangers'. Serials in comics deliberately engineer these so that you will buy the next one to find out what happens. News does the same thing. It promises pictures of the disaster later in the programme. It invites you to watch the next episode on a major story later in the evening, in the next news broadcast.

The notion of structure in narrative has led to various attempts to find something universal in the organization of all stories. Fiske discusses this at some length in *Television Culture* (1987) and refers to the work of structuralists such as Propp who sought to analyse folk tales down to such universal building blocks and rules – the ultimate structuralism. It doesn't work, but the attempt is valuable. For example, such analysis leads to a recognition of **binary oppositions** (as referred to elsewhere in this book). The identification of an oppositional structure leads to a realization that it operates on a literal and a symbolic level in stories. In this case Fiske points out that 'the struggle between the hero and the villain is a metaphorical transformation of that between the forces of order and those of disorder, good and evil, culture or nature. Such a struggle is fundamental to all societies.' In other words, opposing characters stand for opposing ideas. The narrative has a structure that works on the level of character and action, and on the level of concepts, discourses, myths. It is easy to see how mythologies about innocence and evil, about what is culturally valued or disapproved of, can be worked out through this oppositional structure – in crime stories or in romantic fiction.

Furthermore, such a structure relates to notions of resolution and contradiction. That is to say, to an extent, stories work to resolve the opposition. The story of *Othello* is partly about an opposition between duty to parent and duty to husband; Desdemona resolves this by saying that the act of marriage means that the weight of her duty now shifts towards her husband Othello. But, like many stories, this rather avoids other contradictions, which are never resolved. If she had obeyed her duty to her father, she would never have sneaked off to get married secretly in the first place. Anyway there is a related contradiction which is that the Venetians see Othello as a capable general, but also as a Moor; and nice young Venetian girls are not supposed to marry Moors. This opposition based on race is never sorted out. It is in a sense avoided by having Othello murder Desdemona out of jealousy. It would have been far more interesting to have a story in which Desdemona lived on and had children. How would that have been sorted out?! Such contradictions in narratives, in our ideology, are quite frequent. The same story contains one classic opposition, which is about wanting women to be sexy and exciting and pure and loyal at the same time. It is suggested that Desdemona is both lustful to want to marry Othello yet also pure and innocent because of her class background and because she is a victim. Her murder also avoids dealing with this one. On one level this story fits Todorov's (1976) pattern of starting the narrative with equilibrium, moving to some kind of disruption to this situation, and finally returning through resolution to some new kind of equilibrium. But I would suggest that my comments on the contradictions also indicate how this apparently neat approach to explaining the structure of stories may not entirely work.

Structuralism as a critical approach produces some useful ways of understanding how narratives are organized, how meanings are organized, how our understandings may be organized. But it doesn't explain everything about narratives. One popular approach to film criticism has been to look at the work of the director on the assumption that it will reveal structures. These patterns of style and thematic preoccupation may indeed be seen to some extent in the work of many film directors. This is the auteur theory. One example might be the young protagonists in many of Scorsese's films who kick against the culture within which they are trying to make their mark – pool hustling, the Mafia, boxing – often in a violent manner. But they find that they go too far, and hurt themselves and others, some learning wisdom, some dying unwisely. However, this structure does not fit all Scorsese films. So there are limits to how far one may apply structuralist ideas.

2.4 Narrative Cues

Narrative cues direct our understanding of the unfolding story; they may be verbal or visual. They tell us things like: this is a villain, this is a time shift, the story is now moving to another place, something dreadful is about to happen, and so on. To take more obvious examples, the villain is cued by a close-up of an unshaven face, the time shift is cued by a pull-in on the character's eyes as they remember something that happened before, the place shift is signalled by 'and now we go over to our correspondent in Beirut', our anticipation is cued by a cutaway shot to a hand reaching for a gun. Indeed the creation of suspense and anticipation is very much about the manipulation of audience emotions through the use of cues and through the editing that puts them in, and controls the pace at which the narrative unfolds. Near the end of *Blade Runner*, we are cued for the apparent death of the protagonist, Deckard, when he is hanging by his hands from a rain-soaked rooftop projection far above a street. We are shown the distance down to the street. We are shown the straining hands in close-up. We are shown the strained face in close-up. We are shown the 'villain' as from Deckard's view, appearing over the edge of the rooftop and looking down – apparently about to stamp on his fragile grip on safety. We understand these cues in the context of similar scenes that we have viewed. The film maker knows this and plays with our emotions, before actually doing the unexpected and having the villain help him back on to the roof.

2.5   Narrative and Conventions

Narrative is as much bound by rules regarding the way it is handled as are other examples of media content and treatment. We have already noted that narrative cues are, for example, conventions themselves in terms of how they are used and what they mean. They are rules for organizing the narrative and, as with genre or realism, it is important that those who make the communication share the same rules with those who receive and decode it. This creates understanding. Unconventional narrative or unconventional use of the rules can be upsetting, confusing and alienating. This is not to say that the rules cannot be bent, or combined in different ways. It is certainly not to say that people should not experiment with different ways of narration. For example, film makers have tried using black screen to mark a separation between one episode and another. Some have tried killing off the hero halfway and introducing another. Some have jumbled up the proper time order of events (*Pulp Fiction*), or have used flashbacks within flashbacks. It is useful for a media student to watch this kind of film because it really proves that the rules for constructing narrative do exist. But still it also proves that the audience has to learn the rules or make sense of new ones if it is to create meaning from the material.

Conventions underpin mainstream narrative or the classic realist text (see Section 2.7, below). **Conventions work behind continuity** in film and television. For example, one may achieve continuity or a sense of linkage through successive shots that are of different locations, but are 'joined' by the matching of their composition. On a basic level, one achieves continuity when changing angles by, for example, retaining some common feature of background – maybe a wall. And in terms of camera set-ups there is the 180-degree rule, which says that you can't suddenly cross the imaginary line through the middle of a circle around the subject without using a sequence of angled shots. If you think about filming a moving car from one side and then cutting across the imaginary circle to the other side, you will realize that the car would suddenly appear to be going the other way on screen, so the rule makes visual sense!

Conventions of narrative overlap with those of genre or of realism. It is like having one lever that can move different bits of machinery. For instance, you might have a close shot of a hand spinning the chamber of a Colt-45 handgun. The fact that it is a Colt handgun, and therefore an icon of the western, makes it a conventional element of the western genre. This in turn will incline us to drop mentally into a certain mode of realism: straight fiction. But the image also sets up the narrative. We would expect a scene to follow in which the gun is used.

So once more, in terms of the creation of meaning, of the exchange of meaning between the media and its audience, we must not underrate the importance of conventions in making this possible.

2.6 Narrative and the Reader/Spectator

■ *Involvement and Detachment*

Narrative has the power to place us in a relationship to the story. One fundamental relationship is that of the objective or subjective position. In the first case we are standing outside the action, in the second we may be drawn into it. One is third-person story-telling, the other is first-person. Visual and fiction material provide the strongest examples. It is possible that the two kinds of positioning will happen even within one scene. If the heroine is hanging from a clifftop and we are simply viewing this from a distance, then this is objective narrative. But if the camera switches to a view down the cliff as if we were in her eyes and her head, then this is subjective narrative. Print media do the same thing when they use the 'I' form to address the reader directly, or when they simply describe events in terms of 'it happened'. Factual material can use the same device: documentaries may drop in subjective shots to give the experience more impact. Newspapers tend to stick to third-person narrative because they are trying to achieve objectivity. But magazines may well address the reader directly in order to achieve intimacy and credibility.

This last example links with the idea of MODE OF ADDRESS, and the kind of psychological positioning or pseudo-relationship that the text can set up with its audience.

■ *Identification and Alienation*

At an extreme one gets two kinds of position that may be described as identification or alienation. First-person narration, realistic background details, description solely from the protagonist's point of view – all may help us to identify with the feelings, beliefs and experiences of a character in a given story. The more we believe in them the more we may identify. This has been the key to the success of the Adrian Mole series of books and television programmes.

Equally, media narratives can use devices to make us feel separate and detached (alienated) from what is going on. This alienation might be a way of helping us cope with violent scenes that would be unbearable if there was too much involvement. Films like the serial murder thriller *Seven* have used the detached, half-hidden, watching camera. In terms of horror and violence, alienation may also be achieved precisely by an excess of fear and gore, which causes us to hold off emotionally from the material. In Peter Greenaway's film *The Cook, the Thief, his Wife and her Lover* there is a climactic banqueting scene in which an extended right-tracking shot of people dining, followed by explicit views of roast human body, combine to make us horrified and disapproving observers of this satire on human excess.

▪ Spatial Positioning

Narrative can also place us in apparently impossible positions in relation to action. We could have watched our heroine on the clifftop as if from some point in the air looking at the cliff. We accept this godlike position because as with everything else we have learned to accept it from previous viewing. We have learned what are yet more conventions of story-telling.

Then there is the privileged spectator position, when we can see or know things that the protagonists do not. This should remind you in terms of image analysis that it is the power of the camera and of those who direct it that puts us in a certain position. So we may be enabled to see a crucial document on a table, which someone else within the story cannot see. At the same time, this device also draws us further into the drama. It is a sort of participation in what is going on. You can see the same thing happening in a quiz show when the presenter not only welcomes us personally (though he cannot see us) but may show us the prizes, which the quiz show's players cannot see.

▪ Temporal Positioning

Temporal positioning involves devices that affect our sense of 'when' we are in the story, which may make us feel we are in one period of history or another, or even in a different time to that of the main narrative. The television series *Good Night, Sweetheart* requires us to be positioned alternately between the present day and the 1940s. We also have to be given a sense of time moving forward – progress in the plot. One device that is still common is that of captions on screen that tell us where/when we are, when the story has 'jumped'.

▪ Psychological Positioning

There is a writer–reader relationship created by the use of a narrator (see also mode of address). Detective movies have a convention of voice-over in which the hero confides in us about what is happening. The newspaper reporter acts as narrator when she gives us an eyewitness account of some event. The first one is more intimate than the second, but both create a relationship between us the audience and the story that is being narrated.

This kind of positioning is calculated to affect the emotional impact of what is being told, to affect its believability. To this extent these devices of narrative also relate to realism. The kind of realism that we ascribe to the narrative affects how we react to it, affects how we accept the meanings or messages.

So these devices of narration can put us physically (spatially) in a certain place, or they can put us psychologically in a relationship to what is being narrated. This relationship is basically about more or less involvement in what is supposed to be going on. The degree of involvement affects our acceptance of everything on the page or on the screen. This in turn affects our acceptance of the messages and meanings within the material. We are not only seduced into thinking this is believable, for example, but we may also be seduced into accepting meanings such as it is OK for people to exact revenge (in a story), or it is OK for people to do stupid things in public if there are prizes at the end of it (in a quiz show).

But in the end you need to remember that **the narrative is as much in the reader as in the text**. Whatever your notion of 'the story', it is your notion and it is in your head. A page is only a page and a screen is only a screen – with signs on them – until the reader makes some sense of these. The text may cue us to take positions, but we actually do the positioning in our heads

---

Locating Narrative
Is narrative made by the writer of the text?
Is it made by the reader?

2.7   Mainstream Narrative

In all media there is a 'generally accepted' way of making narrative, as described in the previous sections. The conventions of narrative mean that we expect a kind of story unfolding, which helps us know where we are, who we are dealing with, and to believe that one event or action follows plausibly from another. This is the narrative of the mainstream.

There is quite an array of devices available in mainstream narrative, but one thing they all do is to 'get you into the story', to the point where the reader/viewer forgets that it just book or a film – **the narrative becomes invisible.** ·

The way that the creators manufacture this invisibility does have something to do with the particular medium, words or pictures. But in fact there are qualities of mainstream narrative in any media, whether they are achieved by camera or by language – for example, a sense of continuity, linking time and place. Similarly, one would expect a story involving physical or psychological conflict. One would expect some sort of resolution to the conflict or problems of the characters. This last point is known as **narrative closure**.

Realism is so much a part of narrative that another phrase that will do as well as mainstream narrative is the '**classic realist text**'. As Giannetti says in *Understanding Movies* (1993), 'the classical PARADIGM emphasizes dramatic unity, plausible motivations, and coherence of its constituent parts'. We are back to the invisibility of the hand of the creator, and to qualities of realism that enable us to accept the text on its own terms.

In *The Cinema Book* (1985) Kuhn lists features of a classic realist text or narrative as follows:

- linearity of cause and effect within an overall trajectory of enigma resolution
- a high degree of narrative closure
- a fictional world governed by spatial and temporal verisimilitude
- centrality of the narrative agency of psychologically rounded characters.

These kinds of stories are all wrapped up – they seem to make perfect sense, they seem to belong to a real world, they depend on what happens to characters and what they do. Textual analysis reveals that it isn't that simple.

2.8 Narrative and Sound

In the case of audio-visual media, one may fall into the trap of privileging images as carrying the narration, and of underestimating the work of sound. There are, essentially, three kinds of sound that carry meaning: voice, music, effects (FX).

The voice-over (VO) of an omniscient narrator is common in documentary and radio – literally telling the story and perhaps introducing other elements of story structure such as a dramatic exchange or an interview.

In drama we also build the narrative in our heads from exchanges of dialogue: characters reveal feelings, tell us where they are going, and so on. The voice may be reinforced by the images, the pictures may tell the same story. Or the visual narrative may counterpoint the voice in some way, perhaps to produce irony.

Sound may act as a binder to the visual narrative, overlapping the images and drawing them together. FX may contribute to narrative as plot. A classic example is the fatal shot heard, although the murder is not seen. This has a special kind of effectiveness if one is anticipating something like a murder or an execution.

Dialogue usually develops drama, on screen or on sound, over real time or screen time. Such exchanges reveal the development of relationships or the implications of conflict. Sound may therefore propel narrative development in

---

Fig. 6.5 Visual narrative: the final frames from a story of *Buffy the Vampire Slayer*

Comics provide interesting examples of narrative because they mix their own conventions with those of film. Notice the frames, which are also high-angle and low-angle shots; the final frame is typical of the concluding 'departure' shot used in many movies. You may also notice the elements of romance that are typical of the *Buffy* stories, as they bring Point Horror to the screen.

Source: *Buffy the Vampire Slayer*™ & © 2001, Twentieth Century Fox Film Corporation. All Rights Reserved.

terms of both plot and drama. It provides the cues that help us construct what we define as 'the story'.

Music is part of that cueing. It provides emotional as much as rational points of reference. It underlines moments of drama. It relates to emotional positioning. It tells us how we are meant to understand the narrative in terms of feelings. It may relate to a particular character if there is some musical motif linked to that person, but it may also help us understand the emotional state of a character, what is happening with a relationship.

2.9   Montage and Cinema

Montage is a term developed in film criticism to describe the ordering for effect of the shots or of narrative sequences of a film. It is about the building of narrative.

In fact there is no reason why one may not recognize and comment on the effect of exactly the same process in television. This process recognizes the importance of editing in creating narrative in moving-image media. It also identifies the idea of the creation of meaningful sequences of images. If one was taking a semiotic analysis approach, then these sequences would formally be called syntagms. **A syntagm is a meaningful sequence of signs** in any medium. In the case of film one might be talking about a scene, a sequence or an episode from the film.

Film montage criticism tends to concentrate on the cutting of shots to make a scene. It would attend to how this cutting might induce emotions, bring out features of character, generally bring out meaning. So montage attends to the process of editing, the choices made in sequencing shots and to the effects of such a sequence.

In terms of classic Hollywood cinema, montage is designed to make narrative invisible – you aren't meant to see the joins. Loosely, it may be argued that such familiar narrative does this by editing in ways with which we have become familiar (a circular argument!). It does this by using shots and positioning that more or less imitate the way we look at the real world anyway.

Sometimes particular ways of creating montage achieve a distinctive style and identity. The two classic examples of variation on the mainstream are the following.

- **American montage:** this was used a lot in the studios in the 1930s and 1940s. It involved a quickly cut sequence of shots that told a part of the story in compressed screen time, perhaps a bit of history behind the film story. Time and place would be compressed as the pictures rushed through their 'explanation'.
- **Russian montage:** this was a calculated experiment of revolutionary film makers in the 1920s and 1930s, notably Sergei Eisenstein. It involved so-called crash editing, in which shots or sequences were cut together abruptly. The audience would get a visual jolt, but it also gave the films visual energy. The Odessa Steps sequence from *Battleship Potemkin* has been shown to generations of film students as a great example of this

formalist technique. Essentially there are five bits of film of different things happening on the Steps, as the White Russian Guards advance down on the population. These bits are broken up and cut together abruptly. One effect is to spin out the drama of a baby carriage getting loose and bumping down the steps – creation of tension with anticipation; another is to suddenly cut to the shot where a woman is shot in the eye – a dramatic jolt from the unexpected.

In fact the drama of such 'aggressive' montage is not so notable for us today, given the kind of jump-cutting and accelerated narrative that we are more used to seeing.

2.10 Diegesis

DIEGESIS is a useful term, which distinguishes content from form where narrative is concerned. **It describes what is supposed to be in the story and part of it, as opposed to what is outside it and is to do with the way the story is told.** If the hero starts playing romantic music in a radio drama then that is diegetic. But if the director puts in romantic music as part of the backing to create a mood for the drama, then that is non-diegetic.

Music has a long history as a non-diegetic addition to the media text. Comment is usually made in the context of films, but there are plenty of examples in television, not least in advertisements. Bell, Joyce and Rivers (1999) refer to three functions of such music in relation to films. They describe the creation of or support for:

1 emotional qualities of the movie
2 factual aspects of the film – e.g. music that locates the period or year
3 aesthetic dimensions of film such as motif tunes in thrillers, or as background to a rapid montage sequence that helps give it coherence.

See if you can identify television adverts that use music in these three ways, plus an example of the diegetic use of music.

The idea of diegesis also connects with conventions and with realism. Take the example of voice-over. Documentaries can have a voice-over film, which was recorded on the spot at the time (diegetic), or voice-over that is dubbed on the film later (non-diegetic). The first device seems a shade more actual than the second, though both examples are within the collection of conventions that help define a factual, realistic mode of film/television. But, then again, voice-overs can be used in fiction films – the private eye/hero talking on the soundtrack. The hero is part of the film story, so this voice-over is diegetic, but because it is associated with a realist mode of television, which quite often uses it in a non-diegetic, authoritative manner, the audience finds the device of the protagonist one that enhances the realism of the fiction.

So the idea of diegesis helps one concentrate on the ways in which the narrative is shaped and constructed, how we relate to what we think of as the 'story'.

2.11 Alternative Narrative

One could say that **narrative that is not mainstream is in some measure alternative**. The term suggests that at least some aspect of the story-telling is not within the parameters we are used to. Of course, this creates a problem because it depends on what we are used to. Some might say that *Lipstick on Your Collar* (BBC, 1994) is alternative because it mixes up songs with an ordinary story, dream time with real time, but this attends only to realism as an aspect of narrative. In other respects, the structure, the use of cues, the sense of place and time, is all perfectly conventional. In any case it does not make sense that anything that really breaks the rules would appear on mainstream television.

Given that the relationship between audience and producer via the text is a dynamic one, the conventions of features such as narrative are always shifting. The idea of 'alternative' can only be explained in relativist terms. Experiments of 30 years ago are not surprising today, and certain audiences are more in tune with the 'alternative' than are others. So when someone like Bordwell (1993) tries to give an account of alternative narrative in film, one thinks of mainstream movies that have used some of the features he describes. There are also film makers who hover between mainstream and the alternative: Gus Van Sant, Jim Jarmusch, James Toback.

Bordwell's account of the alternative covers the following:

- lack of development of a (traditional) story as such
- lack of closure to the narrative (no neat ending)
- lack of definite connections between events and people
- lack of motivation driving character and relationships
- use of arbitrary events and actions.

Alternative narratives in any medium are likely to be experimental, on the margins and to appeal only to a limited audience. This is not to denigrate them: experimental novels – the work of Samuel Beckett perhaps – are praised and enjoyed, though they are outside what is called popular culture.

Perhaps what is most interesting is work that falls between extremes, or is subversive in some way. For example, there are games on CD-Roms or printed books where the narrative is not fixed in structure and development, but is controlled to some extent by the reader/viewer, who makes choices about how the story develops. There are films like *Koyaanisqatsi*, which is really a montage of images with sound and music, and doesn't have character development or plot resolution.

The existence of the alternative in the media, whether it is to do with narrative or audience or mode of production is very important. It is about experimentation and development. It actually defines what mainstream is, and questions that.

REVIEW

You should have learned the following from this chapter about the nature of realism and of narrative.

1 REALISM: FACTS AND FICTIONS

1.1 There are a variety of words we may use to define realism in factual or fictional material: believable, plausible, actual, verisimilitude, truthful, probable, naturalistic.

1.2 There are different modes or categories of realism, for which we have different expectations in terms of how the material is handled.

1.3 These modes are all based on different conventions.

1.4 Realism can be seen as a function of narrative. It can also be seen as being defined through ideology – what we believe is real to us.

1.5 There are various sources for our ideas about realism, notably our general cultural experience, our personal experience of life, our second-hand experience via the media.

1.6 Media producers prefer to package material within one mode of realism or another, so that it is believable within its own terms.

1.7 Documentary is just as constructed as other modes of realism. It isn't necessarily objective. Television is blurring the conventions that used to separate fact from fiction, at least in principle.

1.8 No mode of realism, whether news or fiction, is absolutely real or truthful.

1.9 Packaging of material in terms of realism is matched by packaging in terms of genres and other categories.

2 NARRATIVE

This is about the story structure and storyline of all media material.

2.1 Narrative defines the place and time in which things are supposed to happen.

2.2 There are two main modes/aspects of narrative: story in terms of events; story in terms of drama.

2.3 Narratives have various structures, or ways of organizing the sequence of story-telling and what the story means.

2.4 Narrative cues are signs within the story-telling that indicate things like where events are meant to be placed, or shifts of time.

2.5 Narrative also has sets of rules or conventions, which producers use in terms of how they tell a drama or a documentary story, for instance. These rules are sometimes also the rules of realism or of genre. These same rules work in more than one way.

2.6 Narrative also includes ways of relating the reader/viewer to the material about which a story is unfolded. Two main 'positions', or kinds of relationship are called subjective and objective; three others are described as spatial, temporal and psychological. Such positions may cause the audience to identify with the 'story', or to be alienated from it.

2.7 Mainstream narrative is that form whose conventions dominate story-telling in our media, and is characterized by the quality of making its own devices invisible.

2.8 Sound in film and television is also important in constructing our idea of the narrative. It has three main elements: voice, music and effects.

2.9 In cinema the putting together of sections of narrative is referred to as montage. This ties in with editing, and the building of visual/sound sequences in order to create plot and drama.

2.10 Diegesis describes what is in the story (content), as opposed to what is outside it (the form of story-telling).

2.11 Alternative narrative is that which 'breaks' the rules. So up to a point anything that works against what we expect of mainstream is likely to be seen as alternative.

This street poster reminds us that not all advertising is about television, nor is it all about selling products. What do you think are the devices of persuasion used by this ad? Who is it aimed at? What is it trying to achieve?

7

Media Product 3: Texts

News and Influence
Advertising and Persuasion

1 MAKING SENSE OF NEWS

This chapter supplements what was said in the previous one about news as genre. It introduces some more concepts that help explain how meanings are put across in news material. **The reason for giving news such a high profile in Media Studies is that it is a prime source of information about the world,** from its geography to its politics. Most people trust the news machine and what it tells us. Often it is endowed with qualities of neutrality and authority which, in fact, it has not got, and could not reasonably be expected to have. So the ideas that follow will help demythologize news. What best puts it in perspective as another piece of media communication is the fact that news material is bought and sold every day just like any other product. This leads us straight in to the matter of where news comes from.

1.1 News Gathering

The term news gathering is commonly used to describe the first stage of the manufacture of news. It implies that news is waiting to be gathered in like fruit, and sorted and packed for the audience. But **news is not something complete and fully formed – it is created.** It is not even 'gathered' by the reporter in many cases, as is popularly supposed. A great deal of material comes through agencies such as Associated Press in the case of the press, and Visnews in the case of television. The material is paid for. Similarly, the television news operations across Europe have a link-up every morning to buy and sell news items. Even where news is collected by reporters it is done in a very routine way for the most part, going to regular sources, using press officers and their press conferences, which front for many organizations, not least the government. In any case, the news item is not just information from the agency sources – **news is constructed just like any communication.**

It may also be argued that news is managed before it can even be gathered. So press releases and conferences will be managed by politicians so that they fit in with news deadlines, and provide soundbites and photo opportunities. This management (see Section 1.12 below, on bias) may be conducted by 'politically correct' groups such as Greenpeace, as much as by politicians. Greenpeace will stage photo-worthy events, and provide press-usable material (including video), as much as any image-conscious multinational.

News gathering can be managed by external forces, as in the Gulf War of 1992. Here, the military press officers physically controlled who went near the front line and who did not. They selected a group of accredited (i.e. favoured) journalists, and fed them information. But journalists may themselves be guilty of creating a 'news pack' in which they borrow ideas and points of view from one another. The coverage of the 1994/95 war in Bosnia is an example of this. There were instances of selective coverage in which Serbia was demonized and atrocities against Serbs were not reported. A collective position had been taken by the correspondents (this is not an apologia for Serbian war crimes). As John Burns, *New York Times* correspondent, said in *Bosnia by Television* (1996), 'journalists cannot expect to be received as impartial observers of conflicts … if they become party to the narrow pack mentality'. Nick Gowing of Channel 4 described the television coverage of this war as 'supermarket war video' – a reference to the abundance of pictures gathered. The problem is that abundance and immediate broadcasting does not make for reflection. In this sense, the press had the advantage of its slower production process, which allowed for rather more consideration of the meaning of what reporters were gathering and sending back.

1.2   Selection and Construction

News, like any kind of media product, is the result of a process of selection and construction. Items are selected in or selected out. Newspapers or news programmes are artefacts that are put together. In effect, meaning is constructed into them. The meanings do not just happen to appear, they are there because someone made them. There are various aspects of news making that reveal how conscious is this making of the communication. For example, the reporter or newsreader interprets events for us. As soon as they talk about 'confrontation', they are actually interpreting what has happened. They are asserting that there has been confrontation, where someone else might have talked about 'disagreement'. The fact that we never see the camera crew on television helps construct a meaning that suggests neutrality and truth. We are not made aware that someone was there choosing the camera angles and indeed the subject matter. Sometimes this construction is very deliberate, as when photo opportunities are set up for celebrities. It is certainly argued that people will perform for the cameras, so that the news event is no longer the real event as it would have been, and obviously the whole process of editing written text or editing news film is a means of constructing a view of the original event. So the concept of construction draws attention to the fact that communication is created. News is created. It follows then that a student of the media must look at why this happens (to sell the programme or paper), how it happens (through an array of devices), and what effect this may have on the audience's view of the particular event or story and of the world in general.

1.3 Agenda Setting

The news organizations set up an agenda of topics that form the news. Once more this opposes the idea that news is somehow a collection of truthful events and facts from 'out there'. The **editors choose the news, and in so choosing also choose an agenda of items that become our view of what is important in the world** that day or that week. Editors decide what their lead items are. In broadcasting they have meetings to decide what their running order of items will be. **Items are selected out and selected in.**

AGENDA SETTING is a process of making priorities. That which has priority is by definition more important than the items that don't. One is also interested in the basis from which news people form such priorities. This says something about how they see the world. At this point one is back into ideology. It may be argued that agenda setting is part of the ideology that is in our heads. If you look at the agenda, it tells you something about that ideology. For example, lead news items are often about people who are powerful in politics and economics; their power is reinforced by being in the news. But the items also contain views that themselves are reinforced. We are 'told' that national identity and not rushing into ties with Europe is important, but some might say that these items should not so frequently be top of the agenda. They might say that sorting out the problems of refugees in Europe is more important than worrying about our national boundaries. They might say that politicians are worried about new kinds of cooperation with the rest of Europe, because this may mean that they lose some of their status and power.

1.4 News Values

News values are concerned with topics that the news makers value as being newsworthy, and with ways of presenting those topics.

■ General Values

- **Negativity**: in general the news machine values the dramatic impact of bad news. Bad news is good news. Events involving a stock-market slump or a crash with deaths are rated above a steady market or excellent safety figures.
- **Closeness to home**: news that is closest to the culture and geography of the news makers is valued most. So a French yacht that sinks in the English Channel may not rate a mention, but if the boat is English it will likely appear.
- **Recency**: recent events are valued above distant ones; hence the competition among news people to get a scoop or to break a story first. This value is well projected on public consciousness: people believe that all the news is up to the minute. This is ironic because, in fact, it is often only the major stories that are recent – smaller items may well be two or more days old. And this value is inconsistent with another one.

- **Currency**: if a story has already been on the news agenda then further details on it are considered valuable, mostly because the audience already 'knows about it'. So stories that run on over days and weeks are not strictly new at all.
- **Continuity**: value is placed on items that are obviously going to have some continuity when the original story breaks. It is attractive to deal with some event like riots or a war, because these are likely to turn into a drama that will run for some time.
- **Simplicity**: items that can be dealt with simply are preferred to those that may be complicated to explain. Particularly, the popular press will prefer a straight story about some act of terrorism to a difficult one about balance of payments problems.
- **Personality**: stories that centre on a personality, preferably a public figure, or that can be developed round a person, are valued above many others because they automatically lend themselves to what is called the human interest angle.

All these general values mean that there are qualities of potential stories that cause them to be chosen above others. To this extent, there is bias built in to the news-making process. This selective approach to encoding communication is emphasized by other kinds of values.

■ Content Values
Certain topics will be valued and therefore chosen in preference to others. Examples are stories about disaster, stars, the royal family, authority figures … you can add to this list for yourself.

■ Treatment Values
These values refer to **what is valued about the treatment of the message**, the handling of the story. Stories that lend themselves to certain kinds of treatment may be preferred above others. Stories may deliberately be handled in terms of these values, even where this does not do justice to the complexity of what has happened.

- **Pictures** are valued – a story may be chosen if it can be given visual impact, especially if the picture is a scoop.
- **Dramatization** of stories is valued as a way of handling the material. Of course, unexpected or exceptional events lend themselves to this treatment anyway.
- **Conflict** is valued: stories may be told in these terms even when the truth is not simply about A versus B. It is more exciting to suggest that the story involves outright conflict, preferably between personalities, rather than being just about shades of disagreement.
- **Human interest** is valued as a way of putting an angle on a story. You will have noticed that, for example, disaster stories are often handled in this way, not least because the bare facts soon run out, and interviews with victims and relatives attract the audience.

- **Actuality** is valued – the news people will put a reporter on the spot, even when the spot is very boring. Pictures of a reporter outside a featureless building saying that nothing much has happened so far are quite common. But it endorses the idea that the news machine is there where it is all happening, where perhaps important political decisions are being made.

News and Predictability
Is all news actually new and unexpected?
Is this an illusion promoted in order to 'sell' news?

1.5 News as Entertainment

When one attends to the fact that news is a construct, then one is more or less saying that **there is little difference between news and fiction**, which is also about constructed stories. The very phrase 'news story' is revealing. It actually suggests that it is something made up – and stories are about entertainment. One can see that at least some news stories have entertainment value, when they are about crime and disaster, when they are about scandal and tragedy, when they centre on the human interest angle. People readily talk about human drama in news, and drama is associated with fiction.

What is more, there are dramatic devices in the unfolding of a news story. There are heroes and villains, the reader is denied information until later in the story. The whole programme in broadcast news is constructed with peaks and troughs in the relative excitement of the news items. Commercial television organizes this excitement around the advertising break, just like a soap opera might. Tabloid newspapers are in no doubt that news must be entertaining, to sell papers. The headlines, the selection of stories, the telling of stories, all contribute to this entertainment quotient.

1.6 Story Angles

The angle of a news story refers to the particular kind of treatment or meaning that is to be privileged. Editors talk frequently about the human interest angle, for example. They mean that they want the event to be dealt with in terms of the people involved rather than just the facts. **The idea of angle contradicts the notion of neutrality**, which the news machine also likes to project as being valued.

This draws attention to the fact that a news article is very much a made thing. Even a serious broadsheet item, full of facts, has to be put together. There is narration. The narrative may be more objective and factual than the stuff of a novel. But still the material is chosen and ordered. And news stories always move into areas of interpretation and speculation, commenting on the significance, in someone's opinion, of events and of statements.

1.7 Conventions

Conventions are unwritten rules about what may be in a newspaper or how it will be handled. This links them closely with news values.

There are also conventions about how the whole story of the news programme is put together and handled. It is a convention that the newsreader acts as link or story-teller. It is a convention that background pictures are put up behind the newsreader. It is a convention that reporters say who and where they are at the end of an item, and hand back to the studio. You can work out why these conventions are used, what effects they have on our views of the news programme as a whole.

1.8 Code

The idea of code has already been dealt with in Chapter 3. You will notice that we read primary codes in the news – speech, writing (captions), non-verbal communication and visual codes. It is also argued that news has its own way of communicating, its own signifiers that we have learned to make sense of, and therefore its own code. For instance, the live link to the place where the story is based is part of that secondary code. It signifies the authenticity of the item. It is used even when it would be as cheap and informative to have someone in the studio telling us the same thing.

So presentational devices are part of this code of news. Don't worry if you have spotted that these devices usually seem to be the same as conventions. They are! They are also talked about in terms of the language of the discourse of news (see Section 1.13, below). This kind of overlap of terminology in critiques of media has happened because media academics have started from different critical positions but ended up talking about pretty much the same ideas using slightly different language.

1.9 Experts

The use of 'experts' in news operations is also part of their image of authority. I use the word 'expert' in a qualified way because it is as much an idea that news people wish to promote as a straight fact. In other words, **they like to use and refer to experts in order to enhance their own credibility.** It is common to refer to reporters as being the 'consumer affairs reporter' or 'our correspondent in Jerusalem'. It is common to see experts in almost anything wheeled on to television news reports to express opinions. I am not saying that there is no expertise, but there is less than is suggested. The question is whether experts do substantially add to understanding of the story by being there in person or by being billed as experts. Most of what they are doing in at least some cases is to contribute to the credibility of the news operation.

1.10 Editorializing

This is the inclusion of an editorial view or opinion on news material. Newspapers have specific sections that express such opinions, which may support political parties' views. Broadcasting cannot do this, mainly on the assumption that it is somehow more influential as a medium and that, by contrast, newspapers at least can offer a choice of views. This idea of choice in the press is itself disputable. What is more to the point is that editorializing may happen covertly. This leads one into the area of bias (see Section 1.12, below). For example, suppose there is on radio news a story about a possible take-over by one water company of another. It is covert editorializing if there immediately follows an item on water pollution perpetrated by one of the companies. A point of view is implied by the association of one item with the other. If the two items are right next to one another, like two pictures in a magazine, then this is an example of **juxtaposition**. Again, it may be that broadcast news deals with material about Iraq in terms critical of the regime. Britain was involved in a war against that country in the early 1990s, so we are not surprised to receive news that is selectively critical. But the fact is that we can get an editorial point of view on the event and related issues. Suddenly neutrality is abandoned as an ideal.

1.11 Impartiality

This relates to editorializing because it refers to the idea that broadcast news doesn't take sides. This is an ideal to be striven for in the way that stories are covered. Editors believe it to be a quality of their programmes. In general terms it is true that broadcast news is not partial to one political party or another (though party leaders have disputed this at various times). But what I have said above indicates that news is not totally impartial about everything, yet it is enjoined to be, by various broadcasting acts and through internal advisory documents: 'each authority ... must ensure that their programmes display, as far as possible, a proper balance and a wide range of subject matter, accuracy in news coverage, impartiality in matters of controversy' (IBA Code of Practice, 1981).

1.12 Bias

News may incline to one view rather than another, to one interpretation of events rather than another. The issue of news BIAS is always being debated (see Chapter 8). News makers talk freely about their lack of bias, but everything I have said denies this – without saying that bias is extreme. **No communication can be totally neutral.** News people write out of their background and their beliefs – their ideology. Newspapers are biased by definition because no communication is neutral or value free. They frequently declare their support for a given view on political and social issues. Bias in broadcast news is less obvious but well documented in critiques of these operations. It has been pointed out that, on a number of occasions, broadcast news does implicitly bias its handling of trades union disputes by giving more time to management views than to those of the union, or by showing the union members as being excitable and disruptive as opposed to the calm talking heads of management.

A number of the critical points discussed in this chapter may be linked to the notion of bias. It can be argued that anything that predisposes the selection of news items (news values) or that frames the making of news (conventions) or that privileges ways of explaining news (picture power) is a kind of bias.

You should be careful, though, not to assume that there is such a thing as unbiased news. There are degrees of bias and kinds of bias. One can set relative benchmarks by which to evaluate bias. There are false understandings created by bias, but that doesn't mean there is some kind of unbiased super-news just waiting to be made.

News and Bias

Does the fact that different newspapers and different news programmes can take different angles on the same story, prove that there must be bias in news?

Are broadcast news stories unbiased because they all deal in the same basic facts?

1.13 News and Discourse

News may represent any number of discourses through its stories. For example, it will use language in particular ways to produce meanings about gender or about crime. But there is also a discourse of news itself. There is **a particular use of visual and verbal language that produces special meanings about the idea of news itself.** Three of these meanings are the ideas that news (especially television news) is authoritative, authentic and promotes consensus.

■ Authority

This lies in the image presented by styles of news presentation. The popular press does not seek this upmarket image of being an authority on news about the world. But the quality papers do convey seriousness in their relatively print-heavy front pages and discrete headlines. It is television, however, that especially seeks to assume the mantle of authority through elements such as the dress of its newsreaders, its reporters on the spot, its up-to-the-minute information. This image is important because it gives the news operation a kind of power – **the power of being knowledgeable and important.**

■ Credibility

Close to the above is **the idea that the news and its newsreaders are to be believed and trusted.** This meaning is promoted by the dress, accent and manner of newsreaders. It draws on our existing notions from our social experience, of who is to be believed. So it is no accident that newsreaders match the image of the middle-class professional.

■ Authenticity

News operations, especially those of broadcasting, like to enhance their trustworthiness and believability by appearing to present news 'as it really is'.

The use of actuality footage, of reporters in real locations, of statistics through graphics, supports **an idea that the news we get is about 'the truth'**. Pictures, whether in newspapers or on television, can be particularly influential in this respect – the cliché that, if you see it it, must be true. News editors will pay money to send news teams to cover an event or just the background to a story, even though they might be able to cover the story without location work, or could buy in material from an agency. Because 'we were there', because one can see the place where events took place or the people who were touched by events, then what they say about the story acquires credibility and authenticity. The 'Dunblane Massacre' story, where young children were murdered at school by a deranged man, is an example of this. The event was over. It served no real function of information to have pictures of the school or interviews with which to bolster the credibility of the news organizations involved.

■ Consensus

This refers to broadcast news only. It defines a tendency in the treatment of social and political issues to deal with them as if **the middle view is always right** and is the agreed view. Clearly this cannot apply so much to newspapers because they are blatantly tied to the views of their owners and are in business to make money. But broadcast news is not set up to make money (though it can influence advertising revenue through the ratings it generates). It should not support political views or any partial views at all, because of the terms of the BBC Charter and of the Broadcasting Acts.

But broadcast news does support this consensus. In the case of stories about kinds of dispute it will always imply that a compromise is the fair solution and is good for everyone. This is not necessarily true.

■ News Discourse and Ideology

News (see also Section 1.4 above, on news values), gives us **a meaning that the activities of those who have power in our social structure are of more importance than what is happening with those who don't have power**. This is an ideological meaning. News actually reinforces this power and definitions of fame through the working of its discourse. So it will, for example, prefer a body-shot picture of a pop star arriving at an airport on a flight that has been delayed by terrorist activity to a general view of tired and anxious members of the public arriving on the same flight.

Taking what is called a political economy approach to making sense of news, the Goldsmiths Media Group (1998) asserts that 'the news media, although a site of social conflict, relay the "dominant ideas" of the ruling classes'. In the group's view, 'economic concerns ... guide the production of news'. This is related to three points:

1 business is a prime funder of news
2 news production is expensive
3 news is a cultural commodity.

So it is argued that in the case of news, as with other media work, economic interests drive what we get and how it is framed.

THE DISCOURSE AS LANGUAGE

Visual code	Non-verbal code	Technical code	Verbal code
The camera POV places us face on to the reporter so that she talks directly to us	The reporter stands straight and her gaze is directly at the camera/at us	The sound appears to be live and immediate because of its quality and because of lipsynch	'Here, at the front line between . . .'

THE DISCOURSE AS MEANING

Produced by the signs used by these codes, it is conveyed that:

- news has the power to put reporters where major events are happening
- the 'live' presence of reporters at such events authenticates the truth of what they say and of news in general
- news has the power to report such events immediately
- the power of news is enhanced by its ability to control advanced technology
- news has authority because of these powers

Fig. 7.2 News discourse in action

For the model above, you should imagine the example of a news item that has the reporter on the spot, on the front line of some war or major civil disturbance.

The meanings of news discourse are the sum of all parts of the programme and of all the other news programmes that have gone before. The examples of discourse as language are at the same time examples of conventions. They are also examples of mode of address and of the relationship created with the audience.

■ *Encoding and Decoding News Language*

However, whether one is looking at news or other material, Stuart Hall (1993) draws attention to the fact that in the process of communication there is a distinction between meanings at the point of encoding and those at the point of decoding. If news has a discourse then **the structures of meaning that are in the minds of those who put it together may not be the same as those in the minds of those who read, view, listen to the news.** I have talked as if the way that the language of the discourse is used, and the meanings it produces, are some absolute 'out there'. But it isn't that simple. As Hall says, 'The lack of fit between the codes has a great deal to do with the structural differences of relationship and position between broadcasters and audiences.' So, to make things even more complicated, what I understand by the idea of news, what I make of a news programme, may not be quite the same as, say, a 'young audience' makes of it. This does not invalidate points made about features of the language of discourse – the significance of the face-on half-body shot of the newsreader – but it does remind us that we have to be careful about generalizing about the meaning of texts.

1.14 News: Social Reproduction

Ideas about discourse and ideology are part of the notion that **news operations in particular help construct social reality**. The meanings in discourse, the values within ideology are part of this reality:

> The social reproduction thesis ... is always based on the assertion that members of the audience obtain from journalism information which will tend to support an ideologically loaded view of the world; one which will contribute to the reproduction of an unequal and fundamentally antagonistic social system without dysfunctional conflict. (McNair, 1994)

But there is a question raised as to whether this is quite true. Can the construction of social reality be seen simply as a reproduction of the dominant ideology, where the news machine expresses ideas about values, about social relations, about power, which we accept uncritically? Perhaps the news does frame off our view of the world to a fair extent, but perhaps it also to an extent raises consciousness of issues, is sometimes critical of dominant ideological positions. Perhaps it does allow us some room to make oppositional readings of its texts, if not much room. After all, some news material does take a critical stance on issues of wealth, class and privilege. There is something called 'investigative journalism', which at times takes on the Establishment.

There is, for example, the explicitly pro-environment position taken by the *Independent on Sunday*. It includes more such stories than other newspapers, with the sometime exception of the *Guardian*. It takes a critical view of government and industry bodies that are not, it believes, working hard enough to deal with problems like global warming. Similarly, this newspaper also runs a campaign against rail service providers and their perceived failures, as well as against the failure of government (it claims) to act in the public interest with respect to transport.

1.15 News: Moral Panics

The term MORAL PANIC was coined by Cohen and Young to describe the hyping of moral issues in the media to the point where a sense of panic is created among the public. It also describes assertions that there is a panic – about youth gangs, for example – when this is not true. Panics sell newspapers: sometimes they are vehicles for the careers of politicians – panics about immigration, for example. You could say that this is also about news values. For instance, if events have to be exceptional, to have significance to make it on to the agenda, then a news organization can give them this saliency by asserting that there is a 'crime wave' or a 'health crisis' or a 'disaster in the making'. The call for further gun laws after the 'Dunblane Massacre' (see Section 1.13, above) was an example of this. It is ideologically 'conventional' to call for more control, more power. On the other hand, there was no such panic over the court case that focused attention on the dismissal of gay personnel from the British armed forces. Certainly some views were expressed that made Attila the Hun look like a pink liberal. Other news coverage gave space to make a critical reading of the unsubstantiated arguments of the Ministry of Defence.

So moral panics fasten on concerns held by one section of society about another. It is argued that they exaggerate those concerns. They foster anxiety. They demonize the social group that is the object of concern. They are therefore socially divisive. A recent example in the media was a campaign by the *News of the World* to 'out' paedophiles by identifying them and where they lived. One consequence of this was mob behaviour on the Paulsgrove Estate in Portsmouth. In various places, individuals were abused and driven out of their homes. In a few cases, people identified as paedophiles simply were not: a case of mistaken identity. From this, it isn't hard to understand how witch-hunts operated a few hundred years ago – though without the support of the press.

1.16 Gendered News

The issues around the gendering of news centre on news workers at the institutional end, on the nature of news texts and, to some extent, on the gender of the audience that finds news appealing. A number of commentators (e.g. Allan, 1999) would argue that news production is male oriented, that news texts are inflected towards masculine interests and a masculine view of the world, and that this is why – for television news in particular – a majority of the audience is male.

The distinction is easiest to grasp if one simply looks at the material of broadcasting and the press. It is possible to make a distinction between 'hard news' and 'soft news': news that is political and economic, dominated by facts and by male players, by ideas about competition and winning and losing; and news that is more social and personal, dominated by stories about personality and relationships. Of course, there is a danger that one falls into another kind of sexism if one simply asserts that gossip news is female news. But, if I give you an example: hard news as provided by most daily newspapers (especially the broadsheets) and by the main broadcast channels, would report stories about the Prime Minster in terms of his performance in Parliament or in international conferences; it would be considered soft news, feminized news, to dwell on his performance as a father. The superior value of the masculine hard-news position is taken for granted. But I would ask you to consider whether his performance as a father isn't just as good a touchstone of his 'worth' as a leader. The notion of a separation between working life and family life is well established for men – and works in the interests of men. It is ideological. It is very convenient for employers to be able to argue that 'naturally' it is not their concern as to what an employee's family circumstances and obligations are. It is convenient to assume that the male employee has a female behind him taking responsibility for the domestic sphere.

Even the reporting of politics has interesting gender assumptions built in to it. Lead stories may be about interest rates, or political sleaze or getting tough on crime. They will be about government policy. But one could argue that the female news audience is more interested in policies and stories that have to do with social and domestic consequences. I say this not to endorse a negative view of women in some domestic ghetto, but in the positive light of female recognition of the value of relationships.

Another touchstone of the divide of gender representation in texts is understood if one looks at newspaper photographs. News photos reproduce inequalities – photographs of the mainly male politicians, military leaders, scientists, and so on. They also endorse difference – photographs of women as fashion objects, sex objects, accompanying articles on health and body matters, figuring in stories about love and divorce.

In terms of news work, the speculation is whether the domination of news production by males creates a masculine view of the world. Would news look different if half the news workers were women? One answer to that (Van Zoonen, 1994) is, unfortunately, probably not. The evidence is that women in news work are assimilated into masculine practices and values. They succeed by going along with existing ideas of what makes good news, both in terms of story and treatment.

In terms of audiences, there is evidence (Silverstone, 1999) that men rather than women prefer to watch television news. Men are also controlling viewers – they like to wield the remote control. They like to watch with undivided attention, and don't like, for instance, to talk about news as it is being screened.

1.17 Technology and News

At the end of this special study of news and related ideas, it is worth looking briefly at a few aspects of new technology that have made great changes in how news is gathered and presented. New technology contributes to news values and qualities such as immediacy and actuality. It contributes to news messages in a number of ways. The advent of **electronic news gathering (ENG)** via video tape and satellite transmission back to the newsroom has enhanced the emphasis on up-to-date news. In the case of television this also means further emphasis on the value of visuals. The audience expects to see up-to-date pictures. The news makers make every effort to show recent pictures or footage. This was evident during the Gulf War of 1992 and in the case of the NATO war on Serbia in Kosovo in 1999, when the evening news showed film from the aircraft of missile attacks made the same day. The use of electronic displays, graphics and captions have added to this visual emphasis and a sense of drama in the case of television.

The 1990s was the decade of 'war through media technologies'. Immediacy and reality had been enhanced, but also the very definition of war and news of war was shifted, so that we now have:

- war from the front – now
- war as a spectacle (the computer game syndrome)
- war as techno-combat
- 'clean' war
- war as refugees.

The globe has shrunk selectively as some parts of it are easily available to satellite links, emphasizing the effect of immediacy and actuality. However, to an extent, new technology has created a sharper line between what is available and what is not. China is one of the biggest countries on earth, but denies access through new technology for the most part, and so is a place little seen. So new technology creates a new kind of geography, new categories of haves and have-nots.

Television news is now marked by the dramatic use of **electronic displays**, driven by the ubiquitous computer. News items drop in mobile graphics, captions, satellite links, almost without pause. Live satellite links with reporters on the spot add to a sense of immediacy, but it may be argued that the array of electronic devices becomes a part of news as entertainment. It may distract from the telling of it 'how it is', as much as it enhances truth-telling.

From this it is a short step to the **computer-controlled news studios** that are now in use. These can be run by one person or can even be run at a distance. Cameras are controlled remotely, news sources are tapped into. Such studios can either be slaves to the main news operations, or in use by satellite television and international news providers. Again, the issue seems to be that new technology is undermining the integrity of news. It is being used by the 'new managerialism' of cost and efficiency in media businesses to provide news on the cheap. Increasingly, regional television news, even the regional press to a fair extent, is only syndicated news. New technology allows standardized material to be accessed and edited easily. New jobs are collapsed into one another. But analysis, reflection, interpretation of events, goes out of the window, because this needs expensive time.

The use of **electronic compositing** of material in newspapers has helped them update their material quickly because it is relatively easier than it was to change page layouts. In effect, this is like using a more powerful version of the computer that was used to write this book. At the same time, technology has made colour photographs relatively easy to produce, perhaps dangerously blurring the line between newspapers and the magazine format. This happens because companies now use electronic process cameras to record images in the production process, and use computers to control **electronic imaging** of the recorded material.

News coverage of the Kosovo war provides an interesting case study in how new technology is changing coverage, perhaps even the meaning of what news is. For a start, both sides could watch satellite newscasts – CNN, SkyNews, BBC 24. The forces involved were also fighting the war via news, so far as they were able to release selective information, to put a spin on what was happening in the military conflict. Governments were involved in a propaganda war, in which news inevitably got caught up.

Philip Taylor (2000) discusses this when he comments on the significance of the Net in fighting the information war. He points out that not only were web sites used to discuss the war as it was happening, they were also used to post partial information about what was supposed to be going on. Allied and Serb governments took part in this activity. There was an elite minority of Serbs who were on the Net, who were perceived as OPINION LEADERS and targets for information. They could also pass out information. Taylor sees the Net as undermining the 'traditionally monopolistic role of journalists'. Taylor quotes a journalist (Mackenzie Wark) who said of new technology, 'the laptop, the modem, the cellphone and the satellite are making it hard for either side to have a complete control over the manufacture of wartime reality'. However, Taylor also comments that the outpouring of propaganda information by both sides – and the determined attempt by the Serbs to 'bomb' allied web sites with hundreds of messages (including some viruses) – all mean that it is difficult to see the Net as a medium of truthful information for the citizen.

Activity (15): Radio News

This activity draws attention to the differences between media and to ideas about news selection.

WRITE A RADIO SCRIPT OF ABOUT 400 WORDS FOR A MUSIC STATION, WHICH PROVIDES A REPORT ON A FESTIVAL OR SOME OTHER RELEVANT EVENT. It is important that you think about your listeners and that you stick to the word limit.

From doing this you should learn something about selection and construction in the media. Why did you leave out or include certain facts and ideas, for example? You should also learn about the qualities of the medium. How did you help the audience visualize what is happening in a sound-only medium?

---

2 ADVERTISING AND PERSUASION: COMMUNICATION AND INFLUENCE

Introduction

This section deals with some definitions, some terms and with techniques of persuasion in particular. It explains ideas that, in turn, help describe how advertising may influence us, and how it shapes our culture and society. Advertising is not a form of communication, but a way of using forms of communication to achieve effects. (Because modes of visual communication are used so frequently in advertising, this section also deals with image analysis, adding to what was said in Chapter 2.)

You should also understand what this section will not do, because there is a great deal of other material around that it is pointless to duplicate within the confines of this book. It will not deal with the mechanics of the advertising industries and the production of advertisements. It will not make an extended analysis of advertising material, nor of verbal techniques.

The reason that advertising is so frequently dealt with in Media Studies is that it is the one type of product that nakedly supports the commercial values of the media. The income it generates underpins all media. Without their income from advertising, popular newspapers would cost 50 to 60 pence each. Without advertising, there would be no commercial television or radio; and it is clear that television is the main medium when it comes down to weight of revenue – an income of £2,777 million for terrestrial television alone, in 1999. Without advertising, most magazines would double or treble in price. Remember too that there are many, many ways of advertising that we take for granted, but that would profoundly affect our environment if they disappeared – posters in the street, material on shop counters, material that comes through our doors. The economic effects of advertising are enormous. Whether we like it or not, advertising does create jobs by creating demand for products. Whatever else the arguments about its effects, there is clear evidence that advertising does boost sales of products when it is present, and that product sales do drop after a while when it is absent. So we have to take very seriously such communication, which affects all our lives in different ways.

Advertising invests huge sums of money in various kinds of research. New technology, for example, helps supermarkets keep track of customer preferences and patterns of consumption – 90 per cent of groceries now pass through barcode checks.

It makes no bones about trying to persuade us, to have some effect on us. **It is very intentional communication.** Its purposes are clear. It is often very well constructed (and possibly effective) communication because the people who create advertisements have invested a great deal of time and money in finding out how its messages should best be treated in order to have an effect.

You also have to remember (see Chapter 4) the huge economic power of advertising in subsidizing media costs and in influencing media content. An example of this influence (January, 2001) is that three major women's magazines, *Cosmopolitan*, *Nova* and *Marie-Claire*, have refused to run an advertisement submitted by the RSPCA. This advert intended to persuade people against the use of animals in the testing of cosmetic products. It shows a rabbit having its eyes sprayed. It is clear that the magazines do not wish to alienate their cosmetics advertisers.

Advertising is also bound up with the increasing dominance of a few companies in the British advertising industry. Among other facts, Brierley (1995) refers to: three ITV companies controlling 72 per cent of advertising revenue; Rank Screen Advertising having an 86 per cent share of cinema screen advertising in 1993; six outdoor billboard companies controlling 82 per cent of sites.

2.1   Some Basic Background Terms

- **Advertising** is paid-for persuasive communication such as appears between programmes in broadcasting, or as point-of-sale (POS) material in shops. Publicity is free communication that may still persuade the audience to judge the product or service favourably. An example would be a film star talking about their latest movie on a chat show. (plugging)

- **Marketing** is the promotion of products (or indeed of things like banking services or a sale of shares in a company). This uses any device to promote its product, such as a staged event, as well as the media.

- A **campaign** is coordinated advertising and publicity across the media and over a specific period of time. It is organized according to a specific schedule. A campaign uses a variety of means of communication at various times in order to get to a target audience and to reinforce its main message.

- The **target audience** is the particular audience chosen for the product or service, defined in terms of gender, occupation, disposable income and socio-economic grouping.

- **Sponsorship** provides financial support to something like sport, or public service television in the USA, in return for which the sponsor gets its name spread around (for example, on racing cars).

- **Product placement** uses the product within media material, often film or television drama, so that it is seen but not nakedly advertised. We have been used to seeing items such as Ford cars featured for years, but now placement of all sorts of items, including things like soft drinks, is big business and is paid for.

- **Brand image** is the impression a particular brand of product leaves in the mind of the audience. This impression can be dominantly about traits such as humour, classiness or value for money.

- **Copy** is the writing created for advertisements in print media.

- **Display ads** are the large advertisements in newspapers and magazines, usually with a picture and in some sort of a box.

- The **rate card** is the table of how much it costs to advertise in a given medium. Rates in television, for example, are extremely complicated, depending on factors like time of day, time of year, national or local screening, whether you are a local advertiser or not, as well as the numbers of your target audience who are likely to see the product.

2.2   The Range of Advertising

People tend to think immediately of products and of high-profile media such as television. But posters are also a successful medium. People also use unusual means, such as balloons and matchboxes, to promote a company name.

The line between advertising and publicity (promotion) is blurred, if we use the idea of 'paid for' as a criterion. Both functions add up to something called marketing, which is generally designed to promote awareness, shift goods and simply to make money. It has been proposed that advertising is the directly persuasive communication that is paid for. Publicity is more indirect, does not involve the advert as object, and is not apparently paid for. However, I say 'apparently' because in fact there is often a huge bill for publicity activities.

For example, launch parties for films or other products are quite common. They are clearly distinct from paying for a radio spot, but again someone has

Table 7.1 Examples of British advertising rates 1998

	Cost in £
Daily Mail full page (black and white)	30,492
Daily Mail full page (colour)	43,974
Daily Telegraph full page (black and white)	41,125
Daily Telegraph full page (colour)	49,500
Sunday Times full page (black and white)	48,500
Radio Times full page (black and white)	13,700
Radio Times full page (colour)	18,500
Just Seventeen full page (black and white)	4,900
Just Seventeen full page (colour)	7,930
Edinburgh Herald and Post full page (black and white)	3,080
Carlton 30-second weekday peak-time spot (1926hrs–2330hrs)	23,000
Grampian TV 30-second weekday peak-time spot (1800hrs–2300hrs)	1,250
30-second spot (each day, one week) in London Cinemas (372 screens)	40,225
30-second spot (each day, one week) in Lancashire Cinemas (162 screens)	10,035
BRMB (Birmingham Radio) 30-second spot, Wednesday–Friday (1600hrs–1900hrs)	700
Virgin FM (London) 30-second spot, Thursday–Friday (1600hrs–1900hrs)	650
Virgin Radio (AM/National) 30-second spot, Thursday–Friday (1600hrs–1900hrs)	1,100

Source: Student Briefing No 6 © Advertising Association

The media fix their advertising rates according to the size of their audience, its age and its social profiles. The rates are highly negotiable, depending on numerous factors, including possible large discounts.

to foot the bill for the party. You will have noticed the spate of interviews with stars that accompany the opening of a major movie. Whether or not a fee is involved, it is obvious that the article that may result is not one that just happens to come up because 'our readers might be interested'. Even the tenth-birthday celebration party given by the Press Complaints Commission is a kind of publicity. It is costing thousands of pounds, and someone is paying for it.

Even means of advertising can be deceptive in the ways that we recognize them. People tend to think of television ads and magazine ads, for example, but another important example is the mailshot that comes directly into our homes as does television. That is paid for as much as the more obvious screen ad at the cinema. There are also the classified ads in newspapers, which though they look very different from an expensive display ad selling new houses, are nevertheless paid for and are trying to sell a product of some sort.

One also gets tie-in and crossover advertising, where an advertisement for one product is used to help market another. A dominant example is music behind film and television ads. In 2000, tracks from Moby's *Play* album were helping to sell cars (Renault and Nissan) as well as chocolates (Thorntons and Galaxy), but of course the ads were also helping to sell Moby's album.

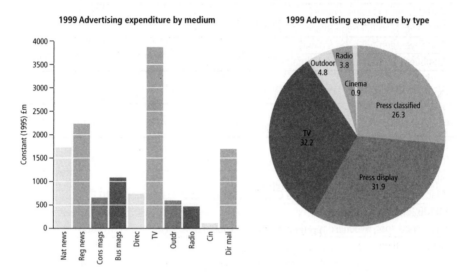

Fig. 7.3 Advertising expenditure by medium and by type, 1999

Source: *Advertising Statistics Yearbook 2000.* NTC Publications Ltd.

2.3   Purposes of Advertising

Advertising can be categorized by its purpose. It isn't just about selling objects. The government is often the top spender on advertising with a range of purposes, such as warning the public about the dangers of drink-driving. When a company like BP spends hundreds of thousands of pounds on television advertising, it isn't trying to get you to buy petrol, it is trying to get us all to see BP as an impressive organization, doing good things like providing jobs and protecting the environment.

Even within a purely commercial environment, advertisers can have a range of purposes:

- to create awareness of the product or service
- to reassure existing customers about the quality of the product
- to reassure the trade and the sales force
- to grab a bigger share of the market
- to hold on to an existing share of the market against competition.

2.4   Advertising as Communication

Advertising provides us with a miniature of the basic process model of communication. It has a **triple source**, which is:

1 the original organization
2 the creative consultancy that creates the advertisement
3 the medium that actually projects the message.

It is created because of commercial needs. It is **encoded** for specific media. It uses specific **media or channels** of communication. It contains messages of both an informational and a value-laden nature. The messages are treated so that they will be attractive to the audience. The **meaning** of the message(s) has to be decoded by the audience. The **audience** is carefully defined (targeted) as the receiver of the communication. There is **feedback**, notably through purchase of the product or service, and through market research. All in all, advertising is a potent subject for Media Studies because it can help you understand ideas about meaning, about values, about ideology, about culture, and indeed any of the topics dealt with in this book. The next few sections look at some of these ideas.

2.5   The Regulation of Advertising

Although I talked generally about media regulation in Chapter 4, advertising deserves a little more space. This is because it notably demands regulation because it is a calculatedly persuasive use of media. All media carry some advertising, even down to the promotional trailers at the beginning of film videos; and advertising in some forms actually extends outside what we conventionally think of as media – street posters, adverts on vehicles, Adshels on bus shelters, and so on. It isn't a separate medium of communication that can be regulated on its own, like cinema. In spite of its avowed intention to influence us and its enormous scope across the media, advertising is mainly self-regulated.

The **Advertising Standards Authority** covers cinema, magazines, newspapers. It has a Code of Advertising Practice. It is a body set up by the Advertising Association, which speaks for the industry across the media. There is also the European Advertising Standards Alliance – another self-created industry body set up, in effect, to protect its own interests.

The **Independent Television Commission** (ITC), also referred to in Chapter 4, regulates commercial television in the UK, including Channel 4, Channel 5, satellite and cable. It works through a Code of Advertising Standards and Practice. This establishes 'rules' about, for example, what kinds of products may be promoted around children's programmes; it will not allow more than an average of 7 minutes of advertising per hour. It has an extensive code of practice that refers to matters of taste, to the use of children in advertisements, to the use of bad language or sexual innuendo. It bans specific kinds of advertising, such as the promotion of betting or fortune-telling – but managed to except the National Lottery! Similarly it bans advertising for political purposes, but has to allow party political broadcasts. Among other rules are those which say that:

- advertisements must be distinguishable from programmes
- drinks adverts can't promote themselves in terms of one being a social success because one drinks
- elite persons may not be used to promote medicines
- subliminal advertising (the used of flashed images) is banned.

The **Broadcast Advertising Clearance Centre** (BACC) is a self-regulatory body for television and radio, set up by broadcasters. It works so closely with the ITC and the Radio Authority that it is nearly indistinguishable from them.

The **Radio Authority** oversees commercial national and local radio advertising. It has its own code of standards and practices. It has a very 'light touch' in its regulation, leaving the largely local stations to be sensitive to what their own audiences will or will not accept.

2.6 Advertising and Representations

Advertisements, like genres, are prone to represent people as types (see Chapter 5, Section 3). If they use stereotypes then they also tend to project the value messages attached to those stereotypes. Such representations are attractive to the makers of advertisements because they are instantly recognizable and so provide a short-cut into the 'storyline'. These images of people are part of the attraction of the advertisement – and it needs to attract attention rapidly. They make the 'story' of television advertisement or full-page magazine advertisement containable within a brief space (perhaps 20 seconds in the case of broadcasting). They carry the audience along with the main message of the advertisement because many of them agree with the value messages within the stereotype – largely because of the way they have been socialized. The nature of stereotypes and the construction of advertisements positively discourages us from stopping to think about them. Particularly if the advertisement invites us to have a laugh, it might seem ill-humoured to criticize it. However, a good student should stop to think about meanings and effects, not least when the same stereotypes are reinforced by being repeated. We may remind ourselves that representation refers perhaps to ideas and institutions, to a version of reality, all of which may be associated with representation as it refers to people.

[handwritten: relates to ideology]

So you should ask yourself, for instance, what it means if women are absent from advertisements relating to banking services. The bankers are often male. The customers, even the newer and younger target audience, are almost always male. This is a view of the world that does not see women as senior bank workers (statistically they are not!); it is a view of the world that does not see young females as potential earners. Such communication, supported by myriad other examples, is likely by accumulation to convince young females that they are never going to be economically powerful, that they are never going to make it in the banking profession. In this way stereotypes can contribute to a self-fulfilling prophecy, a vicious circle in which people end up behaving in stereotypical ways.

These stereotypes in television advertising are quite often set within a narrative borrowed from genre. See if you can spot the miniature soaps, quiz games, westerns, war films, and so on. Remember that, in borrowing the genre, the advertiser also borrows all the themes and messages associated with the genre. Holsten Pils ads used old movie clips, re-edited and with new sound dubbed on. When one of these used an escape scene from a war film, it was also borrowing something of the male, macho associations of such films.

2.7   Advertising and Audiences

Essentially, audiences for advertising are seen in two ways.

1 In terms of demographics: objectifiable categories such as age, gender, occupation, area lived in.
2 In terms of psychographics: more subjective categorization by inferred features such as needs, personality type or lifestyle.

Since advertisers are in the business of tapping into values and seeking to modify attitudes, they have an interest in trying to describe us in terms of how we think and how we see ourselves.

For some years now, **advertising has sought to sell not just images and values but also the whole lifestyle within which the product or service exists.** These lifestyles are not invented but are, rather, sharpened versions of our own lifestyles and aspirations as obtained through market research.

> The function of advertising is to deliver audiences to the market … MASS COMMUNICATION allows them [advertisers] to build up particular class, age and gender related constituencies whose habits can be recognised … so when market research uncovers new social trends advertisers are feeding back to us versions of ourselves. (Hart, 1991)

From another point of view it is all about giving us a story we can drop into, a life we can inhabit and which, of course, is better than our own. It is no accident that in this same period there has emerged a kind of advertisement that tells a story, perhaps one that runs over a number of adverts. The story within which the Renault Clio car was sold existed as one of romantic adventure and Gallic style. It is a world for young women, and reflects the fact that females are now as important as males in terms of car purchases.

The lifestyle is one that gives pleasure and security, and reinforces certain values, notably that consumption is OK and can even be squared with politically correct values such as a concern for the environment.

The identification of audience types and audience behaviours has become ever more complex. BARB has over 100 categories of audience. There are dozens of new broadcast channels. Audiences watching satellite television in pubs can't be recorded by current research methods. Knowing that a sample domestic television set is switched on to a given channel doesn't prove that people are watching it, and now the TiVO device enables audiences to simply screen out the ads. The various industry research organizations, such as the National Readership Survey (NRS) for the press, tend to report audiences in figures, or quantitative terms. Measuring the audience qualitatively (perhaps in terms of psychological profiles) *is* done, but it is a minefield of contradictory evidence about how we perceive and react to ads.

2.8   Advertising and Culture

Advertising in many ways represents key elements of our culture. It is central to our culture and to the ideology behind it because it is about consumption and materialism. It is one of our central beliefs (discuss it with your friends!) that it is a good thing to buy and own goods. These goods can make you happy, can enhance your status, it is believed. You are what your Porsche says you are, and this is good. Since one main business of advertising is to sell goods for consumption, **it is maintaining and promoting beliefs central to that culture.**
Some would say that it even helps to distort them and creates the contradictions to which I refer in Chapter 8. For instance, part of our ideology is about helping other people (perhaps nurtured by religious convictions). But there is at least some contradiction between the idea of being unselfish and helping others, and apparently selfishly pursuing the acquisition of wealth.

Culture is a very complex idea, which includes the artistic and creative sides of the society. So here are a couple more ideas for you about this powerful use of communication. One is that, in a sense, advertising is its own art form within our culture. This may seems odd, given the fact that advertisements shamelessly rip off western art showing a Rembrandt portrait smoking a cigar, for example. But the fact is that just as people discuss other media products as a part of our culture, they also discuss advertisements: 'Did you see the one about ...?'. For example, there is a well-known cigarette poster advertisement that involves visual play on purple silk and the silk being torn by sharp instruments like scissors or knives. The symbolism is very peculiar, the meaning a good one for discussion. It is very much part of our culture, something that is not likely to mean anything at all in Japan, say. A related idea is that just as nursery rhymes are part of our culture – they refer to events and mythical characters that only we could understand – now advertising jingles are too. These are what children sing in the playground. They have become as much part of our culture as Bing Crosby singing *White Christmas* for the millionth time at Christmas.

Advertisers themselves are aware of their place within culture, of their part in promoting and creating cultural phenomena. Market research is now moving into an area described as cultural anthropology. Investigation combines research methodologies to uncover fine details of people's lifestyles. A company named Cultural Imprint conducted research that led to the production of the hugely successful range of Magnum ice creams.

Market researchers are sensitive to developments in cultural theory. They have tried to follow through with audience classification by description of 'cultural group' and related behaviours. As always, they are looking to identify shared values that can be invoked in the ads.

2.9 Advertising and Ideology

I have said quite a lot elsewhere in this book about ideology, so it isn't necessary to repeat definitions and arguments, but it is worth pointing out that **notions of lifestyle and of culture tie in with ideology because they are all about peoples' values and attitudes.** Vestergaard and Schroder (1994) suggest that 'the most coherent, accessible version of the popular ideological universe can be found in the textual messages which people consume regularly, because they find pleasure in them'. People find pleasure in adverts – they are designed to be pleasurable. Adverts have, for example, changed to take account of shifting attitudes towards gender and gender roles. We now hear relatively less about what it takes to be a good mum, and we do see something of young women in an independent role. Having said that, there are still big underlying ideological imperatives that remain – for example, the value of individualism. There is a kind of irony in the fact that cars, mass products on a vast scale, frequently pivot their advertising on appeal to individualism – being different.

It is car adverts, among others, that are referred to by Vestergaard and Schroder when they discuss a particular example of ideology – the ideology of 'the natural'. They talk about 'imposing Nature as a referent system'. They talk about putting the car in some beautiful countryside so that it accrues a kind of value from simply being there. Another common invocation is that of nature or naturalness as an 'ingredient in the product' – in health foods, for example. A third variation is where a product actually claims to be an 'improvement on nature' – hair tints, for example (though the important point is still that nature is a benchmark of value and approval). Finally, there are advertisements that actually 'counteract natural processes' while still invoking naturalness. Here a classic example would again be hair tints that are meant to conceal naturally grey hair, but that claim to restore a natural look. Naturalness is clearly approved of in the ideological context, but its meaning and value is hijacked and grafted on to products that are often a long way from being natural in any respect.

Advertising and Materialism

Is there evidence that advertising has shifted social and cultural values to a belief in things above people?

Does advertising reflect social and economic changes in which people have more money to buy material goods?

2.10 Devices of Persuasion

Advertising is essentially persuasive, and so let us see how communication can be shaped to persuade the audience. You should realize that the devices described below appear in all forms of communication in which persuasion is used. You probably try to persuade someone of something every day of your life, so you can apply the devices to conversation, group interaction, and so on. You should also realize that there is nothing inherently sinful about persuasion. When the word is used in conjunction with advertising people tend to think loosely about brainwashing and sinister purposes, but there is nothing wrong with trying to persuade people not to drink and drive, for example. So if you are going to analyse advertisements for these devices of persuasion, don't imagine you are uncovering some great plot. All you are doing is discovering how communication works. The question of what you are being persuaded of, what you might do or think at the end of it, is another matter. The implications of persuasion operated through one of the mass media are significant because of what is loosely called the power of the media. You can look back to the first two chapters of this book to see what was said about these ideas.

- **Repetition**: people tend to believe messages that are repeated. They take notice of them. Hence the habit of repeating brand names or catchphrases in advertisements.
- **Reward**: advertisements offer rewards in various ways. Free offers are naked rewards, but often the rewards are psychological rather than material. Advertisements for household cleansers offer you the reward of being a good housewife, or perhaps of being a good parent who cares for your children.
- **Punishment**: the reverse of this may be that you are implicitly threatened with punishment if you don't buy: 'Don't miss the opportunity of a lifetime!' Or, if you don't buy this dog food you will feel really guilty because you are not doing the best for your pet.
- **Humour**, whether it is visual or verbal, comic or ironic, can set up a favourable ambience for the product. It can make people feel well disposed towards the ad, and so more amenable to its central message. A good joke can also make a given ad distinctive and different from the rest.
- **Agreement with values**: this is a strong device, because the communication offers value messages you are bound to agree with and then ties them to the product or service, so that you feel you also have to agree to buy this as well. You agree that it is sensible to plan ahead and provide for your old age, so of course you should buy this insurance.
- **Identification and imitation**: this device plays on the status of the source. In this case the advertisement uses, for example, a personality or type that you admire and respect. So you feel bound to order another pint of milk as the advertisement says, because X drinks it. Identification also plays on types of people. If you identify with and approve of the type represented, then you may be persuaded to possess the product they are shown to own and use (see Section 3.1 of Chapter 5, on stereotypes).
- **Group identity**: people have a strong need to be part of groups. This can bring them security and status, as well as a sense of worth and of their place

in the world. So advertisements often persuade the consumer by showing an attractive group member and by offering membership of that group along with the product.

- **Emulation and envy:** in this case the advertisement offers you something like a way of life that you desire. You are shown a Caribbean lifestyle (shown as enviable by previous media material), and so you feel that you should buy this pension scheme that will enable you to retire into the good life.
- **Admiration** is often associated with the use of an elite person such as a sports personality promoting a drink. The identity of the person becomes part of the identity of the product. If we respect the person then we are more likely to accept what the advert is saying.
- **Needs:** most of all, advertisers are adept at appealing to basic needs that we have, and that motivate all our communication anyway. The needs for personal esteem and for social contact are very strong. Many advertisements for beer offer to satisfy these needs. You will become one of the lads and have a good laugh at the bar if you drink this beer. Sex, in various guises, is still one of the most frequent expressions of need that is invoked.
- **Metaphor:** ads are full of transferred meanings and symbols. This common device picks up on connotations, on meanings that are implicit. The car in the advertising image becomes more than just a car: it is a metaphor for status, affluence, comfort, etc.
- **Mode of address:** the 'style' in which many ads address the viewer/reader is direct and personal. It is persuasive in the way that it tries to quickly set up a personal relationship with the consumer.

Generally speaking, all of these devices seek to produce attitude change in the audience (to something favourable), regarding the subject of the advert. After this, it is a matter of hope as to whether the advertiser also achieves behavioural change and a purchase! However, sales figures do prove that consumer action does take place sometimes.

Try looking for these devices in a range of advertisements across a range of media. See if you can pinpoint what it is about the image or the copy that actually triggers the device. Remember that advertisements may well use more than one device at a time.

You might also see if you can relate these devices to the classic AIDA model in which it is said that all advertisements have to grab 'Attention', arouse 'Interest', create 'Desire' and lead to 'Action'.

The basic devices of reward and punishment may be related to theories of cognitive dissonance. This suggests that we always seek a state of mental equilibrium. So if something disturbs us, causes disharmony (dissonance) then we seek to right this – perhaps by agreeing with the message of the ad and by buying the product. If an ad can make us feel guilty or lacking in some way, then we may in theory redeem those disturbing feelings by making a purchase, when there is an opportunity at least.

2.11 Visual Analysis

Advertisements often include visual elements, in newspapers, magazines, television, point-of-sale material, mailshots, and the like. By concentrating on the visual form, I am not running down the importance of words, but education gives proportionately a lot of time to words, somewhat at the expense of visuals as communication.

I would refer you back to Chapter 2 where there was a short section on image analysis (Section 2.5) as a method of studying media material. This focused, for example, on **image position signs** (where the camera is placed and places us), **image structure signs** (how elements such as lighting and focus affect our understanding) and **image content signs** (what the objects in the image may mean). These signs all work together so that the whole is more than the sum of its parts.

You should also look back at the semiotics section (Chapter 2, Section 2.2), and what is said about **denotation** and **connotation**.

Visual analysis of advertising images will make it clear that they are selling values as well as products and services. It will discover the devices of persuasion referred to above. It exposes the use of stereotypes and the covert messages embedded in much advertising material. It reveals what meanings may be in the material and how they come to be there.

Advertising is as significant within the media for its accepted use of persuasion, as news is significant for its position as an informer. In their own ways, both do a great deal to shape our views of the world. Within a limited space I have tried to deal with the 'SO WHAT?' question with regard to advertising. So it plays a vital financial role in the media. So understanding of some descriptive terms helps sort out what advertising is and what kinds of advertising there are. So it tells us a lot about how we use communication in general in order to persuade. So understanding of sign and process can be used to get at the meanings within, and the significance of, this special media product.

Activity (16): Advertising

LIST WAYS IN WHICH A BRITISH STAR OF FILM – HUGH GRANT OR HELEN MIRREN, FOR EXAMPLE – MIGHT BE USED AS PART OF A FILM MARKETING CAMPAIGN.

This activity should bring out points for you about the power of personality in the media, and about the ways in which media interact within a marketing campaign.

REVIEW

You should have learned the following things about news, advertising and persuasion from this chapter.

1 MAKING SENSE OF NEWS

1.1   News is gathered and sorted from a variety of sources and is paid for like any other commodity.

1.2   News is a process of selection and construction of meaning about its material, through various devices.

1.3   News organizations decide on news topics for a day or a week through a process of selection. This is called agenda setting.

1.4   News is selected and handled according to values held by the news organizations. These values relate to content and treatment in particular.

1.5   News is in many ways just entertainment, especially on television.

1.6   News stories are handled from particular points of view with a particular theme in mind. This is called the 'angle'.

1.7   The conventions of the code affect how news material is structured and presented to the audience.

1.8   News has its own secondary code. The signifiers affect how we understand news items, and how we see news material as being truthful and authentic, for example.

1.9   News material is mediated and given authority through the use of 'experts'.

1.10 The presentation of opinions overtly in newspaper editorials or covertly in the way that news material is handled is called editorializing.

1.11 The various news machines believe in impartiality, though they do not always achieve this in practice.

1.12 There are continuing debates about the issue of bias in news, especially in broadcasting. There will always be a degree of a bias because communication cannot, of itself, be neutral.

1.13 News has its own discourse, or special language and sets of meanings about what news is supposed to be. Discourses are ideological. The discourse is encoded by the news makers and decoded by the audience. The sets of meanings in news discourse are produced by its use of visual and verbal languages, especially through news presentation. News is seen as having authority. News nurtures an impression of authenticity, of truthfulness and actuality. Broadcast news tends to present social and political issues in terms of a consensus, or belief that the middle view is always right.

1.14 News helps construct our social reality. It helps reproduce 'things as they are'.

1.15 News manufactures 'moral panics' about various issues of health and public safety through exaggeration and through the selective presentation of many stories on the 'theme' at one time.

1.16 Gendered news refers to ideas about gender bias in the production process and in news texts, as well as in how news is read differently by men and women.

1.17 News making and presentation has been much influenced by new technology, which tends to emphasize the value of recency and of special effects in presentation, at the expense of reflection and impartiality.

ADVERTISING AND PERSUASION: COMMUNICATION AND INFLUENCE

Advertising is not a form of communication, but a kind of use of various forms of communication. Advertising is crucial in Media Studies because it pays for so much material. Advertising is intentional, persuasive communication.

2.1 There are a range of basic background terms that are useful for defining the topic: publicity, marketing, campaign, target audience, sponsorship, product placement, brand image, copy, display ad, rate card.

2.2 Advertising is not all about product. Other descriptive categories include service, company image, public information.

2.3 Advertising has a variety of purposes beyond trying to sell objects.

2.4 Advertising may be analysed effectively in terms of a process model of communication.

2.5 Advertising is specially regulated.

2.6 Advertising tends to use stereotypes to help carry messages about its product, service, etc. These stereotypes also carry covert value messages.

2.7 Advertising constructs whole lifestyles for its audiences, and sells these lifestyles.

2.8 Advertising material is part of our culture and represents ideals (mythologies) about that culture.

2.9 Advertising reinforces the dominant ideology in its value messages.

2.10 Advertising uses a number of devices of persuasion, main examples of which are repetition, reward, punishment, endorsement of values, identification and imitation, group identity, emulation and envy, arousal and identification of needs, the use of metaphor and of certain modes of address.

2.11 Advertising relies heavily on imagery. Image analysis is a very appropriate way of getting at the meanings in advertising material.

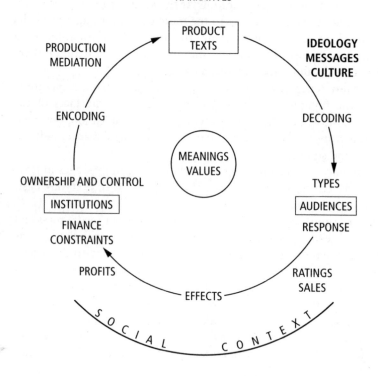

REPRESENTATION
INFORMATION AND PERSUASION
GENRES REALISM
NARRATIVES

PRODUCT
TEXTS

PRODUCTION
MEDIATION

IDEOLOGY
MESSAGES
CULTURE

ENCODING

DECODING

MEANINGS
VALUES

OWNERSHIP AND CONTROL

TYPES

INSTITUTIONS

AUDIENCES

FINANCE
CONSTRAINTS

RESPONSE

PROFITS

RATINGS
SALES

EFFECTS

SOCIAL   CONTEXT

8

Meanings and Issues

In this chapter I want to look more carefully at the kinds of message that are coming through, and at ways of getting to the more covert messages in media material. We need to get beyond seeing the obvious information in a programme or paper as being the message, and understand that within it **there are implied beliefs and values that are also messages**.

This is like the difference between denotation and connotation. A picture in a newspaper of the funeral of some public figure denotes the facts of the funeral procession, of the hearse, of the watching crowds and so on, but what it connotes is much more than this: ceremony, power, significance, cultural distinction, grief, and so on.

There is a difference between making a critical reading of messages in texts and of their possible effects – and what actually happens on an everyday basis when the real audience reads media.

Jenny Kitzinger (1999) says that 'the ability to deconstruct media messages to develop a critical reading in a research setting is not necessarily the same as being able to reject the message conveyed via the media on a day-to-day level'.

One also needs to bear in mind the fact that what we read into media material may or may not fit the ideas and intentions of its producers. I am certainly not saying that there are no intended effects or understandings, but the relationship between producer, text, audience and social/cultural contexts is very complex. We may be affected by cultural values in media material. Yet these values may not have been deliberately 'written in' to what we read and see.

An essential problem in respect of meaning is simply to define its 'location' – where it exists. It is too simplistic to see meaning as something slotted into text and transferred into the consciousness of the audience. It may be seen partly as something pre-conceived in the minds of media producers: 'this is what we want to say'. It is certainly in the heads of audiences: 'this is what we think it is about'. It is something that the audience makes by interacting with the text.

1 MEDIA MESSAGES: READING MEANINGS

1.1   Message and Meaning

So you need to recognize the difference between what is said and what is meant. Messages are not just on the surface. You need to read more carefully to read deeper. For example, a certain advertisement for a bank is seen as apparently carrying the message (paraphrased), 'If you are young, open a bank account with us and we will see that you are all right.' But, in fact, the meaning of the whole advertisement can be a great deal more complicated. It may be telling us that bank managers are of course male. Or that it is quite easy to borrow money from a bank. Or that it is OK to borrow and spend the money on goods, on yourself.

This example also shows how **there are usually multiple messages in any example of media material**. One picture can tell us a great deal, so can one magazine, one programme, one record. There is always more than one point to a story. There is always more than one point of view about some political event.

1.2   Intentionality

It is important to realize that **whatever meanings we may find in the media, they may or may not be there by intention**. We have to steer a course between paranoia about what 'they' are trying to do to us, and a naive attitude which assumes that all messages appear by chance, or that everything is written and produced for essentially benign reasons. It is absurd to suggest that the media producers are intentionally trying to feed us a diet of stereotypes through drama and comedy; it is equally absurd to assume that they are not aware of these stereotypes; and it is stupid to ignore the fact that we do receive value messages through such stereotypes. It is necessary to understand that **even unintentional messages are still the responsibility of those who construct them** into material. Some messages really are there by intention – many of those in advertisements. One would have to be very stupid to spend thousands of pounds on cat food commercials and not realize that one has intentionally encoded messages about cats being females' pets – not least because females do most of the shopping, for pet food among other items.

1.3   Commodification and Meaning

Reference to advertisements provides a good point at which to revisit this idea that the media help a process in which materialism rules, and **everything becomes valued in terms of its financial worth**. An advertisement is about selling commodities or goods, as well as the idea (meaning) that acquiring goods is a proper way to live your life. The advert is also a kind of commodity in itself. It is manufactured by an agency, it is sold into a broadcast or print space. From this view, adverts and other media texts become goods for sale. This is most obvious at media trade fairs, where television programmes or films are sold to distributors. But, then, even people become goods in a way: the audience for the advert is sold to the advertiser; the owners of a magazine have a rate card of costs for advertisers; the rate depends on the numbers of certain kinds of reader that magazine can deliver to the people who want to buy the advertising space.

It may be said that even the social lives of people become defined by commodities. Romantic relationships are tied up with the kind of shampoo you buy, the kind of chocolates you offer your loved one, the coffee you make for them at the end of a meal, and so on.

1.4   Preferred Readings

The way in which the message is handled in a given medium can cause us to prefer one reading of it, one meaning, above other meanings. In effect this is a kind of bias in the way that the message is put across. Once more, this preferred reading could come from a conscious initial intention to make the audience see things in a certain way; or it could come from an unconscious but firm way of seeing things, which the makers of the communication put into the material without realizing it.

Conscious and persuasive mass communication is an obvious example of the intentional kind of preferred reading. For example, a holiday firm might mailshot households giving them colourful, attractive leaflets about beach holidays. On the surface the leaflet just tells us about places and prices. But mainly it tells us about preferred places; it tells us to prefer that company above others, to prefer beach holidays above others. Obviously this is done through a combination of written information and selectively shot pictures, to put it briefly. There is no possibility of understanding holidays and beaches in a neutral way.

But there are also preferred readings to be seen in material that is apparently more factual and objective. To take a reasonably provocative example, we have seen in recent years documentaries about the destruction of rainforests and about the effects of this. If you can bring to mind such aerial shots of destroyed swathes of forest, of miserable-looking dispossessed native peoples, or the voice-overs that comment on the possible effects on wildlife, on the climate of the earth, and so on, then what you are remembering are the cues that prefer you to read the programme and the images as a negative view of clearing the forests. The programme makers prefer you to read their 'story' this way. They leave out any views of the benefit to the economy of the country concerned. There is no question that we are being shown pictures of destroyed forest just out of general interest.

This notion of a preferred interpretation of the material extends especially into news – supposedly the most neutral aspect of media production. The words and pictures that support headlines like 'Travel Chaos' or 'Misery for Commuters' when there is a some kind of transport industrial action clearly prefer us to see that action in a negative light. The news media could prefer the view that this is a healthy exercise of employees' power in support of their rights; or the view that it is all a temporary blip on the economic landscape, or that it is all a necessary consequence of firm management policies. But, in fact, they prefer us to read the material in another way.

1.5 Accumulation and Repetition

Media messages achieve their significance and their effect, it is theorized, by sheer accumulation and repetition of material. A message such as 'A Mars a day helps you work, rest and play' accumulates its impact over a period of time (in this case nearly 60 years) and across a variety of media. Similarly, a message like, 'most doctors are males [and should be]' does not come just from one situation comedy, perhaps, which shows only male doctors, but also from an accumulation of various media sources that say the same thing: romantic stories about the handsome young doctor; advertisements for nursing staff that show a male doctor; radio interviews with representatives of the doctors' professional association, who are usually male, etc.

1.6 The Encoding–Decoding Model

The idea that meanings are encoded into the text by the producer and decoded from the text by the reader is a common part of any process model of communication.

Stuart Hall (1994), produced a model in which he refers to the difference in the meaning structures used by the producer/encoder, as opposed those used by the reader/audience. These meaning structures are, in other words, the ways in which the encoder or decoder makes sense of the material. The result is that different meanings may be constructed. For example, a film that centres around a bunch of young people having a mad weekend clubbing might have been set up within a structure of 'if you're young, it's OK to have fun and do some stupid things', but a given audience might operate within a structure of 'it's not OK to be stupid and young people have to learn responsibility'. One audience sees the film as endorsing a lifestyle, the other sees the film as damning it.

Hall also refers to three other factors that affect how meaning is encoded in and decoded from the text.

1 People operate within frameworks of knowledge. You can only make sense of something as the producer intended if you have enough information and experience to do this. This is also true for the media producer.
2 Relations of production refers to the relationship of producers with audience, in that they share language, including knowledge of media languages.
3 Technical infrastructure refers to producer and audience actually sharing the technology that makes communication possible. For example, a producer might put additional information on an audio CD, but if the listener hasn't got a computer on which to decode this additional material, then all they are going to get is the audio material.

This model places some emphasis on the circularity of the encoding–decoding process, and on the sharing of codes and discourses.

Free Meanings
Are we free to choose what kinds of sense we make of the media?
Are we compelled to understand media material in certain ways?

---

2 MEANINGS AND SOCIETY

2.1   Issues

The media set up issues which they assert are of importance to the public and which they then discuss. One critical position would say that they create a kind of ideological agenda – they tell us what we ought to be concerned about (see Section 1.15 in Chapter 7, on moral panics); they contain debates within their own terms of reference; these terms stay within the dominant ideology. Another position would argue that media offer an arena, a public sphere, in which differing ideas struggle to be heard and to dominate.

One issue, for example, is over whether or not nuclear power is desirable. You could follow this up through the press only and acquire a useful dossier of messages, overt and covert. Overt messages include the various advertisements from special interest groups such as Greenpeace and the Nuclear Energy Authority. These take one side of the argument or another. But you could also look at various articles and opinion columns in newspapers. Sometimes the messages and positions on the issue are interestingly oblique. For instance, there have been articles about the incidence of leukaemia around power stations. Does the relative frequency and scale of reports about this problem in the quality press suggest a basically anti-nuclear power message? Does the relative absence of such comment in the popular press suggest lack of interest, or a pro view on the issue?

2.2   Naturalization

One major message that we receive through the media is that media messages are 'naturally' correct. The media are so seductive in the accomplishment of their communication, especially entertainment, that they gloss over the covert messages. They deliver an assumption that this is the way things are, and should be, these are the ways that things should be done, that what the media say is basically satisfactory and correct. Broadcast news and newspapers carry a view of the world that is never questioned, that is also made natural. It is a view that naturally shows politics in terms of conflict, that refers to government and opposition, and naturally assumes that people have to be on one side or the other of some political argument rather than perhaps agreeing with parts of three or four views. This naturalization works against uncovering what the media may really be telling us, against questioning what they do tell us.

2.3 Normality and Deviancy

Another set of messages in effect define for us what is 'normal' in our society and what is inappropriate or wrong. The media are a significant influence in defining for us what we should regard as normal behaviour and normal people, and what is abnormal behaviour by people who in effect are labelled deviants. This is easy to see in terms of gross criminality. Child murderers are universally depicted as deviants, and murder is abnormal. Again, it isn't just news or factual material that conveys this. We get these messages from a range of material, including drama.

But you should realize that sometimes the messages that help define our view of the world may be more questionable in their validity than is immediately obvious. For example, in Britain, there are Welsh nationalists who have burned down houses owned by English people. The media clearly tell us that these Welsh people are deviants, that their behaviour is not normal. But there are at least some Welsh people who do not agree with this. They would say that such people are patriotic, not criminal. Another example has to do with lifestyle. Those members of our society described loosely as 'travellers' are also generally depicted as abnormal and deviant in respect of their lifestyle and beliefs; they are often dealt with critically when they settle on other people's land or because they may not give their children a regular education. But from another point of view their relative lack of interest in possessions and a material lifestyle could be said to have a positive dimension – one that isn't often promoted by the media. People who prefer to sunbathe in the nude have been represented as mildly deviant or 'odd' in our society. People who support environmental policies above others have been similarly represented as eccentric and untypical. It is interesting that their brand of DEVIANCY has been revalued by media in many parts of the world as it became obvious that Green parties were entering the mainstream political process and were numerically significant.

2.4 Lifestyles

One comes back to the idea that **many messages in the media are about our lifestyle, about the groups we belong to, about our self-presentation, about our beliefs and values.** Think about magazines for young females. They certainly have messages about a lifestyle that is dominantly to do with dressing up, having a good time and being interested in young males. They are about the idea that the young female readers are somehow separate as a group from other females in the population. They often (but not always) assume that young females go out as a group – until they meet a certain young man. They carry a lot of messages about self-presentation, about how to look, since they carry many articles and images that refer to hair, clothes, make-up, and generally to the idea of being looked at. But then it follows that they also carry the belief messages that young women ought to pay attention to their appearance, that they should expect to be looked at. It also follows, then, that they carry value messages about the importance of personal image. Put another way, they are saying that young women are valued according to this image.

2.5   Culture and Subculture

The media help define what our culture is, and what subcultures are in relation to mainstream culture. They define views of and attitudes towards these subcultures. To some extent, minority programming in broadcasting does this, rightly or wrongly. For example, radio programmes such as *Does He Take Sugar* for people with disabilities, define those groups as subcultures within our society. In a general sense all targeted magazines help define subcultural groups – for instance, computer games magazines aimed at young males. To this extent, the media identify and maintain subcultural categories and divisions. They may deal with specific issues, such as the notorious debate about Salman Rushdie's book *The Satanic Verses*, to which Muslims deeply object and over which they have taken to the streets in protest. In this case, there have been innumerable messages in all the media taking different views about British Muslims' right to this protest, and about the degree of their separateness from what is called mainstream British culture.

3 IDEOLOGY

3.1   Power and Meanings

One set of messages that we receive through the media is about power. These tell us, more or less directly, who has power and who ought to have power. If we look at television news programmes and the front pages of newspapers then it is reasonably clear who has power. For the mythical Martian coming to earth it would seem that more men than women have power; that these men are older rather than younger; that many of them are politicians; that quite a number are entertainers; that most of them are white; that a number of them are in charge of countries across the whole globe. It also becomes evident, by contrast, who does not have power: young people, most old people, poor people, female people, people with disabilities, black people. You can make your own analysis to see if you can add any points to this.

In this case, you might also reach such conclusions as: power seems to be about control of government, control of money, control of armed forces, and control of audiences.

The power we are talking about is exerted in relationships between people and groups. The politicians exert power over groups of people. The entertainer exerts power over the audience. Leaders of industry exert power over groups of workers. It is also worth realizing that we may see the media giving messages about power in more personal relationships. Or they may show power as being more personalized between individuals. For example, films such as *Wall Street* or soaps such as *Roseanne* show power struggles in relationships. Sometimes this is about business – white males trying to win take-over battles – but sometimes it is about love and marriage – power struggles for affection, even possession of another person. Sometimes in such dramas we see men trying to own the women in the same way that they own companies perhaps by 'bribing' them with gifts and a good time out. We may also see the women exerting power over men through using or withholding their affections. In this case, we are getting more messages about power in personal relationships, and about how it may be operated.

The important thing to realize is that such **messages about who has what kind of power over whom, are not simply reflections of the world as it is; by being given to us, they actually help make up our view** of that world. This is not say that the messages are totally untrue, nor is it to jump into judgements about whether the situation as described to us is a good or a bad thing, but it is to say that the very act of communicating is one in which a message and its treatment is selected, and therefore cannot by definition be neutral. It is to remind you that the very repetition of such messages, in various guises, reinforces their meaning. You need to be aware of this, because in this way the messages themselves have power over you. You can only take back the power to sort out meanings and conclusions for yourself if you realize what is happening.

3.2 Ideology and Meaning

Discussion of power in the meanings generated by the media leads one directly to the notion of **ideology**. Ideology is a difficult word to deal with because

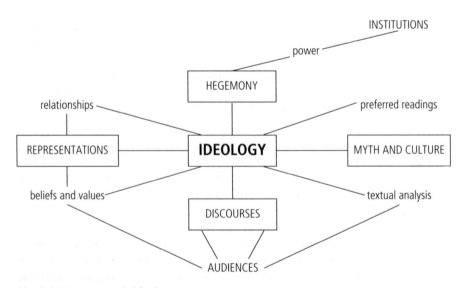

Fig. 8.2 Key concepts: ideology

there have been so many interpretations of it. It is also difficult because it has strong associations for some people – often the idea that it is all about left-wing politics. This is not true. Ideology is, somewhat simply, a **set of beliefs and values that add up to a particular view of the world and of power relationships between people and groups**. All sets of beliefs that have labels or titles are ideologies: Buddhism, communism, capitalism, Catholicism. These '-isms' are often tied to particular cultures, but more than one may exist within a culture. There are at least some Russian people who follow the Russian Orthodox Church and its beliefs, but who are also communists, just as some English people may be Christians and socialists.

All of us have some sort of ideology or view of the world – how it is and how it should be. Our ideology is formed by the culture in which we grow up. In particular, we are influenced by communication that comes from family, friends and school, and also the media. We are influenced by those messages that are about what we should believe in and what we should value as important. This is why any study of communication is likely to come back to value messages, because these become part of the way we think. They affect how we put together communication to other people and how we decode communication from others. Much of this book is about the process of communication through which the media project these values, and so form them or reinforce them (sometimes even question them). The final chapter in particular is about media effects, and so also about how such value messages may or may not be perceived by us, and how they may be taken in and used by us.

The dominant ideology is the dominant view of the world in a given culture. This is the one that the media offer us, for the most part. It will also probably be the view of the world that we hold. This overlap is not surprising, simply because the media seek to please the audience to get readers and viewers in order to sell their product. It is a simple fact, well known to advertisers, that if the messages within communication include those about values the audience holds, then the audience is most inclined to accept that communication and to like it. The 'catch' is, as we have just said, that those same media help form those values in the first place. By the same token, they are not inclined, on the whole, to raise questions about those value messages, about the nature of the ideology, because this would spoil their success as communicators (in their terms). In my terms, I suggest to you the reader that you are actually a better communicator if you are able to question how and why communication takes place, as well as what messages are being communicated.

The value messages about this ideology that we have in our heads are enormous in number. The most important category are those that have to do with power, and this we have already said something about. If you were to write out a list of such messages as statements, it would be very long. I will only give a few examples of what I mean. You can find others by discussing the moral of various media stories. For instance, one message is that the family is a good thing, or that law and order is a good thing, or that it is OK to use force so long as you are on the side of the law, or that it is good to save money and to own things, or that love and courage are good qualities, and so on.

3.3 Hegemony

This term relates to ideology because **it refers to the invisible exercise of power by those who run things over those who do not.** One has to beware of falling into unfounded conspiracy theories, however, it is objectively unarguable that **relatively few people in most societies control (legally, politically, financially) the dominant institutions of government, the military, commerce, the media.** In Britain we would be looking at something like 20,000 people in Parliament and top jobs, who have a tremendous influence over the lives of the other 54 million souls.

Hegemony suggests that the influence does not have to be direct and obvious to be important. It suggests that it has something to do with class and gender (look at the gender and backgrounds of those in top jobs). It constructs the web of values that holds together our ideology.

Hegemony relates back to the concept of naturalization (see Section 2.2, above), which describes the fact that the way media material is put together and the meanings that material contains, are made natural. That is to say it is assumed, for example, that women should be defined in terms of beauty, or that we should be concerned about the exchange rate. It is as if the media are saying, well of course this is important, of course this is true. Not only could one question definitions of importance and of truth, but one could also ask 'Who says this is important?' or even 'Who benefits from saying this is important?'

In fact what the process of hegemony does is to naturalize ideology itself, and all the values and beliefs built into ideology. Hegemony is at its most powerful and most dangerous when people assert that things are naturally true, or even part of human nature. It has been a received truth that men are naturally better drivers than women – but insurance company statistics contradict this; or that the process of law ensures justice for all – when clearly it brings more justice more easily for those with more money.

So from this point of view the messages and meanings within media product like newspapers and films are about some beliefs rather than others. And these beliefs work in the interests of media owners, of advertisers, of something we call the Establishment, rather than in the interests of ourselves, the audience.

Ideology: Change and the Status Quo

In what ways do the media raise questions about how our society is run, and by whom?
In what ways do the media tell us to stick to the same set of values and to obey
    authority?

3.4 Discourse

This concept is again linked with ideology and with the value messages that we get when we read magazines and watch television. The term describes particular ways of using verbal and visual languages to produce particular meanings about the subject of the discourse. In principle, you could have a discourse about nearly anything. In practice, one sees discourses as being to do with 'big' topics such as gender, or law and order. These discourses define what it is to be male or female; they define what law and order means. They are themselves defined by particular words, phrases, camera shots even. Language is not only used by the media, of course – but it can be used with particular effect because of the nature of the media. So, for example, if words to do with softness, scent and colour are used specifically to describe females, then it is the media (e.g. magazines) that especially reinforce the meanings in the discourse. If camera shots and their point of view on females as subject matter particularly directs its 'gaze' at aspects of the physical form of women, then this repeated use of language also reinforces the idea that being a woman means being a body.

In talking about discourses, Turner (1992) talks about 'ways of thinking that can be tracked in individual texts or groups of texts' – ways of thinking about gender. He also talks about 'wider historical and social structures or relations'. In other words, if one wants to understand current ways of thinking about gender, then one needs to take account of where these have come from, of how they may relate to thinking about gender in the past.

Discourses operate within ideology and are a part of it. The value messages of the ideology can also be the meanings of a discourse. The language of the discourse also communicates the value messages. There is a discourse about royalty and the monarchy in our culture. There are dominant ideological values relating to royalty – approval, patriotism, authority. Analysis of the special language used about royalty would lead one to exactly the same words.

Whether we realize it or not we use discourses to make sense both of our real world and of the world of the media. Different ideologies will have their own discourses that both represent how the relevant culture 'sees' the world and frames off how members of that culture make sense of their world.

3.5 Conflicts and Contradictions

One of the interesting things you should come across are messages that contradict or conflict with one another. These tell us something about the contradictions in society itself, and about how difficult it is to make absolute generalizations about the media.

For example, in a previous paragraph I referred briefly to ways in which we get messages about older people that are generally unflattering. There is an interesting contradiction here if you consider the fact that the media also tell us about old people, especially males, who are powerful and respected. Japan is run by men who are what we might otherwise describe as old age pensioners. The USA had a popular president (Reagan) who held office well into his seventies. Newspapers abound with stories of politicians, financiers, film stars who are all old, but who are certainly not incompetent, as others of their age appear to be in dramas and comedies.

Carol took over, guiding her to the squeaky sofa. 'Of course you know, Jenny, he's right in one way,' she said. 'The increase in crime, especially burglaries in areas like this, well it's appalling. I blame all those unemployed boys with nothing better to do.' She leaned forward eagerly, and then back again, frowning as she caught Paul's gaze homing in on her cleavage. 'Have you been in that estate up across the main road? All day long, absolutely heaving with people, all milling about with nothing to occupy them. We're heading for a revolution, that's what I think. They'll come pouring across that road and ransack nice, law-abiding places like this, just like Russia.'

God, she's mad, thought Jenny. Stark staring. Carol would never go across the main road into the estate, in case she was robbed both of her values and her valuables. How could she possibly have a clue what went on over there? But Carol, her spun-sugar hair jerking briskly like a rooster's crest, was just warming up.

'And the children, not a father present between them! No role models. I thank God we were able to send our boys safely off to a decent prep school where they can learn what's what. And there's a lot to be said you know, for joining the cadet force. Channels their energies.'

Into learning how to kill each other, crossed Jenny's mind, but she said instead, 'They could learn what's what here at home, surely, with both parents present?' suddenly keen to defend her own version of family life, 'if all you think they need is a father-figure?' Carol gave her a sly look, something conspiratorial, as if what Paul could teach her sons wasn't likely to be worth knowing.

'You know,' Jenny told her, 'the vast majority of crime by young people is done by boys. The same lone parents are also bringing up girls too. So surely it's the messages that are getting across to boys in society that are damaging, not necessarily their family structure.'

Carol, for a moment looked stumped, but soon rallied. 'Oh well, the girls, we all know what they're doing don't we? Getting themselves pregnant and straight up the housing list, that's what.'

Fig. 8.3 From *Pleasant Vices* by Judy Astley, Black Swan, 1995

This passage shows how discourses inhabit media product everywhere. They intermingle and work together, dominating the way that we make sense of the world. There is the line about the woman's cleavage, in which sexuality appears briefly, naturalizing an attitude about how men look at women. The conversation incorporates discourses about class and masculinity – for example a phrase like 'a decent prep school' belongs to a certain way of looking at the world. Interestingly, Jenny also argues with Carol, and produces an alternative discourse about the young and parenting. But then Carol's dominant discourses roll on again as she talks ignorantly about working-class girls getting themselves pregnant.

Such contradictions of message are interesting in that they prove that the **media do not present a cohesive view of the world,** and useful because they help us be aware that **there are different levels of message in the media.** Messages about values and ideology are often at the deepest level. But they can have the most importance for us personally in terms of shaping our beliefs and in terms of affecting how we behave as members of our society. But before we deal with that important 'SO WHAT?' question – 'So there are these kinds of message, so what?' 'So I can dig out messages – so what?' – there is one more important point to be made about messages and the media. A lot has been said about messages from the media. Let us look at how we may or may not get messages back to the media organizations.

Activity (17): Gender and Ideology

Take one broadsheet newspaper and one magazine for older women. LOOK AT THE NEWS STORIES AND FEATURE ARTICLES IN EACH AND MAKE A LIST OF:

- the types of male or female talked about
- what it is that they do, and seem to have control over (e.g. you might find that a middle-aged male has control over a business or a football team, or that a female is a fashion model and has control over her appearance).

It is likely that this activity will bring out ideological points such as:

- there are ways in which men have economic or political power in a public sphere
- women are talked about in terms of self-presentation and having power in a private or domestic sphere.

---

4 MEDIA ISSUES AND DEBATES

We are going to look at a few of the major issues raised by Media Studies. In fact the media themselves occasionally deal with such issues. In so doing they also send the message that these issues are on the public agenda. This makes the general point that in many cases what we call an issue is only one because the media say it is. This underlines the fact that the media wield considerable power over our view of the world, of what is important or unimportant. What follow then are outlines of debates that you should be able to discuss, offering not only general opinion but also informed judgement from your course and from reading the earlier parts of this book.

4.1   Bias

The issue of media bias usually focuses on their news operations. Journalists –
especially broadcasters – usually conclude that they are neutral. One might beg
to differ. For a start, since communication always comes out of the culture and
values of the communicator, it is impossible for it to be neutral. Whether there
is relative bias or not is another matter.

Questions that one might raise around this issue are as follows.

- How does one identify bias?
- How can one define unbiased-ness?
- Does bias matter in the context of plurality of choice of material?
- Is bias only in text and about areas of form, such as news presentation?
- Is bias something in the heads of an audience as much as in text or
  institution (i.e. could an individual viewer/reader talk about bias, where
  most commentators would argue that it didn't exist?
- How may one combat bias?

Bias in print news may be fairly obvious given the editorial positions of
newspapers, the targeting of readership and the more obvious political
leanings of newspapers like the *Daily Mail*. Bias in broadcast news is more of
an issue because this earnestly aspires to impartiality and neutrality. The
provision of information is not in doubt. The inflection and framing of this
information is something else. Again, it has already been pointed out that
selection out and selection in through the editorial process makes a kind of bias
inevitable. News items are also biased through their priority in the running
order, the time given to the item, its placing next to other items, let alone
through the newsreader's script, which can make crucial choices (and
inflections) when choosing between words like 'demonstration' and 'riot'.
News programmes try to get rid of bias through devices like having both a
Tory and a Labour politician interviewed on a given topic. But the very
assumption of a two-party system or two views is itself a kind of bias. In any
case the interviewer holds the ring and creates another kind of bias saying
things like 'So, could you sum up your position in three or four sentences?'
Perhaps it isn't possible to do this. Simplification can be a kind of bias in itself.
The valuing of pictures when choosing and handling a story can be another
kind of bias. Clearly there is a fundamental issue here surrounding one of our
most important sources of factual information about the world. Did the
Israelis retreat from the Lebanon in 1999 or did they make a strategic
withdrawal? That depends on whose news you watch. Perhaps they are both
biased!

4.2   Control and Regulation

Who should control the media and how? This issue must concern the potential
effects of the media (otherwise it wouldn't matter who controlled them). Key
questions that relate to media regulation are as follows.

- Why do we believe that the media need regulation?
- How do we square the idea of regulation with a belief in freedom of speech?
- How can one moderate the extent of ownership when the global market needs big players?
- How can one regulate to allow for freedom of choice of material?
- Who controls the regulators?

The debate ranges across arguments about who owns the media, under what conditions, and about how the power of ownership should be moderated. In one respect this power can be moderated if the take-over panel of the Department of Trade and Industry is asked to rule on whether or not it is in the public interest for one company to take over another, if that means the new company would have a big slice of a given industry or market (for example, an attempt by Time Warner to take over EMI music was blocked).

So far this has had little effect on the ability of owners to control a number of newspapers or a number of radio stations. When it comes to **cross-media ownership** there are clauses built into the latest broadcasting acts. At the moment a newspaper group cannot have more then a 20 per cent stake in a broadcaster. However, relaxation of this rule is now being considered, and the government has already relaxed the rules relating to ownership of more than one television company. So Yorkshire Television was able to take over Tyne Tees in 1993, and was itself taken over by Granada. In terms of commercial radio and television, there is no argument that a degree of control is in the hands of the Independent Television Commission, set up in 1992 to replace the IBA. Its remit extends across to cable and satellite. It can, for example, give or take away the broadcasting contracts that allow the companies, such as Carlton, to operate.

But there is also the matter of the nature of that control. The dominant model of media institution in this country is a commercial one, with devices for checking and curbing misuse of power (through organizations such as the ITC). But should we look for alternative models of ownership or for regulatory bodies? The *Guardian* and *Observer* newspapers work fine through boards of trustees controlling their destinies.

Allied to this within the main issue of who controls and how, is the further question of the kinds of check of control. I have already pointed out that, in general, the media are self-censoring, but are there enough checks on their freedom of action? Are the checks themselves undesirable? For instance, is the ITC a strong enough body to monitor programming or is it really helpless in the face of the power of the big companies to dominate the whole commercial system through their control of product? How can satellite television be effectively controlled, given the fact that programmes can now be picked up that originate from outside Britain? Then again, are the checks on control and ownership actually too strong? The government licenses all broadcasting, and some people say that it has allowed too few licences too slowly where local and community radio is concerned.

4.3   Public Service Broadcasting

The debates around Public Service Broadcasting (PSB) raise a number of questions.

- Who are the public being served?
- How does one define what a public service is?
- Who is going to pay for it, or how it is to going to be paid for?
- How should it be regulated, and by whom?

For many years the BBC has been the model for PSB, in radio and television. But from the 1980s onwards it has come under increasing attack, first from Tory politicians, but then also from commercial interests who resent the BBC privilege of a licence fee income. The argument of those who support the rule of the market is that if the BBC doesn't enjoy at least half of the available audience then why should viewers and listeners be forced to pay for a service that many of them would do without. It is true that Classic FM has more listeners than Radio 3, that the audience share of BBC1 and BBC2 has dropped below 40 per cent, but then the market argument preserves only those audiences that are profitable – large populist ones, and some specific audiences with high disposable incomes. This is an argument for mass populism and elitist narrowcasting. The counter-argument is that all kinds of public should be served, that experimental material should be tried out, that one tends to guarantee income and policy for organizations like the BBC to do this.

There are also ideological contradictions in the arguments that have taken place in Parliament and the media themselves. At the centre of this is a crunch between free-market economics and cultural idealism. Indeed sometimes the same people face both ways at once, wanting a risk-taking, community serving, creative public service – somehow to emerge from market forces. The contradiction is further exemplified by those people who damn the BBC for going into commercial partnership with Flextech, and for developing a very successful commercial arm, BBC Worldwide, which is into money-making from programme sales, spin-offs and profitable satellite channels. These people say that the BBC shouldn't be playing a commercial game with public money, but then the BBC has been pushed down this road by governments since the mid-1980s, not least because its licence fee rises have been reigned in below the increase in inflation. The BBC has broken up its centralized structure, lost thousands of staff in the last 20 years, and contracts out many of its service needs – just like commercial organizations in many fields.

There is another model for PSB in the commercial sector – Channel 4. This channel has produced innovative programmes for minority interests, and yet has received its share of criticism for also managing to produce some popular successes – imports from the States such as *Friends*. But what one needs to remember here is that Channel 4 is not simply a commercial television channel. Even the big companies that dominate ITV (Channel 3) are constrained to serve the public with educational, documentary, news and regional programmes – by contract – and the ITC makes sure they do. Even more,

Channel 4 is required to contract out production and to present programmes for minorities. In other words, the commercial sector isn't in a totally free market, either – and where it serves different kinds of public this is at least partly because it is made to.

If PSB means having radio and television that is sometimes for small, unprofitable audiences, and that produces some unusual material, and provides educational and informational material regardless of audience interest because it is thought to be a good thing, then this has to be paid for regardless. It has to be insisted upon by the politicians who are supposed to represent our interests. In all the debate that surrounded the formulation of the Broadcasting Act 1990, no one wanted to abandon the ideal of PSB and no one came up with a better agreed system than the one we have.

What does seem clear is that the PSB model represented by the BBC until the 1990s is dead. That kind of quasi-monopoly is inconsistent with a belief in the free market. National public broadcasters cannot easily be preserved in the face of competition from global media working via satellite and international acquisitions. So the BBC has to a fair extent taken the line of 'if you can't beat 'em, join 'em'. It has done various deals to get out into the global market-place. It has gone on to satellite. It has gone digital. It has gone into 24-hour news. Equally, it seems that government intervention can still enforce a degree of public service on commercial providers. The British commercial broadcasters are squealing about unfair competition from the publicly funded BBC, but presumably in a democracy the public can insist on whatever public service model it wants. If it wants to 'subsidize' the BBC then the rest will have to lump it. There is no law of nature which says that commercial models for media finance and production have to prevail.

4.4   Access

In this case one can identify a number of key questions surrounding the idea of the audience/public having access to the media, especially their means of production and distribution.

- Should anyone have right of access to our media?
- If not anyone, then who, or what interest groups?
- What exactly does one mean by access?
- For broadcasting, is it the right to make programmes in a community slot? The right to have distribution at certain times?
- Does access include the right to reply if one has been the subject of an article or programme?
- Does such access include the right to editorial control?
- Who would monitor and control such access?

The Home Secretary has the right to demand air time any time he pleases if he judges it is necessary in the public interest. Those who feel wronged by the press have no right of access to explain those feelings; they do have a Press Complaints Commission, set up by the industry, which controls that access.

Those who feel wronged by broadcasters have no right to anything – no apology, no space. Local and regional broadcasters are awarded contracts on the understanding that they will provide local and regional programming, but local people do not have a say in this. They do not have a say in what committees are set up by the BBC and the commercial contractors to advise them. They certainly don't have a right to any air time, any more than they have a right to space in what is often proclaimed to be 'your newspaper'.

The question of access for political purposes is a very difficult part of this debate. Small parties frequently complain that they cannot get enough air time. The amount of air time for party political broadcasts around general elections is fixed by the broadcasters and the Whips of the Labour and Conservative parties. Smaller parties, such as the Liberal Democrats, are involved in discussions, but they have no legal right to any particular amount of air time. The problem remains of who is to decide who gets on to say what. There is no right of access for local political views either. At least we can see and read about national political events and issues, but matters of local government are not talked about as of right – only when the local editor decides there is some mileage in them. So far as newspapers are concerned, one special problem has to do with distribution. You could produce a local paper as a way of getting access to the audience (whether to present political views or anything else), but you might not be able to distribute it because distribution is largely a monopoly of WH Smith (which also owns the publisher of this book) and Surridge Dawson. They could decide not to handle your newspaper if they thought it was too political. This would mean that it wouldn't get into their shops either.

4.5 Invasion of Privacy

This has been a very hot debate for the last decade – when pictures and stories about the famous and sometimes their failings can help sell papers and magazines. The take-over (2000) of the Express group of newspapers by the publishing group that also sells *OK!* magazine is a good example of the merging of interests on the common ground of gossip journalism. The questions it raises are difficult ones and can affect people very personally.

- At what point does the taking of photographs and the seeking of information about individuals become an invasion of their right to privacy?
- Do public figures have any right to privacy?
- How does one balance a sense of people's right to privacy with a belief in investigative journalism and in the public's right to know?
- If one justifies investigation as being in the public interest, then who defines what that interest is?

There has been much talk in recent years about creating a new Act of Parliament to curb the activities of the news operations of the media, and of the press in particular. There was a particularly notorious instance when pictures were printed of the late Princess Diana working out in a private gym.

Newspapers claimed it was a matter of public interest. Certainly it would be difficult to construct an act that did not then protect corrupt individuals from having their sins exposed. Equally, there is well-founded criticism of the press in particular for indulging in what is called cheque-book journalism in order to bribe people to expose the private lives of the famous, or perhaps even to exploit their connections with those who are the victims of tragedy.

There is a code of practice from the PCC (1997) that seeks to protect privacy and to protect the children of the famous in particular, but given the fact that editors can always invoke the let-out clause of the 'public interest', it is not surprising that nothing has changed.

4.6 Freedom of Information

This debate centres around questions such as the following.

- How much freedom should the media have to obtain and communicate information? About what or about whom?
- What kind of information, about whom or what, should be available to the news media?
- At what point does any such freedom threaten national security or the public interest?
- Who defines such a point?

The debate here is a sharp one because, unlike many other countries, Britain does not have a Freedom of Information Act. Organizations can be very obstructive about releasing information that might be of interest to the public, and there is no easy means of compelling them to do so. Even where, for example, there is a clause in local government acts, which insists that people have a right to see minutes of council meetings, some councils resort to devices such as charging for the service and demanding that the enquirer (a local reporter?) has to say which pages they want to see or have copied before they will be released. This of course is an impossible demand.

It has been argued that this kind of secretiveness by officialdom, and the lack of rights of journalists to see documents produced by public servants, allowed the cover-up of sexual abuse in children's homes to go on for years unreported. This story finally broke in 1999–2000.

These issues are important because they raise essential questions about who runs the means of communication called the media and how, and about the rights of governmental and public institutions to control and deny information to those media that wish to communicate with the public.

Activity (18): Age and Naturalization

Before attempting this activity, it may be useful for you to have a discussion with your friends about older characters in soap operas or sitcoms, and what they are like in the stories.

MAKE A LIST OF ANY FEATURES OF THESE CHARACTERS THAT THEY HAVE IN COMMON – PERSONALITY TRAITS, BEHAVIOUR, ATTITUDES, ETC.

Then consider older people you know in real life, and tick off any of the features that fit these people.

Look at what you have ticked and not ticked. Look at the common characteristics you have written down of old people in television programmes.

This should bring out points for you about how representation can make certain views of people seem 'natural' and true, when in fact this doesn't really fit real life.

REVIEW

You should have learned the following things about media messages and meanings from this chapter.

1 MEDIA MESSAGES: READING MEANINGS

1.1 The meaning(s) of a piece of communication are also its messages to us. Media texts create multiple meanings.

1.2 Messages may not appear in the media by intention. But even if they are covert and unintentional, one should still be aware of them and their importance.

1.3 Media promote meanings about the value of material goods. This materialism is transferred to the valuation of our lifestyles and of our social relations. It is a process known as commodification.

1.4 Messages may be framed in such a way that the audience is caused to prefer one meaning or reading above all others.

1.5 Messages accumulate their effects and impact by being repeated over a period of time.

1.6 The process of producing meanings through the media may be understood through the encoding and decoding model. Media producers are encoders. Audiences are decoders. They share some factors such as common knowledge, but they also have differences which mean that intended meanings and decoded meanings may not be the same.

2 MEANINGS AND SOCIETY

2.1 There are dominant categories of message that may be described as being about issues relating to ideas about such things as gender and age, power, ideology. This is rather like the media setting up the news agenda. These issues also reveal the workings of hegemony and discourse.

2.2 Media messages are presented in such a way that it is assumed that their meanings are 'natural' and correct.

2.3 Another set of messages define for us what we should think of as 'normal' and what is not (deviant).

2.4 Common messages that we receive through the media are about lifestyle, group identity, self-presentation, and our beliefs and values.

2.5 Some messages help define cultural differences, dominantly between what is defined as mainstream and what is defined as a subculture. Such messages tend to devalue subcultures.

3 IDEOLOGY

3.1 Media messages help define to us who is and who should be powerful or lacking in power within society.

3.2 Ideology and its meanings are about a particular set of values and a particular way of looking at the world. The dominant ideology works in the interests of those who control things, and against the interests of those who are controlled.

3.3 Hegemony describes the invisible exercise of power by ideology. It describes the power of the dominant set of ideas about how the world should be. These ideas are made natural and indisputable through the ways in which they are put across in the media.

3.4 Discourses are part of ideology and hegemony. They are ways of using languages or codes that produce a particular set of meanings about their subject – about what it is to be a woman or a teacher, for example.

3.5 Some messages that we receive through the media contradict one another. Contradictions reveal the strains within the ideology.

4 MEDIA ISSUES AND DEBATES

- There are a variety of issues concerning the operation of the media, which are sometimes also discussed in the media.
- Major examples are about bias in media material, who has control over media production and message making, Public Service Broadcasting, how the audience may have access to the media, how far the media should invade people's privacy, how free the media should be to use information.

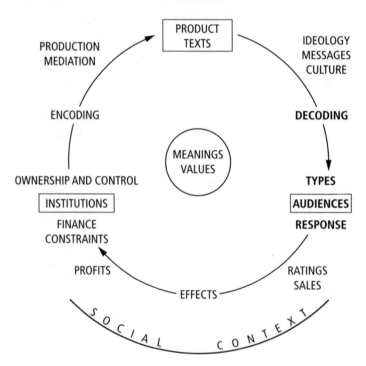

REPRESENTATION
INFORMATION AND PERSUASION
GENRES REALISM
NARRATIVES

PRODUCT
TEXTS

PRODUCTION
MEDIATION

IDEOLOGY
MESSAGES
CULTURE

ENCODING

DECODING

MEANINGS
VALUES

OWNERSHIP AND CONTROL

TYPES

INSTITUTIONS

AUDIENCES

FINANCE
CONSTRAINTS

RESPONSE

PROFITS

RATINGS
SALES

EFFECTS

SOCIAL CONTEXT

9

Audiences

We have reached the point in the communication process where we are dealing with those who are both the receivers of messages and the ones who pay for it all, however indirectly.

In terms of mass media, the question of who the audience is and what effect it has on communication is a complex one because of the size and variety of audiences involved. Perhaps the first thing to realize is that the **audience is not something separate from us**. It is not some abstract idea. We are all the audience or different audiences. **The people who make media material are at the same time part of the audiences for their own material.** Press editorial teams also read other newspapers – avidly. Music A&R people also listen to records, and so on.

At the same time, it is silly to pretend that these people are just the average person in the street. In terms of their skills and their position they are also special. People who edit film and television have a special power to shape the material we spend a great portion of our lives taking in. They are in unusual jobs. There are not many of them. They have special skills. So to this extent they do have a special place in the media communication process. It has been said that they are also special in other ways – for example, they are predominantly white, male and middle class. Those in senior positions of power are also dominantly middle-aged with the background of a university education. To this extent, while actually part of the audience, they are not like the majority of that audience.

So we need to start looking at audience by taking on two opposing, yet equally valid, truths. In one sense there isn't a gap between producer and audience, and we shouldn't think in terms of them and us, but on the other hand 'they' actually are rather separate from the audience in general by virtue of background, skills and their very power to produce these pieces of communication.

There are interesting questions about how media workers see their audiences. In spite of the apparent weight given to 'audiences as statistics' – viewing or circulation figures – media workers are often sceptical as to what such figures really say about the popularity of the material they create. Some (creators of advertising) would say that the audience doesn't really know what it wants. They do not necessarily see the audience as discerning or discriminating. Then there is the much-quoted example of the Anglia radio producer who talked about the audience as being a housewife called Doreen. We think of Doreen when we are writing and producing material.

In general, it is unclear as to how media workers conceptualize their audiences. They are much concerned with what their peers or their line managers think of what they have made, rather than any notional audience member.

In fact it is possible to argue that 'audience' is as much an idea as any specific group of people. There are no coherent bodies of people out there who buy a magazine. All they have in common is that they buy the magazine – and possibly enjoy the activities that some magazines are specifically about. Audiences only exist as long as they are together, consuming – e.g. in the cinema. When the film audience goes home, it is no longer an audience.

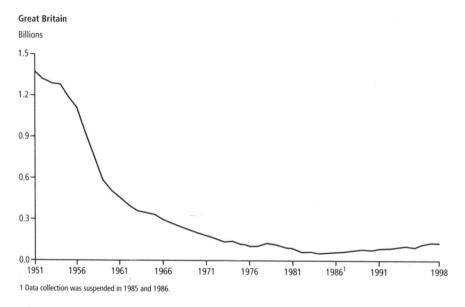

Great Britain

Billions

1 Data collection was suspended in 1985 and 1986.

Fig. 9.2 Cinema admissions

Source: National Office of Statistics.

1 MASS AUDIENCE

In general we can describe the audience in terms of scale and of specificity. Scale relates to what is loosely called the mass audience. This mass audience is a particular phenomenon of the media and of the twentieth century, especially huge numbers of people all reading or viewing the same product. The significance of this lies in the possibility that so many people might make the same reading of the same material and end up with the same views. Of course they might *not* take the same meaning from the material, and they might *not* do anything specific as a result of taking in those views. Nevertheless, we cannot ignore the possibility.

The audience figures in Table 9.1 look generally impressive. Those that run into millions stand for an enormous consumption of messages. Those from broadcasting represent a simultaneous consumption – a sort of mass behaviour that the electricity and water providers know about when enormous numbers of people flush the toilet and make tea in the advertising breaks. Figures like these – *reception of such media material* – look significant on grounds of sheer scale. How far they really are significant has to be determined. But at least it is clear that, without needing to argue whether a 100,000 or 20 million is large, **media audiences are not only huge but distinctive because they are huge.**

We will look at potential effects later on, but it is worth saying now that this matters because of the possibility of informing or persuading or influencing such a large proportion of the population at one time. It matters because, given this scale, we can reasonably talk about the media as a socializing influence. That sort of proposition would not make sense if, as in 1937, there were only 100 television sets in the country (all in London). It matters because **economies of scale mean that there are huge profits to be made from these mass audiences.** The media have become colossal industries, as vital to our economy as manufacturing industries. As mass audience we not only put millions of pounds in the pockets of media owners, but we also indirectly pay the wages of thousands of our fellow citizens who work in those industries, making equipment, making programmes, making communication artefacts such as tapes and discs.

This view of mass audience is tied in with notions of the audience as consumers of commodities. Richard Hooper (1996) raises questions about what exactly we mean by this 'consumption'. He refers to the work of Shew in a piece of research for News International. Shew came up with the following information:

- the average UK adult spend 40 hours a week consuming media
- measured by the hour, the average division between three main media is 24 hours for television, 11 for radio, 4 for newspapers
- at the time (1996) the BBC had 44.1 per cent of media use, as measured by hours spent
- News International (with 35 per cent of British national newspaper circulation) had no more share of media use than a single commercial radio station in London (Capital Radio).

Shew concluded that, looked at in terms of media use, there wasn't a case for concern over the concentration of ownership with respect to national media.

The term mass audience has passed into common speech. It is central to various Marxist critiques of media and culture. The argument that the mass media influence the mass audience and create kinds of mass culture is well embedded in people's minds. Indeed, I have just pointed out that viewers, listeners and readers do exist in considerable numbers for a given channel or publication. But I would now like to move on to an argument which points out that the mass audience and influence idea is marginal to really understanding the relationship between media and audience. These large audiences are in fact of very variable size. Nor are they necessarily coherent. It is pretty meaningless to talk about 'the television audience' or 'press readership'. So I would suggest that it is the definition of audience in specific terms that really matters, especially if you want to argue the case for any kind of influence.

Table 9.1 The consumption of British media: typical audience figures

Television	Average peak programme viewing figures	18 million
Radio	Average peak programme listening figures	4 million
Daily newspapers	Average total sales figures	16 million a day
Cinema	Average admissions a week	2½ million
Records/tapes/discs	Average sales figures × units sold	3⅓ million a week
Books	Average sales figures × units sold	10 million a week

The Invisible Audience
Are media audiences just collections of individuals who are all different?
Are media audiences groups of people with something more in common than being a
　listener, reader or viewer?

2 SPECIFIC AUDIENCES

These audiences in their various categories still involve vast numbers of consumers. It is important to realize that there are few examples of mass communication that address a real cross-section of the population by age or background, or any other criterion. **Television has many different audiences for different programmes.** The same people do not consistently watch the same programmes even, say, a drama series. On the other hand, there are similar types of audience for given programmes.

Audiences are specific in three complementary ways. That is, they may be defined by:

1   **the particular magazine, record, film that they consume** – so we talk about the audience for *Time* magazine or the audience for records by Travis
2   **the type of product** – computer magazines, modern jazz music, romantic films, and the like
3   **the audience profile,** in terms of standard factors such as age, class, gender, income, lifestyle, and so on.

So there is a specific audience for a given magazine for women. There is a specific audience for women's magazines in general. There may be a describable audience for media material thought to interest women in particular. Similarly, there is an audience for a specific section of an upmarket newspaper – say, on science or books. There is a specific audience for the newspaper as a whole. There will be a type of audience that prefers to buy that type of newspaper.

We have had an example of the economic importance of specific audience in the explosion of European-wide magazines for women, like *Hello* and *Best*, which work to a formula and just vary some of the material for some specific national audiences. Another example is the *Independent* newspaper. This broadsheet, quality paper was started in 1991 to target a well-off, politically aware, middle-class audience that does not identify with the right wing in politics. It has a Sunday sister paper. It has been quite successful, has profitable advertising rates, because it has found a market niche, a particular audience.

An interesting example of the specific audience – and one that relates to following sections – is the female teenage audience for the Point Horror books series. According to Angela Werndly (MeCCSA conference paper, 2001) in 1996 65 per cent of this audience (aged 14–16) opted for horror as its most popular genre. It appears to be a very specific phase through which these girls pass. The books are often based on or linked to, school life. The 'school story' is the reading that 75 per cent of the girls surveyed said had previously been their favourite. The Point Horror books incorporate relevant themes – romance, loneliness, parenting – as well as horror conventions. Many stories show awareness of the passage from childhood to adulthood. Respondents to the survey said that they liked the realism – the way that girls really are 'horrible to each other'! Clearly this is a product tailored for and targeted at a specific audience.

3 PRODUCT AND AUDIENCE

It is a principle of effective communication that the way one says something, what one chooses to say, is shaped for the receiver. The volume of material and the range of forms in the media, allow us to see a lot of that audience in the communication. To make an obvious point, magazines for young females almost literally represent their audience in their pictures of readers or of young models, in relation to fashion and confessional stories. This kind of identification helps the audience relate to the product. You can get hold of these magazines, and see what other points of identification there are. For example, what is said in such stories about lifestyle, values and dreams? Should we believe that the audience already has these in their heads and is therefore attracted to them in the product?

The media have considerable financial and skills resources, as well as time and experience with which they can make their words and pictures recognize and define the audience. This last point is important.

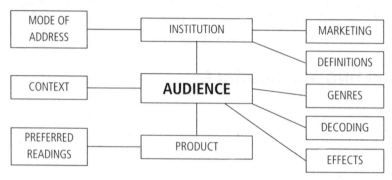

Fig. 9.3 Concept diagram: audience

3.1   Audience in the Text

By saying things that are relevant to a particular audience, by bringing that audience into the material, **the product actually defines the audience for whom the communication is intended.**

Heavy metal magazines contain photographs of clothes, of fans, of performers that define their largely male audience in the product and by providing a model for a lifestyle that is assimilated into the behaviour and habits of that audience. They are shaping the material for an audience they have already shaped through previous material. Obviously there are other inputs into the lives of heavy metal fans – concerts, group talk, and so on – but still there is a sense in which that circle is a very tight one.

Ask yourself, from a reading of a given magazine, how do I know:

- what kind of audience it is intended for
- what kinds of audience is this magazine certainly *not* intended for
- what do I know about the characteristics of this audience from the magazine?

More formally you can ask yourself:

- how is the audience represented?

Look at elements such as appearance, lifestyle, occupation, relationships, beliefs and attitudes.

The English daily newspaper the *Daily Mail* is another example in which we can see the audience in the choice of typical articles and sections, in the style of address, in the editorials, as well as in the news photos and advertisements. It is a middle-class, middle-of-the-road paper, with a slant towards a female audience, and assumed affluence signalled by sections on money matters.

This newspaper does have an audience that can be read into the material, and that is targeted through the choice of content. The repetition of similar items and the proportion of space that they occupy suggests that their inclusion is intentional, though this may be an unintentional expression of values. Whatever, as the audience reads the paper it is arguable that it is accepting a stereotypical view of its own composition and interests.

4 MARKETING AND AUDIENCE

Marketing seeks to promote the value of a product and to sell it as profitably as possible. Mass media are marketed, usually in terms of specific books, tapes or programmes, though sometimes in terms of the medium (for example, the Adshel campaigns to market bus shelter advertising space). As part of this marketing, the audience themselves may be marketed. Indeed, in many ways, marketing has defined the term audience, and put it into common currency (see also Chapter 7).

4.1 Marketing of the Audience

In the case of television the marketing people talk about delivering so many TVRs to the potential advertiser. These TVRs (television ratings) represent the percentage of the target audience that is watching when the advertisement is run. If the percentage is low then repeats may knock up the TVRs. The number of TVRs promised can be delivered by picking the right time of day or the right area, or by simply repeating the ad enough times. So what the ITV company is saying to the advertiser is, we can sell you an audience – perhaps children aged 6 to 12, or married women aged between 20 and 40. Of course they will not know that only these people are viewing at the chosen times, but their market research will have pinpointed viewing habits accurately enough for them to be sure that a significant number of the target audience will be viewing, and can be 'delivered' (like produce) to the advertiser.

In fact **the audience (or audiences) become a product to be marketed to advertisers in all the mass media,** and advertisers nowadays do not just want mere quantity of audience, they also want to know what type of audience will be reading or viewing. Advertising space in magazines and newspapers can only be sold if the people paying for it believe they are getting to a specific target audience, not just any old audience. That audience may be described in some detail. Media marketing executives can describe the buying habits, social habits and most importantly average disposable income of typical members of their target audience to the potential advertiser. They can describe them according to the government classifications (see Table 9.2), through which we are all rated in terms of types of occupation (and therefore income).

Table 9.2 UK adult population by social group, 1999

Group	NRS social grade definition	% male	% female	All
A	Upper middle class Higher managerial/professional	1.6	1.3	2.9
B	Middle class Intermediate managerial/professional	10	9.2	19.2
C1	Lower middle class Supervisory/clerical Junior managerial/professional	12.7	14.5	27.2
C2	Skilled working class Skilled manual workers	11.8	10.2	22
D	Working class Semi-skilled/unskilled manual workers	8.6	9.1	17.7
E	Subsistence level Casual/low grade workers Pensioners/students	4	7	11

4.2   Marketing to the Audience

The audience is recognized as a factor in the way that it is sold the product, as well as in the way that the product itself is shaped. The best example is again television, where **programming and scheduling are used to define broad types of audience.** For example, there is a peak-time audience from 7.30pm to 10.30pm. Children's viewing runs up to 9pm (in theory!), but there is a crucial audience of young people from 4pm to 7pm. The daytime audience previous to this is dominated by elderly people, the unemployed, students and by women looking after children – for obvious reasons. Then there is the late-night audience, which has a greater proportion of males than earlier in the evening. The Saturday-night audience is smaller because of leisure habits (people go out) and so the costs on the advertising rate cards go down slightly. There is the audience for religious programmes on Sundays. There is the child audience during school holidays. There are the mass family audiences during bank holiday times, especially Christmas.

These are defined and recognized, and are being sold to through programming and scheduling. What this means is simply that **certain types of programme are put out at certain times for certain audiences.** You can prove this by going through the television schedules over a week, looking at the times and the types of programme. If you do this, you will find yet more types of audience that are identified, for whom the programmes are being marketed (such as the weekend audience for sport). In fact you should look at the schedules and ask of any programme, why is it placed here?

None of these programmes appears by accident. Senior executives are paid a great deal of money to programme material so that it will attract the right audience at the right time. They use devices like putting on generally popular soaps early in the evening to pull in the viewers, since there is some evidence that people are lazy about switching channels. They 'hammock' a 'weak' programme such as a documentary between popular ones such as a comedy and the main news. They try to hold the audience for the whole evening by having two or three popular comedies or dramas in the first half. They try to pull the audience back the next evening by having a 'blockbuster' spread over two evenings. And, of course, they market directly by having attractive previews for the evening or the week repeated between programmes.

4.3   Targeting the Audience

Essentially this notion is about, first, actually identifying and describing the target audience, and then about shaping the marketing strategy and materials to the lifestyle and needs of that audience.

There is a Target Group Index (TGI) produced by the British Market Research Bureau (BMRB), which interviews thousands of people in order obtain information about their social behaviour and habits, as well as, of course, their preferences for certain products. From this information it is then possible to devise categories or descriptions of target groups, which may have nothing to do with conventional socio-economic descriptors. Some of the slickest descriptions are contained in phrases like 'the pink pound' for the gay market, or Dinkies for households with double income, no kids.

Targeting is most obvious when one sees different adverts for the same product. The advertiser is trying to match the attitudes and values of the target audience. Vestergaard and Schroder (1994) talk about a 'signification process whereby a certain commodity is made the expression of a certain content (the lifestyle and values)'. The advertisement is trying to link values to the product, and vice versa, so that in the minds of the target audience the product is the lifestyle and has value. (You should tie in these comments with what I have explained about the idea of commodification, elsewhere in this book.)

4.4   Marketing to Find an Audience

Sometimes attempts are made to use marketing as well as new products in order to find and define an audience of a type that did not exist before. Of course we are not talking about suddenly finding a section of the population who never read magazines, but finding a section who will take to a new magazine because it offers things that others do not. When *Cosmopolitan* first came out it was sold, like *Options* after it, to a 'new' kind of woman. It recognized, implicitly, social and attitudinal changes. These meant that there was a female audience for a magazine that at least varied the formula for women's magazines enough to take account of independence of thought, of lifestyle and of income. The product was marketed to find an audience.

Another famous example was the 'discovery' of the television audiences for snooker. The general principle of a good audience for sport is well established. So, once again, we are not talking about some dramatic feat of marketing and audience discovery, but the BBC did identify a potential audience, offered the product to it and then more positively sold that product, especially when it was discovered to be really successful.

4.5　Marketing Across the Media

This is akin to discovering and building variations on the audience by selling basically the same product to an ever-expanding audience across different media. For example, Disney movies, such as *The Lion King*, are certainly not sold to one audience just as a film. The soundtrack albums are also sold to that audience and to a wider one (people who have not seen the films) and, again, the videos are sold to a wider audience beyond those who have seen the films. After this there is the matter of selling spin-off products. Marketing across the media can sell more products to a greater number of the same audience. It is also possible to pick up different audiences in this way.

Another longer-running example is Sue Townsend's *The Secret Diary of Adrian Mole* series, best known through two books that have sold over six million copies. But in fact the story started as a short play for the theatre, then became a short radio play, then became the first of the books. It has since been made into a longer theatre play and a television series. In other words it has crossed over the audiences for the various media concerned. It has expanded its audience in terms of number and profile, moving from something relatively cultish for a smaller audience to communication that has mass appeal. The same thing has happened to the popular children's novels about the young magician, Harry Potter. There are film and stage versions too.

5　MODES OF ADDRESS

In this case one is looking at something like style, at **the way in which the media text 'talks to' the audience verbally or visually.** This is all about making a connection, about being attractive to that audience, about defining the relationship of the text to the audience.

For example, television programmes for young people such as *SM:TV Live* on a Saturday morning, talk to their audience in a very particular (and peculiar?) way. The presenters talk very fast, move around a lot and fool around as if they were hyperactive teenagers – in fact they are nearly 30 years old. They appear to be generating the persona of an ideal older brother or sister for the young audience. This mode of verbal and non-verbal address is supplemented by the use of visual address, which is characterized by rapid editing, bright colours and brief bites of items. The mobile camera and changing camera positions create excitement, but are anchored by the presenters' determined direct address to the audience 'out there'.

This mode of address, these characteristics, can be seen in other media – chatty, bouncy, colourful, 'noisy' magazines for teenage girls are an example. The layout and graphics create a cheerful, excitable style. The editorial segments 'talk' to the reader in a best-mates, streetwise manner.

In one sense this sounds all very well as a way of appealing to the audience – talking to them 'on their level'. However, Gill Branston points out in *The Media Studies Book* (1999) that one could be looking at the idea of audience address the wrong way round. Perhaps teenage girls respond to targeted magazines and programmes because they have become conditioned to respond in this way. Perhaps media material that repeatedly assumes that its audience has the attention span of a gnat, ends up convincing the audience that this is all it is capable of. Another negative aspect of mode of address would be when an audience member feels disturbed because they perceive the material as being aimed at them, but the person being addressed is not really like them at all. What about the teenager who actually feels guilty or alienated because she knows that she is not like the female that the magazine is talking to, but believes that perhaps she ought to be?

All examples of media address the audience in some way. Some modes of address have a more distinctive identity than others. It is relatively easy to pick out the authoritative, firm voice of broadcast news, for instance.

But, to take one more example, modes of address permeate advertisements. In fact, if one turns the pages of a magazine or watches a sequence of television commercials, then one is addressed in different ways through different 'voices'. Some adverts are intimate and whisper in our ear, some are strident and assertive. Some talk to us very reasonably about why we should use the services of a certain insurance company, some talk to us as if we are concerned parents.

This last point draws attention to the fact that mode of address does position the audience in relation to the text – we, as audience members, are responsible for making sense of the media text, but it also creates for us particular positions from which to understand it. We are addressed as if we are a certain kind of person, as if we have a certain kind of role. This positioning helps set up a preferred reading; it takes away at least some of our freedom to read the text as we please. It is all part of the persuasive manipulation of advertising in this case.

> We need to be concerned with the modes in which programmes address us, as audience, and with how these 'modes of address' construct our relation to the content of the programme, requiring us to take up different positions in relation to them. This emphasizes the role of television discourse not just in reinforcing pre-established subject positions but rather in actively constructing these viewing positions. (Morley, 1992)

Audiences are invited to become participants – literally in the case of the studio audience for a game show – but even as a viewer at home, we are set up to participate, to indulge in a kind of false interaction, because that performance as viewer resembles life, and it makes us feel comfortable.

Table 9.3 Modes of address

Mode of address	Audience relationship	Audience role	Example
Initial (sets up main mode)	Introductory/exploratory	One who is met	Radio intro pieces
Direct	Semi-formal	Acquaintance/client	Consumer affairs programme
Objective	Formal (but equal)	Listener	Political documentary
Authoritative	Formal/submissive	Learner	News
Familiar	Friendly	Friend	Talk radio
Intimate	Close	Confidante	Girls' magazines

6 ACTIVE AUDIENCES

We have looked at various ways in which audiences may be defined, including through the media product, and at ways in which they are addressed through the marketing of product, but now we must dispel any notion that audiences are simply passive receivers, that they are lumps of clay to be dug out and moulded. Although their scope for providing influential feedback on production itself is very limited, in terms of doing something with the communication that they receive, audiences are not as slothful as the mythology of the couch potato might suggest.

Kilborn (1992) in talking about soaps, refers to the ways that viewers tap into 'a whole range of reading skills that they have acquired over a period of time'. He argues that soaps in particular encourage social discussion and reflection because there are different ways in which one can make sense of their narrative.

But one may not assume that an 'active' audience is necessarily a critically acute one. Kitzinger (1999) says that, 'the "active audience" is not immune from influence'.

6.1   Processing Information: Perception

For a start, audiences are receivers of messages, they are processors of information. They may be sitting and reading or viewing in a passive sense physically. But in fact a great deal is going on in the mind. And people do many things while keeping an eye on the screen, including talking about other things!

The stream of information that comes from the pictures and print on a newspaper page requires active involvement to decode it. Reading is an activity; it requires us to recognize symbols, to make sense of them, to assign meaning to them. We assimilate those meanings into our store of knowledge, into our opinions, into our views of the world.

In another sense we are always learning from the media when we process this information. Examples such as *Sesame Street* make it most obvious that this learning is taking place.

Sometimes the activity involved becomes externalized so that it is very clear just how much is going on inside our heads. Cinema audiences can become so active (so involved) that they actually throw comments at the screen, make noises of protest or approval.

6.2 Indirect Active Response

Another kind of audience activity that is not immediate but that clearly shows a response to the communication, is the increase in participation rates in certain sports after exposure in the media. Obviously, media sports programmes may not be the only factors causing people to join sports clubs in greater numbers, but sometimes they seem to have been the major factor (as in the case of snooker and the rise of local halls and clubs in the late 1970s). American football is a more recent example, where the development of active club interest has coincided with the featuring of the game first on Channel 4, and then on satellite channels.

6.3 Uses and Gratifications Theory

USES AND GRATIFICATIONS THEORY says that, far from being passive consumers of media material, **the audience actually uses media material to gratify certain needs that it has.** Viewers choose to watch a certain programme because it satisfies particular needs that they have at that time – perhaps for information. Or readers select from a newspaper, turning past the hard news to a gossip section on the aristocracy or stars because they need entertainment. Needs also colour the interpretation of material. One person may understand their favourite soap opera in terms of conflict because they are relating their own needs for power to what is happening to the characters. Another person may understand the same programme as being mainly about love and understanding because they have strong needs for security and choose to bring out those aspects of the story in their minds.

In essence this theory suggests that we have the following kinds of need that we may gratify through kinds of viewing, reading and listening:

- the **need for information,** based on sheer curiosity as well as the practical advantages of building up a picture of the world
- the **need to maintain a sense of personal identity,** by checking media role models for behaviour
- the **need for social interaction,** developing a notion of one's social behaviour and relationship with others by using examples from the media
- the **need to be entertained and diverted,** to escape from immediate anxieties or achieve kinds of pleasure.

This theory relates ideas about people and their motivation to ideas about mass media. It relates interpersonal and mass communication. It helps integrate an essential principle of communication that **we are all driven by communication needs in any area of our communication activity.**

So from this point of view the audiences for various media communication are indeed active users. They don't just take anything that they are given, though they can only choose from what they are offered. They use what is on offer to suit their needs. They select what they want from among whole programmes, newspapers or records. They play an active part in creating meaning from the communication. They decide what the messages may be. They interpret them.

But this theory has to be taken alongside other ideas such as preferred readings and covert messages. You should realize that media producers (not least those who create advertisements) are well aware of ideas about audience needs. They are certainly capable of arousing needs and using them to sell their product, and perhaps other messages carried along in the material. So the truth, as far as we can understand it, lies somewhere in between extreme notions of audience as passive victims of cunning media producers, and audience as active controllers simply using media material as they please. One cannot generalize about audience anyway. Individual audience members may be more or less active or passive. Even the needs themselves are a kind of assumption, read into people's psychology by observing their behaviour. But then their behaviour includes media consumption – so does media product recognize a need or does it actually create it?

In so far as the audience uses the media to gratify needs, various needs can be gratified at one time. Certain tracks on a CD may satisfy personal needs (for instance self-insight) as well as providing relaxation and entertainment. A need for information can be met by a fictional serial on television. At the same time, this material could also satisfy social needs, perhaps as a substitute for real-life friendship.

The relationship between female audiences and soap operas has been discussed in terms of gratifications (and pleasure). There is evidence that women use soap watching not only for diversion from routines and domestic labour, but also as a way of satisfying psychological needs to work through comparable situations in their own family life. There is gratification to be had from seeing women, in these stories, succeeding in work and being valued in the domestic sphere.

7 THE AUDIENCE AS READER

You need to relate the following brief remarks to Section 6, above, where audience reading positions are discussed. In line with what I have said about active audiences, you need to bear in mind that audiences 'read the text' and are not simply 'read to'. They engage with, for example, the magazine or radio programme. They read things into it, selectively. They attend to items that are relevant to their experience. They *choose* to read or to listen. They have a pseudo-relationship with the talk radio host – that of confidante. They make sense of what they read or hear in a dynamic relationship with the text.

That reading happens in a context. The context of reading (or reception) may vary physically – reading a magazine on a bus, reading the television in the living room, reading a film in a cinema. Such environments allow and disallow different possibilities of reading. Television can be discussed as is it is watched, for example. **Context may also be cultural.** Talking about a CD track with a number of people at work is not the same as 'reading' it on one's own through a Walkman. **Different contexts of reception set up different meanings.**

Passive/Active Audiences

In what ways can one see the media as controlling their relationship with the audience and encouraging passive consumption?

In what ways can one see the audience as taking an active role in its listening, reading and viewing?

---

8 THE GENDERED AUDIENCE

Interest in audiences by gender distinctiveness has largely looked at women and at specific genres such as romance and soap opera. Women are the majority audience for soaps (see also Chapter 5). There has been much discussion of this viewing preference, as of the role of female characters in soaps. This discussion has included identification with character, uses and gratification (see Chapter 10), and the involvement of soap plots with the working through of episodes from female viewers' own lives and problems.

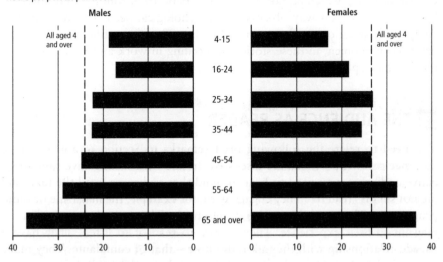

Fig. 9.4 Television viewing: by gender and age, 1998

Source: BARB; AGB Ltd; RSMB Ltd.

Critiques of romance have been both positive (romance as a private space for women, resisting domestic demands) and negative (romance as escapist commodity, produced for the benefit of male-dominated media).

The readership of women's magazines is clearly female dominated. But beyond this, attempts (Hermes, 1995) to determine how women read or reasons for their preferences have been inconclusive.

What does seem clear, however, is that it is more interesting to determine how women consume, rather than what they consume most of. Typically, evidence is contradictory. Some shows that there is no difference between gender viewing preferences and behaviours. Some suggests that there are distinctions: for instance that men prefer events and action, where women prefer narratives that involve emotional release.

Table 9.4 Reading of national daily newspapers: by gender

| | % Males | | % Females | |
	1981	1998–9	1981	1998–9
Sun	31	24	23	17
Mirror	27	15	22	12
Mail	13	12	11	12
Express	16	6	13	5
Daily Telegraph	9	6	7	5
Star	13	5	8	2
The Times	3	5	2	3
Guardian	4	3	2	2
Independent	n/a	2	n/a	1
Financial Times	2	2	1	1

Ages 15+   July 1998–June 1999

Source: National Readership Surveys Ltd © Crown Copyright 2000

9 AUDIENCE, MEDIA, CULTURE

Notions of media affecting audience or of audience using media may not be the best way of understanding the relationship between the two elements. Perhaps **they both exist in a dynamic, interactive relationship within the context of culture and the meanings produced about that culture.** For example, teenage magazines for girls certainly are part of their subculture. Readers can share the culture through the magazines. They can find out who is 'in', who is 'out'. The magazines help perpetuate the argot referred to by Michael Brake in *Comparative Youth Culture* (1985) as one of three defining factors (together with 'image' and 'demeanour'). But those same female readers do have a subculture without the magazines. They go to certain clubs and pubs, they talk about certain topics, they engage with those who are selected as belonging to

Table 9.5 Reading of the most popular magazines: by social grade and gender, 1994–95[1]

	Percentage reading each magazine[1]							Readership[2] (millions)
	AB	C1	C2	DE	Males	Females	All adults	
General magazines								
Reader's Digest	15	14	12	9	13	13	13	5.7
Radio Times	17	13	8	6	11	10	11	4.9
Sky TV Guide	9	11	13	9	13	8	10	4.8
TVTimes	7	9	10	11	9	10	9	4.3
AA Magazine	16	10	8	4	11	7	9	4.2
What's on TV	5	8	9	11	7	10	9	3.9
Viz	6	8	7	5	10	3	7	3.0
TV Quick	3	6	6	6	4	7	5	2.5
Women's magazines								
Take a Break	5	11	13	15	5	16	11	5.0
Bella	5	9	10	10	3	14	9	4.0
Woman's Own	6	9	10	10	2	15	9	4.0
M&S Magazine	14	10	6	3	4	12	8	3.6
Woman	4	7	7	8	2	11	7	3.1

Note: 1. Data are for the 12-month period ending in June 1995. 2. Defined as the average issue readership and represents the number of people who claim to have read or looked at one or more copies of a given publication during a period equal to the interval at which the publication appears.

Source: National Readership Surveys Ltd

their subculture through social processes – not just because the magazine or record industries say this is their niche. As a consuming audience they could be defined as buyers and readers. But as an audience and subculture they exist with, but not because of, the media product. Lisa Lewis in *Television and Women's Culture* (1993) talks about 'the dynamic relationship between mediated texts and social practice'.

Such social practices are exemplified through the audiences for and the contents of teenage girls' magazines. These practices are to do with appearance and adornment, the admiration of celebrities, the development of sexual behaviour. In *The Times Education Supplement* (28 January 2000) David Mosford and Julie Henry discussed the cultural nuances of such magazines and their audiences. *Sugar* is described as being upfront about sexual issues and environmental issues related to compassion (the fur trade etc.). *Just Seventeen* is seen as being for older (typically A, B, C) teenage readers. *Big!* is more concerned with the world of stars and celebrities. The significance of magazines for this age group may be judged from one piece of research, which reveals that 72 per cent of girls read magazines (as opposed to 58 per cent of women).

Lorimer (1994) asserts that 'a straightforward and comprehensive method for understanding audiences does not exist'. He talks about approaches to audience study that 'conceptualize audience/media engagement' in terms of 'elements such as gender and cultural identification'. One needs to look at how audiences behave, as much as at what audiences are. Institution, audience and

Table 9.6 Reading of popular consumer magazines: by age, 1998–99

			Percentages		
			Age groups		
	15–24	25–44	45–64	65+	All
Sky TV Guide	17	15	12	4	12
M&S Magazine	6	12	14	8	11
Take a Break	11	11	9	7	10
Reader's Digest	4	7	12	11	9
What's on TV	15	11	7	6	9
Radio Times	9	7	9	9	8
AA Magazine	3	8	11	7	8
FHM	28	9	2	..	8
TVTimes	10	6	7	6	7
Cable Guide	11	9	5	2	7
Woman's Own	5	6	6	5	6

1 July 1998 to June 1999

Source: National Readership Surveys Ltd © Crown Copyright

Table 9.7 The most popular magazines and newspapers read by children in the UK: by age and gender

Percentage aged 7–10		Percentage aged 11–14	
Males		**Males**	
Beano	28	The Sun	22
Match	25	Match	18
Shoot!	22	Shoot!	18
Sonic the Comic	18	The News of the World	17
Dandy	17	Beano	15
Females		**Females**	
Smash Hits	16	Just Seventeen	41
Barbie	13	Sugar	39
Girl Talk	13	Big!	34
Beano	12	It's Bliss	34
Live and Kicking	12	Smash Hits	32

Note: For 7 to 10 year olds data are the percentage of children who said they read the publication; for 11 to 14 year olds data are the average issue readership.

Source: Youth TGI, BMRB International

text are, from this point of view, part of one thing, one phenomenon. All of these elements could be said to give or to produce meanings about our world. But they don't do this independently. What we think love/romance really is does not come simply from the romantic novel industry. It doesn't come only from romantic texts. But nor does it come independently from the minds of the audience. It is created by the interaction of all three.

10 AUDIENCE AND PLEASURE

One proposition about this interaction is that it depends on kinds of pleasure where the audience are concerned. Critics have talked about the **pleasure given by the text**. They have discussed **pleasures obtained from the text** – not necessarily the same thing. This pleasure idea is not far from that of uses and gratifications. For example, one could talk about the pleasure of recognition and identification that women may obtain from their experience of soap opera. There has been much discussion of male pleasure in looking where pornographic magazines or licentious film scenes are concerned. The pleasure is something that involves the audience in the text, perhaps binds the audience to the text, especially in respect of people being, for example, 'glued' to a series on television. The meaning and nature of pleasure is complex. For example, if the audience enjoys a happy ending where a love relationship is confirmed, is the pleasure one of emotional warmth in the shared and approved-of experience, or is it a more intellectual satisfaction that comes from knowing one had predicted this outcome, and now the plot seems to be neatly tied up?

John Fiske in *Media Texts* (1993) writes about various aspects of this pleasure. In respect of my last point, he refers to Barthes' work and the idea that we get pleasure from playing with the text. He refers to the pleasure of voyeurism in the visual media, made sense of through psychoanalysis. He talks about the pleasure of experiencing texts that both confirm rules, but that also allow the audience to safely challenge rules. This idea of 'safety' may contain a key point about pleasure and text. Whatever the pleasure achieved by engagement with the text, it is only a text. This is not to argue that texts have no involvement with our 'real' lives, no influence – but they are after all only about representations, they are not the same thing as life. If the camera invites us to peek at the woman undressing in the window, then it is a safe experience – we could not get found out and embarrassed or prosecuted. If we gain vicarious satisfaction from the death of a villain and the restoration of moral

Table 9.8 Participation[1] in home-based leisure activities: by gender

	Percentages		
	1977	1987	1996–97
Males			
Watching TV	97	99	99
Visiting/entertaining friends or relations	89	94	95
Listening to radio	87	89	90
Listening to records/tapes/CDs	64	76	79
Reading books	52	54	58
DIY	51	58	58
Gardening	49	49	52
Dressmaking/needlework/knitting	2	3	3
Females			
Watching TV	97	99	99
Visiting/entertaining friends or relations	93	96	97
Listening to radio	87	86	87
Listening to records/tapes/CDs	60	71	77
Reading books .	57	65	71
DIY	22	30	30
Gardening	35	43	45
Dressmaking/needlework/knitting	51	47	37

Percentage of those aged 16 and over participating in each activity in the four weeks before interview.

Source: General Household Survey, Office for National Statistics © Crown Copyright

order, then we are in no real danger from the bullets that kill him in the story. If it turns out that we are wrong about the denouement bringing the marriage of two protagonists, then it does not matter in the way that it would if these were people we really knew and really engaged with.

Audiences are an integral part of the whole process of communication through the media. In many ways they are the *raison d'être* for the media industries, because no audience means no profit means no reason for running the organization. It is the audience that makes sense of the communication. And this sense becomes all the more important because of the size of the audience, given the potential for influence, and the part the media play in the socialization of that audience.

Activity (19): Audience

MAKE A LIST OF ALL THE EXAMPLES OF MEDIA MATERIAL FOR WHICH YOU HAVE BEEN AN AUDIENCE FOR OVER THE LAST MONTH. This might include programmes, magazines, films and CDs.

- Now, put an R (for 'regular') against all those items you nearly always or often read/watch/listen to (like reading a magazine regularly, for example).
- Put a C (for 'concentration') if you stay with the whole programme/magazine/film/CD/etc. until it is finished.
- Put an A (for 'attention') if you did something else while watching/listening/reading.

As an option at this point, you could compare your list with one made by a friend or friends, and ask them where they agree or disagree with your choices.

This activity should bring out points for you about:

- how audiences (including you) are not regular in what they consume
- how they can be active in various ways
- how they may not be particularly cohesive as a group.

REVIEW

You should have learned the following things about audiences from reading this chapter.
- The people who provide media material are also members of the audience, though their position is special because they create and shape this material. Media producers see their audiences sometimes in terms of statistics about them and sometimes in terms of a typical member of an audience.

1 MASS AUDIENCE
- Media audiences are both large and specific in their characteristics. The size of such audiences is what makes them very profitable to the producers.

2 SPECIFIC AUDIENCES
- May be defined in terms of the product that they consume, of the type of product that they consume, of their audience profile.

3 PRODUCT AND AUDIENCE
- One may 'read' the kind of audience targeted into the product that is produced for that audience.

4 MARKETING AND AUDIENCE
- The audience affects the ways in which the product is marketed.
- 4.1 Specific audiences are sold to advertisers, and are identified through examples of material that will appeal to that audience.
- 4.2 Audiences are also the objects of marketing through such devices as television programming and scheduling.
- 4.3 Audiences are targeted by marketing strategies.
- 4.4 Sometimes marketing is done in order to identify a new audience.
- 4.5 Marketing is something that is done across the range of media. This means that the messages within the marketing campaign are reinforced all the more.

5 MODES OF ADDRESS
- Are special ways of talking to the audience, are used to identify and to attract a particular audience.

6 ACTIVE AUDIENCES
- Audiences take an active part in media communication.
- 6.1 Part of the activity includes the decoding of the material within the mind of the audience (intrapersonally).
- 6.2 There is evidence of indirect active responses to the media, as when people appear to be taking up sports as a result of exposure in the media.
- 6.3 The uses and gratifications theory suggests that audiences make use of media material to gratify needs that they have within them. This means that the audience is not a passive receiver of communication. The essential needs that have been identified are: for information, for a sense of identity, for social interaction, for entertainment and diversion.

7 THE AUDIENCE AS READER

- Audiences engage with texts as involved readers. The context in which they do the reading affects the sense that they make of the text.

8 THE GENDERED AUDIENCE

- There are issues to be raised about the different ways in which men and women may make sense of texts, and about the reasons why they have preferences for certain genres of text.

9 AUDIENCE, MEDIA, CULTURE

- Audiences, the media, and the culture which both share, exist in a complex relationship in which the one affects the other.

10 AUDIENCE AND PLEASURE

- Audiences get different kinds of pleasure from media texts. These attract them to certain texts and are part of their relationship with that text.

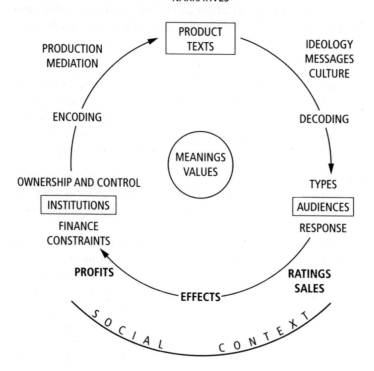

10

Effects

This chapter focuses on the reasons why it may be thought worth studying the media – the proposition that **the media affect our beliefs, attitudes, values and behaviour, directly or indirectly**. This proposition is an expression of a belief in the power of the media.

As Taylor and Willis put it (1999):

> The more commonly known strand of the effects tradition argues that the media have effects which in turn have the power to influence the thoughts of individual audience members to such an extent that they might 'act out' the ideas and activities that the media have exposed them to. This approach is often characterized by its focus on the negative impact of the media ...

The media are special in various ways, not least because of the technology, the economics, the scope of their operations. They are special because they are so very conscious, in some ways, of how they carry on communication – because it pays them to be aware.

In all this, the biggest irony is that, **for all the research into effects it is extremely hard to prove any.** There have been many propositions made about media effects, some of which seem acceptable at least on grounds of sense and logic. A great deal has been established about conditioning factors, but there is very little which absolutely proves that if one communicates in a certain way through a particular medium of mass communication one will have a particular effect on the audience. Indeed, Curran and Seaton say (1997) 'there is no adequate vocabulary to describe the relationships between the media, individuals, and society'.

It is worth remembering that, as we look at the possible effects of media material on the audience, there are also influences on that material.

McQuail (2000) refers to Shoemaker and Reese's summary of five ideas about what influences the media content that is supposed to influence us:

1 the routines of media organizations
2 media workers, in respect of their socialization and their attitudes
3 social institutions and forces
4 social reality and attempts to reflect society
5 ideology (the workings of hegemony).

1 WHAT SORTS OF EFFECT?

There are a number of theories that provide some kind of label for effects. Then there are a number of descriptions of supposed effects that provide another set of categories.

1.1 Short-term Effects

In the early days of media research it was supposed that one could apply a simple stimulus response model, in which the media or perhaps even a particular newspaper provided the stimulus, and the response was a change in the audience voting patterns, or something like that. This short-term behaviourist approach has been discredited. People don't act immediately – if they act at all – and there are too many variables to take account of, apart from the media.

Sometimes this approach was referred to as the '**hypodermic effect**' theory, as if people were being injected with some media material and responded accordingly. Such theorists liked to quote the famous panic in 1939 when Orson Welles radio broadcast a docu-drama version of H.G. Wells's *War of the Worlds* so that some people believed there was a Martian invasion, and thousands took to the roads. But in fact it has been demonstrated that there were other crucial factors – such as people's knowledge of the imminence of real war – that had them in a state of high anxiety anyway.

A typical and shocking example of a well-publicized claim as to this effect relates to the sexual abuse of an 8-year-old Florida girl by her 15-year-old brother (September, 2000). He claimed that he got his ideas from the *Jerry Springer Show*. But in fact there was no relevant material broadcast on the show at the time in question, or indeed at any other time. This is a typical example of claimed **imitation** or **copycat effects**, which are rarely found to be valid, and never in isolation from other major social and familial factors.

1.2 Long-term Effects

What is proposed is that, whatever the nature of the effects (see below), they take place over a long period of time, and are more to do with changes in ATTITUDE and belief than with immediate behavioural changes. This idea is plausible and underpins much existing research. There is still a problem of conducting the right kind of investigation of audiences over a long enough period of time in order to be sure that their attitudes have indeed changed. There is an even greater problem in this case of separating media influence from other influences. There is also a problem in objectifying the nature and degree of attitude change. One basic difficulty is that one has to find some external behaviour that represents the internal change in attitude. So, often, one comes back to asking the audience more or less direct questions and replicating experiments in order to 'get inside their heads'. One basic question, then, is how far one can accept, or even fairly interpret, what people say. What they think and what they say they think may be two different things.

1.3   Inoculation Theory

This theory proposes that continued exposure to media messages causes us to become hardened to them, to become desensitized. The theory was popular with those who wished to believe that the media made us insensitive to violence. The same people were not so ready to believe that it might also follow that we would become immune to persuasive devices of the media, for similar reasons. Anyway, research has found no evidence to support this theory, though as a point of view you will still hear it tossed around.

1.4   Two-Step Flow Theory

This theory proposes that the media influence us indirectly in two stages. The first stage involves the media activity (and perhaps OPINION MAKERS): the second stage involves opinion leaders (see Section 2.4, below) who are respected members of our peer groups. We listen to what they have to say more than perhaps the media themselves. If the media have influenced them in the first place, then in fact we can be indirectly influenced. This theory owes much to the work of Katz and Lazerfeld in the 1960s. One important offshoot of the work was to generate propositions about how active or passive we are as receivers of the communication. It suggested that, in talking with people around us about what the media offered, the theory indicated that we were quite active in dealing with the material, not passive sponges.

1.5   Uses and Gratifications Theory

This has already been dealt with (in Chapter 9) because it is all about the active audience. This theory assumes that there are effects but does not really engage with measurement of them. You will remember that the idea is that the audience uses media material to gratify certain needs, described generally as needs for information, entertainment, personal identity, social interaction. The theory deals with how the audience may be affected, as much as whether they are affected or not. This is not to say that the propositions have been developed in a vacuum. It is thought that people are affected within these areas because the headings classify the kind of response given to questionnaires, for example. But again, the research does not really question the existence of the needs themselves – they are there because researchers say they are there. Nor is there enough questioning of why they are there – i.e. what part do the media play in generating these needs in the first place?

1.6   Cultivation Theory

This idea is ascribed mainly to the work of George Gerbner (1986). It relies heavily on content analysis of media texts, but includes analysis of institutions and production, and correlation between degrees of exposure to television and audience beliefs. It has concentrated on the representation of crime and violence on television. It distinguishes between light and heavy users of media – the latter of course are more likely to be influenced, it is argued. It pays attention to television above other media. It proposes that audiences can come to believe the mediated reality they experience through television. Audiences are seen as actively engaging with material. But the conclusions are much the same as those theories that assume passivity – that heavy television viewing cultivates a particular and negative view of the world as being a violent place.

However, it has to be said that, as with other theories of media effects:

- it makes a correlation between media activity and audience behaviour that is assumed, not proven
- it ignores inconsistencies in research evidence.

Gauntlett (1995) cites various studies that undermine Gerbner's conclusions. He also points out that one explanation for a marginal correlation between heavy television viewing and a fear of crime is that heavy viewers can be shown to live in more crime-prone areas and to watch more crime drama.

1.7   Cultural Effects

Researchers here are more concerned with collective audience effects than with reactions of individuals, with how the media define and circumscribe culture, and with the perpetuation and reinforcement of cultural divisions – stereotyping by race, for example. This work also relates to views of media functions.

This position is much the same as when one looks at the dysfunctional effects of media systems. It should be said that there are opposing and positive views of the constructive functional influence of the media. In this case it would be argued, for example, that the media have the effect of maintaining cultural individuality and of bringing it to a wide audience. This in turn could be opposed to the view that the media undermine and deny cultural and subcultural differences by creating a mass culture.

If we now look at types of effect in terms of what may actually happen to audiences, as groups or individually, then you should remember that this is a list of categories that has been proposed on the basis of some research. These have not been conclusively proven.

1.8   Types of Effect (Various)

- **Attitude change:** the media have the effect of changing people's way of looking at the world in that they modify their attitudes towards others and towards issues.
- **Cognitive change:** the media have the effect of changing the way that people think, the way they value things – it changes (or modifies) their beliefs.
- **Moral panics/collective reactions:** the media have the effect of generating unfounded anxiety about issues such as law and order or public health.
- **Emotional responses/personal reactions:** the media affect people by evoking emotional reactions (as much as rational ones). This is next door to 'moral panics'. For example, it could be argued that the question of personal and body image, especially for women, is raised emotively by the media. The

audience does not rationalize about the effects of messages about the value of anti-ageing creams. It ignores the fact that the product cannot work because the skin cannot rejuvenate cells. The effect is to create anxiety and aspirations about appearance.

- **Agenda setting**: the media have the effect of setting up an agenda of important topics through news activities in particular. We come to believe that this is what the agenda ought to be.
- **Socialization**: the media have the effect of socializing us into the norms and values, and accepted behaviours of our society (see also cultural effects and media functions).
- **Social control**: the media have the effect of controlling the audience by advancing arguments for consensus, and for law and order, and by suppressing arguments and materials that question the ways in which our society operates. This goes back to the views of those social theorists and Marxist critics of the 1930s and 1940s, known as the Frankfurt School. They saw the media as an agency of social control and as undermining the capacity of the audience to think critically about the media, or indeed about any other institution. But they also proposed the mass effects view, that the media do things to audiences.
- **Defining reality**: the media define social reality for us. Social reality is what we take to be real, normal, proper, concerning the way we run our society, and the way that we conduct our social relationships with other people.
- **Endorsement of dominant ideology**: the media do have the effect of endorsing this dominant way of looking at the world, this dominant view of power relationships between groups in society, this dominant view of how things are run. To this extent the media become an important part of hegemony – the social and cultural power the elite and privileged members of society have over the rest. Hegemony naturalizes this power to the extent that it becomes invisible. It may endorse notions of high art or of good taste, as taught in schools or colleges. It may create assumptions – for example, that Channel 4 has a 'better' type of programme than Channel 5. It underpins notions of class and social difference as being 'natural'. Ultimately, the concept of hegemony underpins the authority of Parliament itself, creating an assumption that what it does must be right and good for society as a whole.

Finally one may usefully look at effects as categorized by McQuail (2000), in respect of beliefs and opinions held by the audience:

- cause intended change (conversion of views)
- cause unintended change
- cause minor change (form or intensity of views)
- facilitate change (intended or not)
- reinforce what exists (no change)
- prevent change.

McQuail has also produced a useful summary of various kinds of proposed effects (see Figure 10.2).

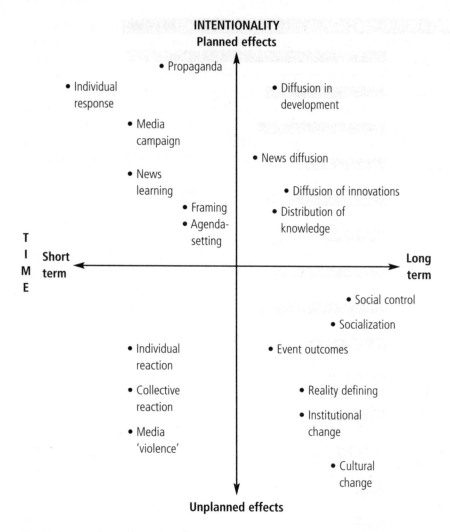

Fig. 10.2 A typology of media effects

McQuail's version of categories of media effect located within the parameters of long term–short term, and planned–unplanned.

Source: D. McQuail (2000) *McQuail's Mass Communication Theory* (4th edn). London: Sage.

2 STUDYING EFFECTS

2.1 Methods of Research

First of all it is worth looking briefly at some ways of investigating and measuring effects on the audience (see also Chapter 2). This presumes we know what we want to measure. Usually this has to do with behavioural change, or most likely nowadays, attitudinal change. In other words:

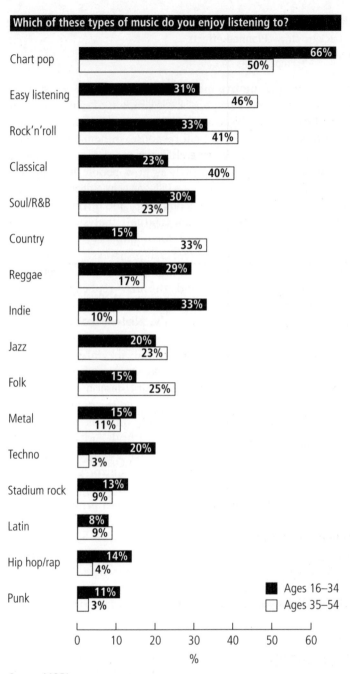

Which of these types of music do you enjoy listening to?

Chart pop — 66% / 50%
Easy listening — 31% / 46%
Rock'n'roll — 33% / 41%
Classical — 23% / 40%
Soul/R&B — 30% / 23%
Country — 15% / 33%
Reggae — 29% / 17%
Indie — 33% / 10%
Jazz — 20% / 23%
Folk — 15% / 25%
Metal — 15% / 11%
Techno — 20% / 3%
Stadium rock — 13% / 9%
Latin — 8% / 9%
Hip hop/rap — 14% / 4%
Punk — 11% / 3%

■ Ages 16–34
□ Ages 35–54

Source: MORI.

Fig. 10.3 Audience appreciation: enjoyment of music by categories and by age

Figure 10.3 shows another way of looking at audiences and effects. You could also look at ways in which marketing strategies relate to the information in this chart – how are these different audiences targeted?

- can we prove that the media (or some part of their output) have affected the way that people act or think?
- how can we prove this?

There is an attraction in **quantitative methods** of research. These ask very specific questions that demand closed responses, the simplest of which is yes or no. They appear to be factual and objective in their approach. Their attraction lies partly in being able to achieve a statistical response, in being able to talk about percentages. However, **qualitative research** is just as valid, even if it deals in looser and more immeasurable factors, such as how people feel about a particular media product.

Research can deal with the *audience* by **questionnaires and interviews**. It can deal with the *product/text* separately by **straight (textual) analysis**. It can deal with the *interaction between the media and their audience*, through, for example, research into media institutions or readership surveys.

It can deal with the *interaction between text and audience* either first hand (e.g. **ethnographic surveys**) or second hand through **replication of, or accounts of, the viewing/reading experience**, e.g. Broadcasters' Audience Research Board (BARB) surveys). For instance, the Nielsen market research organization in the United States supervises film previews during which the sweat and pulse rate of the audience can be measured; they also turn knobs by the viewing seat to register liking or dislike for certain scenes or characters. Replication asks sample audiences their opinions of material shown to them. This is not, of course, the same as seeing the communication on the screen or at the point of sale. The difficult thing is to make the experience authentic and therefore the reactions truthful and the evidence accurate. There are various other details of method that attempt to make the evidence objective. The classic detail is the use of a **control group**, which seeks opinions from those who have not heard the radio programme in question, and then compares their reactions with those of a group of people who have.

Closed experiments are those where the research may be done in a laboratory or a very specific place and concentrate on particular aspects of the material and of audience reaction. For example, children have been shown violent acts [sic] on screen, still or live, and have then been monitored for their style of play behaviour. The experiment is controlled, but it is also essentially artificial because normally we read and view in many places with all sorts of things going on around us.

Field studies are those where researchers go out to the audience, trying to obtain evidence of behaviour as it happens, or trying to obtain opinions and reactions soon after the media experience. One example of the former was based on video cameras fitted in television sets to watch the viewers' behaviour, and then on discussions with these people afterwards. In the case of the latter, straight audience questionnaires would be a staple approach.

Ethnographic research is a kind of field study in that, broadly, it involves the researcher being with the audience as they interact with the media. It takes account of contextual factors, such as (in the case of television) how viewers interact with each other, or whether lifestyle affects viewing.

Longtitudinal studies describes an approach that uses 'natural' settings, the same group of respondents and a replication of enquiry over a period of time, often years. These may be useful, for example, in dealing with assumptions about long-term effects. In relation to aggression and violence, for example, such studies suggest that social environment is a better predictor of violent behaviour than is media consumption.

Content analysis has already been described as a quantitative analysis of media material fastening on content (and possibly treatment and structure). In this case one is making particular assumptions about effects on the audience. It is jumping to conclusions to say that because the material contains, say, a high proportion of images of a comfortable material lifestyle, therefore it generates a longing for that lifestyle in the reader/viewer.

Correlational studies are, like content analysis, based on quantitative research. They seek to correlate or make connections between sets of statistics. There are two problems here. One is the assumption that there is a connection between one piece of exceptional information and another. The other is that it cannot be assumed that such a connection is causal. So, for example, if there is a correlation between television violence and aggressive behaviour, then it could be as likely that aggressive people like watching aggressive television, as much as that aggressive television causes aggressive behaviour.

Gauntlett (1995) reports on a fairly complex piece of research (by Lynn, Hampson and Agahi, 1989) involving 2,000 children in Northern Ireland. This seems to suggest that personality traits, not television viewing, are the crucial factor in predicting aggressive behaviour.

Table 10.1 Radio listening in the UK: by age and gender, 1998

Age group	Hours and minutes per week		
	Males	Females	All
4–14	5:13	6:42	5:57
15–34	18:11	15:14	16:45
35–64	19:56	16:39	18:15
65 and over	16:54	17:34	17:18
All aged 4 and over	16:42	14:59	15:50

Source: RAJAR/RS Ltd © Crown Copyright

2.2 Media Audience Research

Our opinions about media material (and issues of the day) are constantly being sought by a number of research organizations, both independent and attached to the various media.

The aforementioned **Broadcasters' Audience Research Board (BARB)** is jointly owned by the BBC and ITV. It samples which age groups are watching which programmes and when. The audience is sampled across age, class, geographical spread, and so on. Nearly 5,000 homes are electronically monitored every day to see which channel the television set is switched to; 3,000 different people are interviewed each week around the country, via a viewing booklet. There have also been special surveys of audience attitudes to violence on television or their attitudes towards particular channels. But, generally, BARB and those working in the broadcasting industries are concerned with ratings. It is true that now they are well aware of the importance of numbers within a target audience. The high proportion of young male viewers for American football is important to those selling the advertising space: consumer products such as jeans will be tied to such a programme. It is also the case that the BARB researchers produce what they call an **audience appreciation index** (AI), but the fact is that, particularly in commercial television, the programming executives don't care much about a high AI index for a programme that is losing its total audience figures. That programme is still likely to be moved out of prime time, or even axed.

Radio Joint Audience Research, like BARB, covers both the BBC and commercial radio, and is funded by them. It covers nearly 20,000 people a week, asking them to record their listening preferences in diary form.

The **National Readership Survey** is funded by newspaper owners and advertising agencies. It conducts 28,000 half-hour interviews a year in people's

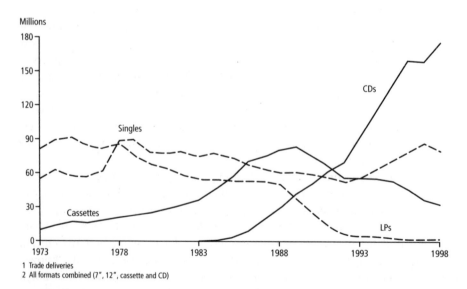

Fig. 10.4 UK sales¹ of CDs, LPs, cassettes and singles²

1 Trade deliveries
2 All formats combined (7″, 12″, cassette and CD)

Source: British Phonographic Industry

homes. These cover 200 titles of newspapers and magazines, and deal with reading habits, topic preferences and audience background.

The **Audit Bureau of Circulation** (ABC) monitors, via retailers and audience research, the sales and circulation figures for newspapers. An example of an independent research organization would be Gallup.

The **Joint Industry Committee for Regional Press Research** is, as its title suggests, a specialist organization set up by and for the regional press.

Cinema and Video Industry Audience Research (CAVIAR) is an organization funded by the Cinema Advertising Association. This in effect means a mixture of advertisers, distributors and retail chains. As with other organizations, such as BARB, much of the actual work may be subcontracted to market research organizations, even if CAVIAR controls the objectives and the methodology.

This kind of 'official' research is clearly exhaustive in its scope, and careful in its identification of audience samples. Yet it is often as much concerned with audience size and with what attracts audiences as it is with audience thinking and ATTITUDE FORMATION. Necessarily, it is not seeking views and reactions that could show serious criticism of the material or indeed of the whole structure of media communication as it is set up in this country.

2.3 Problems Surrounding Effects Research

The basic problem with identifying and measuring media effects is that there are so many **variables** in the process through which material is constructed, transmitted and decoded. There is also the issue of trying to deal with all the media at once – which most research does not do. Obviously one is not comparing like with like: different means of communication have different qualities. But then it is also a problem if one ignores all media but one because, as has been said, many messages actually do come through more than one medium at a time. There is a tacit assumption that visual aspects of media are 'powerful' because the images are directly decoded (they are iconic), but one cannot really say that, for example, reading about pornographic acts [*sic*] in a book does not endorse them just as film viewing is supposed to. So one has to recognize that, as a term, 'the media' covers multiple channels of communication, with various characteristics to the nature of each medium.

The **context of communication** matters a great deal. Television is seen as 'powerful' (i.e. influential) because it reaches into the home, but then there may be counteracting influences in the home, where other people can offer opinions on the material. Perhaps reading comics on the bus coming home from school is influential because it is an isolated activity. Then again, perhaps cinema viewing as an isolated activity is not so influential because everyone 'knows' that one goes in to this dark room to experience a fiction, which is not a general part of everyday experience.

Assumptions made by researchers are another problem. I have commented on this with relation to 'official' research. But then academic research is equally open to the error of assumptions. People are likely to approach research with some propositions or hypotheses that they would like to prove. The industries of academe are not perfectly neutral by contrast with the commercial industries of audience research.

Separation of the influence of the media, in particular from other influences in general, is extremely difficult. People are, for example, influenced by the opinions of family and friends. Certainly, attempts to demonstrate direct or immediate effects are fairly useless; in 1984 McQuail observed that 'Numerous investigations have by now seemed to establish that the direct effects of mass communication on attitudes and behaviour are either non existent, very small, or beyond measurement by current techniques.'

Closed experiments (e.g. laboratory) tend to be restrictive. They exclude the range of social experience, the complexity of real life as it is lived, and as it must affect the decoding of media material. Artificial conditions may lead the subjects into guessing how they are 'supposed to' respond to questions, or to behave. Such conditions diminish, for example, real-life inhibitions against behaving violently.

Field studies are only as good as their methodology and the interpretation of results. Belson (1978), for example, has questioned children, asking them to remember programmes they have seen some years before (when trying to demonstrate the influence of television with regard to violence). Anyone who has asked people questions about what they watched last night will see the flaw in this one. Barker (1984), during a particular furore about children watching video nasties, demonstrated that children would actually lie about what they had seen in order either to please the researcher or perhaps to boost their own sense of status.

Content analysis, as has been said, is essentially divorced from the audience. Frequent use has been made over the years of this approach, but to enumerate the number of shootings on television over a month, or the total acts of physical violence in children's programmes, proves nothing about how the audience perceives these acts – it only assumes an effect, attitudinal, emotional or behavioural.

Research methodology as such needs to be looked at carefully. There was a well-known and still sometimes reported piece of research in the United States into television and social behaviour. This was interpreted especially in terms of violent behaviour and was produced as the Surgeon General's Report. On the face of it, a research programme costing US$1 million should have been significant. But other commentators have remarked on the fact that the 23 separate projects involved were not in fact coordinated in any coherent way, that there was no distinction made between social and personal violence or collective and individual violence, that there was no sense of the social context to the violence described.

So there are clearly considerable problems surrounding the administering and interpretation of effects research.

The Value of Research
Is media research so problematic that it is a waste of time?
Are there good reasons for trying to develop approaches to media research?

2.4 A Process Model Critique of Effects

■ *The Source*

Power held by those who deliver the messages affects what kind of message goes to whom. This refers especially to those who create the material and who present it to the audience (as opposed to the owners who control a given medium).

Referent power is that where viewers may identify with a presenter as someone of their own 'type' and with their views. They will then be predisposed to believe what that person says.

Expert power would be exemplified by magazine readers who are inclined to believe what they are told because a source is billed as an expert or is someone whom they believe to be (probably from reading about them!) an expert.

Opinion makers in the media are respected individuals who are seen to be knowledgeable and trustworthy, and so are readily believed. Newsreaders or current affairs presenters would be examples of such people. The whole style of their presentation, the history of their appearances in the broadcasting media, inclines the audience to accept what they say, not to question it.

The medium as source also makes a difference. Radio news programmes are perceived as being more 'reliable' than, say, a satirical programme based on news items. The judgements and criticisms made by the latter could be piercing and worthy of consideration, but the former will be seen as having more status.

The monopoly enjoyed by the source will make a difference. For example, a great deal of hard news material, especially in regional papers, comes from the Press Association (collectively owned by the major regional newspaper groups). Regional papers cannot afford to have their own reporters in the field – they buy in their news. Regional populations receive essentially the same hard news from this source. There is a process of repetition and reinforcement going on. The audience has, because of this degree of monopoly, a relatively limited ability to check out what they are told, to seek alternative versions of main news. So the effect of presenting a particular view of the world is strengthened.

The credibility of the source is crucial.

■ *The Context*

This would cover:

- the immediate physical environment in which media consumption takes place – such as the home

- the immediate social (group) context of consumption – such as friends or family
- the broader social context – that is, society at large.

Opinion leaders relate to social context. Research has demonstrated that **most people within their social groups are inclined to listen to certain respected individuals** (it could be your mother or your best friend or your teacher). If these people endorse some opinion articulated through the media, or offer some opinion on the material, then the audience is inclined to listen to them. If these people confirm a media opinion or endorse the value of some programme or magazine, then the audience will be the more affected by that material.

Social conditions will affect how far some media item will influence the views and values of the audience. If the audience member has been a victim of crime in an inner-city area that is plainly suffering from some kind of neglect, then the likelihood is that they will pay attention to media information and views on the subjects of urban crime and urban decay.

Media events and media issues are also part of the context. This is a kind of self-fulfilling prophecy, where the media condition their own effects by setting up conditions. For example, in 1989 a spate of stories about problems with food hygiene put this issue on the agenda, made it an issue in the first place and also predisposed people to pay more attention to further items on the subject. An atmosphere of anxiety, and criticism of the monitoring of food hygiene, predisposes people to feel anxious and critical when any new information on the subject comes their way.

■ *The Message and its Treatment*

That which is absent: what is not said, what is not known by the audience because it is not said, will condition the effects of the communication. For example, you might buy a single by a favourite group, not knowing that the group was going to break up. If you did know then your attention to the music and its effects would be different.

Repetition of messages tends to enhance their effects. People tend to believe something if it is said often enough (provided it isn't too outrageous!).

Media currency is about whether or not the message is about something that has already been presented in the media. In other words, once something has been made an issue – such as aircraft crashes and air safety – then another item about this subject is likely to get attention because it fits a pattern. Again, there is a kind of irony that the media themselves have created this heightened awareness.

Conventions in presenting the message: it is obvious that if a news item is presented through banner headlines and dramatic photographs, then this will condition the readers' responses.

Message structure could refer to the way a story is told in a magazine or to the composition of a photograph or to the structure of a piece of music. To take a simple example, if one has a photograph in a brochure that carries a message about happy holidays, and the children playing in a pool are out of focus (in the background), the effect of the message will be different from that of them being clearly in the foreground. There is a shift of emphasis.

■ The Audience (Context and Reading)

The place of the audience in the social structure (including status) makes a difference. Those who are well off are likely to be affected differently from those who are badly off by a message about increases in taxation.

Prior beliefs are to do with what the audience believes already. Someone believing in self-sufficiency and independence will respond to an advertisement encouraging people to start up small businesses in a different way from someone who believes in job protection and a job for life.

The greater the match between the views and knowledge of the audience and what is said in the communication, the more the communication will be believed.

The needs of the audience at one time, or over a period of time, will condition how it is affected by given items. If one is feeling depressed and lonely then one will interpret a situation comedy about the trials of life on one's own in an apartment differently from someone who can't wait to get into their own place.

Perception will condition the way the audience understands a text and makes meanings from it. All media material, like all communicative experience, has to be perceived. The experience, the material, the person, the image of a person, has to be judged and assimilated into one's way of looking at things. To pick up the last example, one person will view a sitcom scene showing a man making a mess of domestic chores in one way – perhaps perceiving it as not too serious a comment and typical of male incompetence anyway. Another audience member might perceive it as an annoyingly stereotypical view.

Morley (1992) discusses his work and that of others when he takes a view of how audiences may decode or read texts.

- A **dominant reading** is the same as a preferred reading, where he argues that certain social groups will make sense of a text in the way that it 'wants' us to make sense of it, a way that fits the dominant ideology.
- A **negotiated reading** is one where the audience member is able to stand back from the text to make certain choices about what they think it means.
- **Oppositional readings** are those that actually make sense of the text in quite the opposite way to how it was intended to be taken.

Research suggests, not surprisingly, that what we make of a text depends on where we are coming from. For a start, you may develop a capacity to negotiate readings with texts as a result of reading this book and taking on board at least some of its implications. But, in any case, you will already have certain positions, sets of attitudes and values in your head as a result of your upbringing and of the norms of those groups you value. To pick up an example from Morley, you are going to look at a television news piece about some industrial dispute rather differently if you are a trainee manager in a bank, than if you are a trades union official working in a factory.

> **The Emphasis on Violence in Effects**
>
> Is it valid and beneficial that a lot of attention is paid to violence as an area of media effects?
>
> Should research look more widely at other kinds of effect (for example, the influence of representations of relationships, as these may affect young audiences)?

3 BRIEF CASE STUDIES

It is worth noting that, **when effects are discussed, specific issues are often raised,** such as the effect of television on children, or the effect of television on family life. While it is useful to fasten on a particular issue and a particular audience, there are a lot of assumptions behind all this.

In both cases the exclusion of other media ignores important influences. What about comics or videos where children are concerned? What about the effect of tapes and records on family life?

3.1 Children and Television

Propositions about children in relation to television need to take account of many things. What do we mean by a child? The programmers or the film censors clearly realize that **different age ranges are likely to be affected in different ways.** Again, there is a weight of evidence which shows that children are able to distinguish between modes of realism by about the age of eight. So cartoon violence, or indeed any fictional violence, is less likely to affect the older child because it is seen as being of a special world apart from the one in which they live. So, as always, one has a problem in defining violence in the first place and, second, in defining which programmes children are actually watching.

There is also concern about various **kinds of role model** offered to children through television, not least in programmes made for children. *Grange Hill* is a well-known British series about a fictional state school. There have been anguished comments about its depiction of elements such as bullying, young romance and racism. One proposition is that children may adopt the worst role behaviour and the least attractive attitudes from the drama (even though it takes a clear moral stance). This is about **effects as imitation and effects as attitude change.** There is no evidence that either effect or consequence takes place. It does seem that adults are uncomfortable with a relatively truthful view of the child's school world that does not fit their ideals. Children have been heard to comment that reality can be worse, that the programme makers have cut out the swearing anyway!

The view of children and how they experience television often says more about the adult commentators than it does about the children. This is not to argue that parents should not have attitudes and values regarding the content and quality of television, that these parents should not try to impart these values to their children. One would expect this to happen as part of the usual process of parental socialization. But these parents underestimate their children if they believe that they have no powers of discrimination or judgement. They are overestimating television and its effects if they really believe that, on its own, it is going to make their children passive or will in some way 'control their minds'.

For example, a study of children's ability to distinguish between programmes and adverts showed that even three year olds made a 66 per cent correct distinction (Gauntlett, 1995). Other studies show that children between the ages of five and nine, are well aware that adverts are trying to sell something.

One also has to look at the **context of violence** before making assumptions about its effects on children. This might refer to endings, for instance, in which narrative closure makes it quite clear that whatever violence has gone before, it isn't approved of and doesn't pay off.

David Thompson (*Independent on Sunday*, 18 June 2000) makes typically anxious claims about television (and all visual media), while also making an impassioned plea for teaching visual literacy. He quotes the content-based extrapolation that the average eighteen year old will have seen 20,000 acts of violence on visual media – as if this tells us something about the nature of that violence, the nature of its effects. I suggest that it is other representations that he should be more concerned about. He is entering interesting (and insufficiently researched) territory when he speculates about how children may read images of people. They may indeed be more concerned about the emotional behaviour of actors on screen, in particular contexts, than about killing and wounding as such.

3.2 Violence and Television

Many people have opinions about this subject, but little has been proved. In one survey the IBA (the Independent Broadcasting Association – now the Independent Television Commission) found that 60 per cent of sample viewers asserted that there was too much violence on television, but when questioned more closely very few of these people could actually name specific examples. Another IBA survey asking about a possible decline in the standards of television found only 5 per cent who thought this was because of excessive violence. Yet, another survey by the IBA (December 1987) suggested that as many as 6 per cent of viewers sometimes felt violent after watching violent programmes on television. The actual question was about whether or not the viewer agreed with the statement 'sometimes I feel quite violent after watching crime programmes'. Apart from the fact that violence is not confined to crime programmes anyway, the answers to such questions in no way tell us how long the feeling lasted, nor could they prove that these people then behaved violently.

The media themselves are prone to raise media violence as an issue (often asserting that it is excessive), and so perhaps falsely affect public opinion of

Table 10.2 Children's viewing: most popular programmes, 1994

TVRs

All children

Honey, I Shrunk the Kids	41
Gladiators	38
National Lottery	37
Do it Yourself, Mr Bean	36
Neighbours	36

Girls

Neighbours	40
Honey, I Shrunk the Kids	39
3 Men and a Little Lady	38
EastEnders	37
Gladiators	37

Boys

Honey, I Shrunk the Kids	42
National Lottery	41
Ghostbusters II	39
Gladiators	39
Do it Yourself, Mr Bean	37

Aged 4–9

Honey, I Shrunk the Kids	46
Gladiators	40
ET	40
Ghostbusters II	37
Do it Yourself, Mr Bean	36

Aged 10–15

Neighbours	42
National Lottery	38
EastEnders	38
Twins	37
Casualty	37

Source: BARB/AGB in *Spectrum*, spring 1995, ITC

Table 10.2 shows the top TVR ratings for programmes that children like to watch. You could draw conclusions about their tastes and interests. You might also consider the ideology of the programmes concerned, and the potential effects on these young people.

how much violence there really is. It is notorious that the popular press asserted that the killer behind the 'Hungerford Massacre' of 1988 was influenced by violence in Rambo films. There was no evidence that the person concerned had ever seen these films. Still this notion of effects through 'imitation' remains a popular one.

These comments are not meant to ignore people's anxieties. There is concern about long-term effects of the media – perhaps that of desensitization, especially where children are concerned. But in terms of there being a connection between television portrayals and human behaviour, as the Director General of the IBA said in 1987, 'a direct causal link has never been convincingly established'.

However, this same organization clearly does assume the possibility of a link because it has issued guidelines to steer the programme makers. These include being careful about the possible effect of material on the young, not assuming that violence that is condemned is therefore harmless, and not showing kinds of violence that can easily be imitated. One clear precept is 'If in doubt, cut!'

As I have said earlier in this chapter on possible media effects, there are many conditions and influences that surround possible effects. A survey by Portsmouth Polytechnic lecturers reported in *New Society* (18 August 1987) suggested that, for example, where people live relates to violent behaviour as much as what they view.

I have also pointed out that research methods (and even researchers' possible predispositions) can cause problems. Belson in *Television and the Adolescent Boy* (1978) purported to find a connection between violent behaviour and viewing of violent programmes when people are young. But the problem was that he was looking at youngsters chosen because they had committed crimes in the first place, and then asked them for comment based on a list of programmes that seem to have been pre-selected because many of them were relatively violent compared with much television material. Such selection of samples and of materials was bound to produce a correlation.

One survey of violence on television – *The Portrayal of Violence in BBC Television* (Cumberbatch, 1989) – is very useful in its content analysis approach, and to this extent is objective. It appears to prove some interesting things – for example that, measured in terms of acts of violence, British television is actually growing less violent, and is certainly less violent than US television. What the study does not and cannot do is to connect the evidence covering types of violence and their performance in certain types of programme with actual violent behaviour by the audience.

Another point you might consider with relation to effects on children in particular is that concerning the distinction between fact and fantasy. Children may talk violently or play violently, to an extent, after watching certain television material, but this does not mean that they are going to think violently or act violently some time after this experience is over.

In terms of fact and fiction on television, it is clear that people distinguish between violence in each of these modes. This does not mean that violence in news, for example, is considered to be automatically OK. Gauntlett and Hill

(1999) in a report of a diary experiment, refer to concerns expressed about the level and nature of violence shown in the Bosnian war. One major dimension of 'the problem of media violence' – also shown in their work – is the sheer inconsistency of people's responses to, and opinions about, violence. Three things that do seem to make a difference to perceptions of violence are:

1 the context in which it takes place
2 whether the audience has prior knowledge/experience of such violence
3 what consequences are as a result of the violence.

In 1985 some research into children and their viewing of violence suggested that as many as 40 per cent watched so-called violent programmes (films) sometimes. In 1988 another team replicated this research, but in its questioning slipped in titles of films that did not exist; 68 per cent of children surveyed claimed to have seen these non-existent films. So, again, one has doubts about the supposed links between types of violence in the media and violent behaviour in life.

Some critics argue that their concern for the effects of media violence on the young is in respect of its causing emotional disturbance (as much as violent behaviour). This seems to be a modest and more plausible proposition. Such disturbance may in itself lead to some violent behaviour. All the same, it proves no easier to define what is meant by 'disturbance', and then to link it to specific media consumption.

Those who choose to believe that television shows too much violence will continue to believe this. Whether they can define what is 'too much', and of what, is another matter. There is also evidence that people draw some of their concerns about violence from ongoing debates about violence, which are presented through the media (see the section on moral panics in Chapter 7). One may remain concerned about the possible effects of what violence there is on television. But you as a student of the media should be cautious about accepting the assertions of researchers without looking at their methods. You should ask yourself basic questions about how one defines violence in the media (what about psychological violence, for example?), about how one measures the extent of such violence, about how one measures audience reactions to that violence, and about whether any of this proves a connection between the screen and the mind of the viewer.

4 CONCLUSIONS

It is clear that there is no straightforward causal relationship between media consumption and social behaviour, let alone the acquisition of specific attitudes and values. Television viewers must, for example, be discriminating to a degree, or there would be no need for alternative listings magazines, or videoplus, or TiVO.

However, the fact that there is only very conditional evidence of effects is neither an argument for asserting that there are none at all, nor will the kind of refutation I have offered simply stop people worrying. Beliefs are powerful.

So I am arguing that concerns are valid, research should continue, but that panicky and unfounded assumptions should be questioned rigorously, or even rejected.

It is fair to say that one should take account of the long-term and indirect effects of the media on ways in which we think about ourselves and about our society.

We are back to the meanings that we may construct by interacting with the media. These meanings are generated from the process that has been discussed throughout this book.

Media Studies is not simply about facts – who owns what or how newspapers are made – it is about the significance of those facts: how we think and how we live our lives. If it is about the production of meaning then it is also about the values by which we live and the beliefs that inform our actions, about the part the media may play in constructing and invoking these.

This seems to me to be a pretty good reason for making the media central to study. So, carry on …

Activity (20): Children, Reading and Effects

This activity should bring out points about how, in respect of ideas about media influence, there are assumptions made about effects and audiences that need to be questioned.

First, you need to TALK TO A NUMBER OF PARENTS AND/OR TEACHERS ABOUT CHILDREN AND READING. You will have to pick a particular age group of child. Try the following questions.

- What do they think that children read?
- What do they think children should read?
- Why do they think that children should read the kinds of material given in answer to the second question?

Second, you need to TALK TO SOME CHILDREN FROM THE AGE RANGE YOU HAVE CHOSEN.

- Ask them what they read and why.

See what you can learn from the similarities and differences between the answers given by adults and those given by the children. Do the answers tell you anything about the assumptions made by adults about children as children, as well as about their reading? Do the answers contain any assumptions about the effects of reading on children?

REVIEW

You should have learned the following things from this chapter on media effects.

- It is often proposed that the media affect our attitudes, beliefs and values, directly or indirectly.
- There has been a great deal of research into effects on the audience, but much of it is inconclusive or depends on certain conditions.
- There are many factors that may influence people's attitudes and behaviour. The media are only one of these. It is difficult to separate the media from those other factors when conducting research.

1 WHAT SORTS OF EFFECT

- Types of effect may be summarized as follows: short-term effects, inoculation theory, Two-Step Flow Theory, Uses and Gratifications Theory, Cultivation Theory, cultural effects, attitude change, cognitive change, moral panics and collective reactions, emotional responses and personal reactions, agenda setting, socialization, social control, defining reality, endorsement of the dominant ideology.

2 STUDYING EFFECTS

2.1 Types of research may be marked by quantitative or qualitative approaches. Methods of research notably include closed experiments, field studies, content analysis.

2.2 The media conduct a great deal of audience research of their own. Examples of organizations doing this are the Broadcasters' Audience Research Board (BARB) and the Audit Bureau of Circulation (ABC).

2.3 Problems surrounding effects research, and trying to prove effects, notably include the following: the number of variables to take account of, the context in which communication takes place, assumptions made by researchers, separating the influence of the media from other factors, the unrealistic nature of closed experiments, the quality of methodology and interpretation of field studies, the separation of content analysis from the audience.

2.4 A process-based critique of effects leads to the following conclusions: the status and credibility of the source of the message matters; media authority figures, known as opinion makers, also matter; the essential nature of the medium influences how the audience is affected; the degree of monopoly of information or of material in general possessed by the medium (owners) matters; the context in which the messages are received influences how they may affect the audience; opinion leaders in social groups may be part of that context; social conditions matter; events and issues raised by the media themselves are also part of the context in which the messages come through; the nature of the message matters; what is not said is as important as what is actually said; repetition has an effect; messages about subjects that are already in the media matter; the use of conventions of presentation affect the impact of the message; how the message is structured matters; the audience's powers of perception, their beliefs, their knowledge, influence how messages affect them; they may make dominant, negotiated or oppositional readings of texts.

3 BRIEF CASE STUDIES

- Some discussion of effects is related to specific issues and audiences, such as the effect of television on children, or the effects of violence on audiences.

3.1 The effects of television on children depend on many factors, such as the age at which they distinguish fiction from reality, and on the preconceptions that adults have about children.

3.2 There are many opinions offered about violence in the media and particular effects, but no direct relationship between media material and habitual violent behaviour has been proved. The media themselves often raise violence as an issue and perhaps cause anxiety about it. The most plausible effects proposed are long term and to do with attitude change and desensitization towards the depiction of violence. There have been many problems with research methods in terms of proving violence effects. Recent content analysis demonstrates that, in terms of acts of violence depicted on television, there are fewer than there used to be and fewer in Britain than elsewhere.

4 CONCLUSIONS

- Problems with research do not mean that the media do not affect us and that we should not be concerned. In terms of media effects, we need to be most concerned with possible effects on our attitudes, values and beliefs.

Glossary of Terms

The following is a list of terms used in this book, with a brief definition for each one. You may also come across some of them in your further reading, especially if you take on more 'difficult' books. For further references and information see O'Sullivan, *et al.* (1994).

Agenda Setting refers to the process by which the news media define which topics (the agenda) should be of main interest to the audience, by selecting these topics repeatedly for news material.

Anchorage refers to the element of a picture that helps to make clear (anchors) its meaning. In many cases it is actually the caption underneath the picture that does this.

Attitude, Attitude Formation refers to the hostile or friendly view that we hold towards a person or an issue presented in the media. Attitude formation refers to the ways in which the media shape our views on a given topic.

Audience defines the receivers of mass media communication (also readers and viewers). It may be measured in terms such as numbers, gender and spending habits.

Bias describes a quality of media material which suggests that it leans towards a particular view of a given issue when it should be more neutral. The term is often discussed in relation to news treatment.

Binary Oppositions refers to a frequent pattern in texts where characters, ideas or plot elements are set one against the other; the text is organized around the idea of opposites.

Campaign describes the organized use of advertisements and publicity across the media and over a period of time, in order to promote such things as sales of a product, the image of a company, the views of a pressure group or political party.

Censorship refers to the suppression or re-writing of media material by some person or committee that has power over those who created that material. The reasons for carrying out censorship are often based on religion (as in Eire) or political beliefs (China).

Channel is simply the means of communication. This general term could apply equally to speech or to television.

Code (*see also* Secondary Code) is a system of signs held together by conventions. Primary codes include speech made up from word signs, or visual communication made up from image signs.

Cognition refers to the mental process by which we recognize what is going on around us and then make sense of it in our heads. For example, when we decode a magazine for its meaning.

Consensus refers to the middle ground of beliefs and values agreed within a society. It also refers to the compromise position that is taken on issues raised through the media.

Conspiracy Theories refer to the idea that the media represent a plot by someone to influence our beliefs and attitudes.

Constraints are factors such as lack of finance or legal obstacles that limit the power of media producers to do what they want.

Content Analysis is a way of analysing the meaning and significance in media material by breaking it down into units and measuring how many of each type of unit appear. The more one item appears, the more likely it is to have some significance.

Context refers to the circumstances in which a media text is produced or understood. Context could refer to place, to production conditions or to cultural surroundings.

Conventions are rules that organize signs in a code, and so help bring out meaning. These rules are unwritten but can be worked out if one observes repeated patterns in human behaviour or in media material. So there are conventions that govern how we talk with one another, and there are conventions that govern how a soap opera is put together. We know these rules subconsciously; this is what helps us work out what a conversation or a soap opera really means.

Cultural Imperialism describes the way in which selling the media products of one country (USA) to others is rather like creating an empire of ideas that influences those other countries.

Culture (*see also* Subcultures) is a collection of beliefs, values and behaviours that are distinctive to a large group of people, and are expressed through various forms of communication. It is common to see culture in terms of nations, but in fact culture can cross national boundaries (e.g. Jewish culture). Culture is represented through dress, religion and art forms in particular, as well as through language. The media show these things and so also become part of the culture.

Deviancy refers to the idea that certain groups within society (and representatives of these) are branded as deviants by news in the media. This means that they are shown in varying degrees as odd, rebellious or even criminal. It also means that such people do not fit in with what are also defined as social norms – accepted attitudes and behaviours.

Diegesis is the text itself and everything that is part of its content (rather than how it is expressed).

Discourse is a difficult term, used to describe how certain kinds of understanding are created and perpetuated within various institutions in society. These discourses are about ideas and meanings that are made apparent through the way in which the subject of the discourse is 'talked about' through visual as well as verbal languages. So, there is a set of ideas and there are ways of communicating them that are special to medicine or education or television or even television news in particular.

Dysfunction describes negative or destructive ways in which the media can be operated or used.

Feedback is communication in response to a previous message. In terms of mass media, feedback is often delayed because those taking part in the process of communication are not face to face. It is also largely ineffective because the audience giving the feedback has no means of insisting that the producers should change their communication in some way in response to that audience.

Genre refers to types of media product that are recognizable through having a number of common and identifiable elements that add up to a kind of formula for the creation of story and characters. Genres are also, by nature, popular and commercially profitable. Many genres are also narrative fiction (e.g. the detective story), but not always such (e.g. quiz shows).

Globalization refers to the process by which media ownership, media production and media use is expanding on a global rather than on a national scale.

Hegemony describes the exercise of power by elite groups in a society over the rest of that society. The institutions of the media are important in expressing and maintaining that power. This is especially true because the exertion of that power is not necessarily obvious, e.g. it may not be noticed that the media still present it as natural that people who are important in our society are white, middle class and speak with received pronunciation.

Icon is a symbolic element within a genre, which is highly charged with meanings relevant to that genre. An icon is, in effect, a symbol for the genre, e.g. the trench coat and trilby hat for the detective genre.

Identity refers to the sense of self that is constructed for a group through media representations.

Ideological State Apparatus refers to those institutions controlled by the state that act as a power for representing (and communicating) this dominant ideology, e.g. education and schools. It is not necessarily obvious that they are doing this because the values comprising ideology are often shown as being naturally correct and therefore made 'invisible'.

Ideology is a term that refers to the coherent set of beliefs and values that dominate in a culture, and that are particularly held by those who have power. Ideology is concerned with social and power relationships, and with the means by which these are made apparent. The media communicate ideology to their audiences. This ideology can be found in the material by looking for covert messages. The dominant ideology is that ideology whose views and values prevail.

Image Analysis is the analysis of the signs within the image (photography, painting, cartoon) in order to deconstruct the meaning these signs create.

Impartiality is the notion of not taking sides or a particular view on a given issue. Broadcast news in particular believes in the idea of impartiality, though it does not always achieve it.

Institution is the word identifying any type of media business or organization that owns the means of making media material.

Intertextuality describes the ways in which texts and their meanings are intertwined, from one medium to another or perhaps within a genre. We understand one text partly from what we know about others.

Mass Communication is the general term for means of communication that operate on a large scale, i.e. in terms of the geographical area reached, the numbers of people reached, the numbers of pieces of communication that are reproduced.

Meaning is what you think it is! The meaning of communication, printed or broadcast, is what you believe it is trying to tell you. The meaning in a piece of communication is signified by the signs that make it up. The meaning that is intended by the sender of the communication may not be the same as the meaning that is decoded or 'read' by the receiver or audience.

Media Power refers to the power of media institutions, through ownership and control, to shape messages that, in turn, may influence the attitudes and behaviour of the audience.

Mediation describes the way in which the media come between the audience and the original material on which the programme or printed matter is based. The media provide their own version of this original material. In mediating it they change it.

Message is any item of information, of opinion, of value judgement that we believe we are being told through an example of media material.

Mode of Address refers to the way in which any media text 'talks to' the audience, to how it sets up a relationship with the audience through the way it 'talks'.

Moral Panic is a term that describes a collective response to events in society as shown through the media. The original work that helped coin the term was about news coverage of mugging. The suggestion was that the news people created a panic about mugging by reporting it frequently, and implying that it was a more serious problem than it really was.

Myth is a story or even part of a story that is not really true, but that says something about what a culture wants to believe in. Genres are full of myths about heroic deeds or even about ideas such as the 'American dream' that everyone can be a great success if they really want to.

Narrative refers to story making and story structure. The narrative of a programme or article is not just its storyline. It is also about how the story is organized and about how the understanding of the reader is organized by the ways in which the story is told.

Naturalization refers to the way in which the messages within much media material are made to seem naturally 'right' or 'true'. The messages that make up ideology are usually held to be naturalized, so that one is not aware that the ideology is there.

News Values are the news topics and ways of treating those topics that the news makers judge as important.

Opinion Leaders are those people in groups that we belong to whose opinions we respect, and that we are likely to agree with because of this. The effects of the media depend partly on these opinion leaders.

Opinion Makers are media figures such as the presenter who fronts a documentary series, who thus have the power to interpret information and represent views to the audience.

Paradigm is a collection of signs that 'belong together' but that then need conventions to turn them into a working code. The alphabet is a paradigm of letter signs that need conventions to organize them into words (syntagms).

Preferred Reading refers to the way in which an article is so written or a programme is so constructed that the audience is subconsciously pressured into preferring (reading) one meaning into that material rather than any other meaning.

Propaganda refers to communication that is intentionally manipulated by a powerful source in order to project influential political messages. This source is also powerful enough to exclude alternative messages. It is a misuse of the term to call advertising propaganda.

Realism is a quality of a piece of communication, fictional or factual, that causes the reader or viewer to judge it to be more or less truthful or lifelike.

Regulation refers to the mechanisms, formal or informal, legal or economic, through which media production is controlled. (*See also* Censorship and Constraints.)

Representation refers to both the creation of a likeness of something through using signs and to the creation of meanings through those signs. Representations of people are constructed through image signs in the media. What those images mean or stand for is also represented.

Role is a particular pattern of behaviour that we take on because we see ourselves in a certain social position in relation to other people. Roles are also taken on because others assume we should do this. The positions are defined in terms of factors such as job or place in the family. So we talk about the role of daughter or the role of reporter.

Secondary Code is a particular code of signs and conventions that works on a level above the primary codes of speech, non-verbal communication, etc. The media are full of such codes, which belong to genres in particular, e.g. the news.

Semiotics refers to the study of signs, of sign systems and of their meanings.

Sign: anything can become a sign if we agree that it has a meaning. The particular meaning of a sign or set of signs is something that is agreed and learned through experience. Signs have no particular meaning of themselves, so gestures or elements of pictures become signs because we agree that they have a meaning.

Signification has two possible meanings. One refers to 'the signification' – what the receiver believes that a sign actually does mean, out of all the possible signifieds. The other refers to the 'process of signification' – the making of meanings through signs.

Signified is that part of the sign that is its possible meaning. In many cases the signifier could refer to a number of possible meanings.

Signifier is that part of the idea of sign that actually signals something – a wink, a camera angle, a word.

Socialization describes the processes through which a person becomes a participating member of society. It is learning to live with others. It includes the idea of acquiring beliefs, norms, values, conventions, and of ways of interpreting experience, including our experience of the media. The media help socialize us.

Source is where the message comes from.

Stereotype is a generalized and simplified social classification of individuals or groups. This classification includes untested assumptions and judgements about types of people. So stereotypes are also often about prejudices or negative attitudes towards the type of person or group represented.

Structural Analysis is a process of looking for the structure or organizing principles within a text. (*See also* Textual Analysis, Binary Oppositions, Narrative.)

Structuralism is an approach to studying experience that looks for organizing principles and structures within that experience. In the case of the media it assumes that there are structures to be found in media products. If one finds those structures, it is believed that this helps us to find out how the programme or printed item (the text) comes to have meanings.

Subcultures are cultural groups within a main culture. Often they define themselves by opposing that main culture in various ways. For example, Rastafarians see themselves as disagreeing with at least some of the values of mainstream British culture and certainly have distinct characteristics of their own.

Symbol is a type of sign that bears no literal relationship to what it refers to. Words are symbolic. Pictures are generally called iconic because they usually resemble their subject. The word 'tiger' doesn't look like a tiger, but a picture of a tiger does. The word symbol is complicated by the fact that it is used in different ways. So it is also possible to talk about a picture of a tiger being symbolic in another way – the Esso tiger, for instance, becomes a symbol of that oil company as well as a symbol of strength.

Text describes a piece of communication that may then be analysed for its signs and its meanings. A conversation, a photograph, a programme, an advertisement, a news article may all be treated as texts for analysis.

Textual Analysis is the process of analysing a text to see how it is put together, what meanings are in it, and how they are built into the text.

Uses and Gratifications Theory is about how the media may affect the audience and about how the audience may use media texts. It suggests that the audience actively uses the media to gratify certain of its needs.

Values include the idea of taking an attitude towards an issue, of seeing particular ideas as valuable and important. The idea of value includes the idea that we have made a judgement about the relative importance of whatever it is that we value.

Select Reading and Resource List

There are many, many books on the media. But a lot of these are about specialized aspects of media study. There are quite a few on areas such as news and effects, but again, many of them can be tough going. This list is deliberately selective, and tries to make clear why the book is worth reading by having a few lines on each. General texts may cover specialist areas to some extent, as well. Your tutor can suggest even more background reading to suit the course that he or she has put together. (I have added a section that covers any other books I have referred to in the text.)

I have also listed some trade magazines that are worth getting hold of if you can. These will give you inside information on things like advertising campaigns, on changes of ownership in the media industries and on costs. You will need to look for them in school or college libraries, or in the bigger public libraries.

There is also a select list of some web sites you may find useful.

COMMUNICATION AND MEDIA: GENERAL

Dimbleby, R. and Burton, G. (1998): *More Than Words: an Introduction to Communication Studies* (3rd edn). London: Routledge.
  Read Chapter 5 for a potted version of major media topics that may help you get into this book if you have problems. Chapter 1 could be useful if you want to understand more about the basic theory of communication as a process.
Fiske, J. (1982): *Introduction to Communication Studies*. London: Methuen.
  This is an introduction for the able A-level student and for tutors. It adopts a semiotics-based approach and has a lot of theory in it. It is very good in what it does, but is not necessarily the first book to read on a communication course.

MEDIA STUDIES: GENERAL

Bell, A., Joyce, M. and Rivers, D. (1999): *Advanced Level Media*. London: Hodder & Stoughton.
  Although this book does have a 'tools for analysis' section, it is mainly organized generically. It has sections on the music industry, for example. It also has very useful film and film genre case studies, e.g. film noir and African cinema.
Branston, G. and Stafford, R. (1999): *The Media Student's Book* (2nd edn). London: Routledge.
  A popular and compendious work covering many aspects of the media, and key concepts in media study and critical theory including postmodernism and globalization.
Briggs, A. and Cobley, P. (1998): *The Media: an Introduction*. Harlow: Longman.
  Probably most appropriate for degree-level students, especially in the critical sections. But there are also some really useful snapshots of the state of various media industries.

Burton, G. (1999): *Media and Popular Culture* (Access to Sociology series). London: Hodder & Stoughton.

I wrote this short book (130 pages) as a way into key ideas about media and culture for sociologists. It includes activities and study points. It has an explanation of what is meant by mass media and popular culture. Covers key topics such as news, institutions and representations.

Lusted, D. (ed.) (1991): *The Media Studies Book*. London: Routledge.

Although this book is written for teachers, it is perfectly readable by A-level students. It covers key topics such as narrative, institution, audience, representation. Obviously it is angled towards helping teachers deal with these topics, but it provides explanation and information along the way.

Nicholas, J. and Price, J. (1998): *Advanced Studies in Media*. London: Nelson.

Necessarily covers core concepts such as institution and audience, but this one has quite a number of activities, case studies and practical production sections towards the end. Generously illustrated, including colour.

O'Sullivan, T., Dutton, B. and Rayner, P. (1998): *Studying the Media* (2nd edn). London: Edward Arnold.

A thorough, useful text, which covers most major topics and provides useful examples.

Skeggs, B. and Mundy, J. (1992): *The Media*. Walton on Thames: Nelson.

A sociology textbook based on readings or extracts from various sources, and covering key areas of Media Studies. A very useful little book, not least for the lucid introductions to sections.

Taylor, L. and Willis, A. (1999): *Media Studies: Texts, Institutions and Audiences*. Oxford: Blackwell.

This one is clearly aimed at a degree-level readership. The title speaks for itself. It also covers areas such as reading images and media consumption.

You might also like to look at the *Guardian* newspaper media supplement on Mondays – you never know what you are going to find.

MEDIA OWNERSHIP: INSTITUTIONS (INCLUDING DEVELOPMENT)

Crisell, A. (1997): *An Introductory History of British Broadcasting*. London: Routledge.
Simply, very useful and thorough.

Curran, J. and Seaton, J. (1997): *Power without Responsibility: the Press and Broadcasting in Britain* (5th edn). London: Routledge.

This book is good because it provides a concise and informed history of the press and broadcasting, which also brings one up to date with current developments. The chapter on the sociology of the mass media is similarly concise in packing in issues and concepts.

Eldridge, G., Kitzinger, J. and Williams, K. (1997): *The Mass Media and Power in Modern Britain*. Oxford: Oxford University Press.

An intelligent, well-argued critique of the nature, effects, and developments in media power and influence.

Seymour-Ure, C. (1996): *The British Press and Broadcasting Since 1945* (2nd edn). Oxford: Blackwell.

Simply, a thorough, informative history. With chapters on audiences and on the government's changing relationship with broadcasters.

Williams, G. (1996): *Britain's Media – How they are Related*. London: Campaign for Press and Broadcasting Freedom.

Although certain matters of fact get overtaken by the frequency with which the big fish gobble up the smaller ones, still this slim work provides some thought-provoking comment on the march of globalization and the exercise of power by Britain's media owners.

Who Owns Whom (Dun & Bradstreet) is a useful reference work through which to check on which media company is owned by which other one. Usually the thread leads back to the same few names.

▉ MEDIA REFERENCE WORKS: THEORY AND PRACTICE

Dyja, E. (ed.) (2000): *BFI Film and Television Handbook 2001*. London: BFI.

Also covers video. Packed with addresses for production companies, cinemas and libraries, among many others. Lots of useful statistics relating to film and television material and organizations.

Gauntlett, D. (ed.) (2000): *Web Studies*. London: Arnold.

As the title suggests this book is about the uses and possibilities of the web. It is difficult to place in that it does contain some useful references, but it is also full of descriptive and critical work. It isn't exactly about studying the web in a formal sense, but it tells you a lot about what people are doing with this relatively new medium. For example, I used Philip Taylor's chapter on uses of the web.

Hayward, S. (2000): *Cinema Studies, the Key Concepts*. London: Routledge.

A very thorough book of reference, which explains everything from schools of film to theoretical positions.

O'Sullivan, T., Hartley, J., Saunders, D., Montgomery, M. and Fiske, J. (1994): *Key Concepts in Communication and Cultural Studies*. London: Routledge.

This is the best reference work for defining terms and cross-referencing them.

Peak, S. and Fisher, P. (2000): *The Guardian Media Guide 2001*. London: Guardian and Matthew Clayton.

A reference guide that seems to be dominated by addresses and telephone numbers for media companies. It also includes useful information about the law, and sections on topics such as ethnic media, as well as valuable media statistics.

Price, S. (1997): *The Complete A–Z Media & Communication Handbook*. London: Hodder & Stoughton.

The title makes excessive claims, but it offers a pretty concise explanation of a good range of key terms in the subject areas.

Watson, J. and Hill, A. (2000): *Dictionary of Media & Communication Studies* (5th edn). London: Arnold.

A thorough, well-established, sometimes quirky reference work.

In terms of journals, and apart from what is mentioned elsewhere, you should find the following in your library, in print, or on CD-Rom or on an intranet.

British Humanities Index: this takes a lot of ploughing through and refers to many American journals that are hard to obtain. But large public libraries will, for example, carry *Sight & Sound*.

Social Trends (HMSO) is also published in a variety of formats. It contains the results of continual government surveys into our economic, social and leisure habits, as illustrated in material in this book.

▌MEDIA THEORY (INCLUDING EFFECTS AND VIOLENCE)

A lot of theory – key concepts, debates, issues – is covered by the books referred to under Media Studies: General (above). You will find the following books useful to add to that list.

Barker, M. and Petley, J. (eds.) (1997): *Ill Effects: the Media/Violence Debate*. London: Routledge.

This is a useful book for taking a robust view opposing various suppositions about media violence.

Cumberbatch, G. (1989): *The Portrayal of Violence in BBC Television*. London: BBC Publications.

This slim book represents research carried out on the basis of content analysis. It includes tables of findings from the research. It leads to interesting conclusions such as the apparent decline of violence on television at a time when public debate inclined to believe there was more.

Cumberbatch, G. and Howitt, D. (1989): *A Measure of Certainty: Effects of the Mass Media*. London: John Libbey.

This small but expensive book is useful for its summary of effects research, including that relating to violence.

Gauntlett, D. (1995): *Moving Experiences, Understanding Television's Influences and Effects*. London: John Libbey.

A thorough and extremely useful survey of effects research and conclusions.

McQuail, D. (2000): *McQuail's Mass Communication Theory* (4th edn). London: Sage.

Although some may object that this is written by a sociologist (as opposed to a Cultural Studies person, for example), it really is very comprehensive. A number of the topics that I have discussed are dealt with at greater length and with more explicit theory behind them. It is now a massive work.

▌THE PRESS

See also 'News', below.

Keeble, R. (1998): *The Newspapers Handbook*. London: Routledge.

McKay, J. (2000): *The Magazines Handbook*. London: Routledge.

UK Press Gazette (weekly).

Willings Press Guide has addresses and other information relating to these journals.

Benn's Press Directory gives details of who owns what in publishing, and of newspaper and magazine circulation.

The Audit Bureau of Circulation's web site may be found at: www.abc.org.uk/electronic.

▌FILM

Cook, P. (ed.) (2000): *The Cinema Book* (2nd edn). London: BFI.

This is a well-established and valuable work, which nevertheless sits a little uneasily between being a reference book and one that explains terms and critical approaches to film.

Giannetti, L. (1993): *Understanding Movies* (6th edn). Englewood Cliffs, New Jersey: Prentice Hall.

A thorough, well-illustrated book – rather expensive – covering all aspects of film criticism.

Nelmes, J. (ed.) (1998): *An Introduction to Film Studies*. London: Routledge.
   The title is misleading! This is a huge book, and it doesn't provide an introduction to concepts and critical approaches to film in general. But some of these ideas are in there, within a wide range of chapters covering form, genre and examples of national cinema.
Independent on Sunday newspaper – particularly David Thompson's articles on film.
Sight & Sound (BFI): despite the tensions between the academic and the populist in its articles, this remains a useful magazine for its ongoing critical take on movies and the cinema industry, and for its reviews of films.

MUSIC

Longhurst, B. (1995): *Popular Music and Society*. London: Polity Press.
Negus, K. (1992): *Producing Pop, Culture And Conflict in the Music Industry*. London: Edward Arnold.
   Although a touch dated – nothing about the Net here – this is still a good account of production and promotion in the pop industry.
Shuker, R. (1994): *Understanding Popular Music*. London: Routledge.

RADIO

Crisell, A. (1994): *Understanding Radio* (2nd edn) London: Routledge.
   Radio is a lost child among the media, usually lumped under broadcasting. This book covers radio background, history, genres and critical approaches.
Wilby, P. and Conroy, A. (1994): *The Radio Handbook*. London: Routledge.
   Like all others in this series, useful for its mixture of practical information and at least the elements of critical approaches.

TELEVISION: GENERAL

Burton, G. (2000): *Talking Television: an Introduction to the Study of Television*. London: Arnold.
   This is a comprehensive work covering established critical areas such as realism, narrative and representations. It describes and discusses critical concepts and the nature of television, including reference to cultural and postmodernist approaches. It has chapters on television history and futures.
Fiske, J. (1987): *Television Culture*. London: Methuen.
   This book is aimed at degree-level students, but it is invaluable in providing a critique of television material and television audiences, with a Cultural Studies inflection. The chapter on 'news readers, news readings' covers a lot of relevant ground.
Holland, P. (2000): *The Television Handbook* (2nd edn). London: Routledge.
   This book emphasizes the production of television, and is in this respect practical. But it also has a useful second part that does look at, for example, narrative television and documentary on television, with explication of critical approaches.
McQueen, J. (1998): *Television, a Media Student's Guide*. London: Arnold.
   Covers a range of television genres such as game shows and sitcoms. Has a wide-ranging section covering concepts such as audience and ideology. Includes readings and sample essay titles.
Selby, K. and Cowdery, R. (1995): *How To Study Television*. London: Macmillan.

This book is not informational or critical in the conventional sense, but it does deal with some key ideas, and it does demonstrate how to deconstruct the texts of television.

MAKING TELEVISION (INCLUDING DOCUMENTARY AND REALISM)

Hart, A. (1989): *Making the Real World: a Study of a Television Series*. Cambridge: Cambridge University Press.
This book also appears as part of a teaching pack (with a video) called *Teaching Television: the Real World*. *The Real World* is a documentary series on aspects of science produced by Television South (TVS). The book talks about how the programmes were made, as well as about the knowledge of science that we get from such programmes. It is interesting because it goes further into how our understanding of what science is can be influenced by the way programmes are put together. It deals with narrative and audiences, and with facts about the ownership of TVS and how it comes to produce such a programme series.

Strathclyde University: *Brookside Close Up*.
This is a very useful video tape in two parts, which looks at the making of this Liverpool soap and at issues surrounding it such as the question of its authenticity. (Available from Audio Visual Services, University of Strathclyde, Alexander Turnbull Building, 155 George Street, Glasgow G1 1RD.)

NEWS

Allan, S. (1999): *News Culture*. Buckingham: Open University.
This is aimed at degree-level students, so it isn't a soft read, but it does cover a lot of ground and usefully talks about the press as much as about television. It covers, among other topics, gender issues, racism and news discourse. There is also a historical/development of news section.

Eldridge, J. (ed. for the Glasgow University Media Group) (1993): *Getting the Message: News, Truth and Power*. London: Routledge.
Although the case examples are getting a little dated, the content and discourse analysis approach is still hard-hitting in its objectification of news bias and the construction of meanings for audiences.

Hartley, J. (1990): *Understanding News* (2nd edn). London: Routledge.
This is an excellent and thorough approach to understanding how messages are embedded in news material and how those messages may affect our view of the world. It includes a good semiotics-based chapter on reading the news.

McNair, B. (1994): *News and Journalism in the UK* (2nd edn). London: Routledge.
This covers history, debates about news and a range of media including radio.

ADVERTISING

Brierley, S. (1995): *The Advertising Handbook*. London: Routledge.
This is full of practical information about the industry, but also covers items such as devices of persuasion and measuring effects.

Dyer, G. (1982): *Advertising as Communication*. London: Methuen.
   This compact volume includes chapters on the development of advertising, but it is
   more useful later on, as the author deals with effects, creation of meaning, semiotics
   and language in advertising. There are useful examples.
Goldman, R. (1992): *Reading Ads Socially*. London: Routledge.
   Some of the theorizing you may find difficult, but it is stuffed full of telling analyses
   of actual ads.
Vestergaard, T. and Schroder, K. (1994): *The Language of Advertising*. Oxford:
   Blackwell.
   This is a higher-level kind of book, but it is good at analysis of adverts and their
   meanings, making connections with important concepts.
British Rate and Data (BRAD) (monthly) – directory giving advertising rates for the
   press and broadcasting, as well as information such as circulation figures.
Campaign (weekly).
Marketing (monthly).
Advertising Association: *Finding Out About Advertising*: a pack of sheets and leaflets
   that describes types of advertising, gives facts and figures, and includes case studies.
   The Advertising Association also publishes sets of leaflets on other aspects of
   advertising. For further information, contact: The Public Affairs Dept, The
   Advertising Association, Abford House, 15 Wilton Road, London SW1V 1NJ.
The Advertising Standards Authority publishes various booklets, including the Code of
   Advertising Practice, which covers all print media. Contact: The ASA, 15/17
   Ridgmount Street, London WC1E 7AW.

◼ INSTITUTIONS: BACKGROUND

The BBC Annual Report and Handbook – note that you cannot buy this from the BBC,
   only from bookshops designated by it.
The Broadcasters' Audience Research Board (BARB) publishes reports on television
   viewing. Contact: BARB, Knighton House, 56 Mortimer Street, London WIN BAN.
The ITC Television and Radio Year Book – very entertaining for a trip around its
   productions.
The ITC Annual Report and Accounts – gives you a lot more hard information about
   programme hours and expenditures. The commercial sections of big public libraries
   will have this.
   The Independent Television Commission (ITC) also publishes various journals and
   leaflets, most useful of which are *Television: the Public's View* and *Spectrum*.
   Contact: The ITC, 33 Foley Street, London W1P 7LB.

◼ OTHER BOOKS REFERRED TO

Barker, M. (1984): *Video Nasties*. London: Pluto Press.
Barker, C. (1999): *Television, Globalisation and Cultural Identities*. Buckingham:
   Open University.
Barthes, R. (1977): *Image, Music, Text*. London: Fontana.
Belson, W. (1978): *Television and the Adolescent Boy*. Farnborough: Saxon House.
Berger, A. (1992): *Film Art: an Introduction* (4th edn). New York: McGraw-Hill.
Brake, M. (1985): *Comparative Youth Culture*. London: Routledge.
Brown, M.E. (ed.) (1993): *Television and Women's Culture*. London: Sage.
Buckingham, D. (1987): *Public Secrets, EastEnders and its Audience*. London: BFI.

Burns, J. (1996), in Gow, J., Paterson, R. and Preston, A. (eds) (1996): *Bosnia by Television*. London: BFI.

Curran, J. (ed.) (1999): *Media Organisations in Society*. London: Arnold.

Evans, J. (1998), in Briggs, A. and Cobley, P., *The Media: an Introduction*. Harlow: Longman.

Fiske, J. (1987): *Television Culture*. London: Routledge.

Fiske, J. (1992), in Allen, R. (ed.): *Channels of Discourse Reassembled*. London: Routledge.

Fiske, J. (1993): Television pleasures, in Graddol, D. and Boyd-Barrett, O., *Media Texts: Authors and Readers*. Clevedon: Multilingual Matters/Open University.

Feuer, J. (1987), in Allen, R. (ed.): *Channels of Discourse Reassembled* (reprinted 1992). London: Routledge.

Gallagher, M. (1988): Negotiations of control in media organisation, in Gurevitch, M., Bennett, T., Curran, J. and Woollacot, J. (eds): *Culture, Society and the Media*. London: Methuen.

Gauntlett, D. and Hill, A. (1999): *TV Living*. London: Routledge.

Gerbner, G. (1986): Living with television – the dynamics of the cultivation process, in Bryant, J. and Zillman, D. (eds): *Perspectives on Media Effects*. Hillsdale, NJ: Laurence Erlbaum.

Gow, J., Paterson, R. and Preston, A. (eds) (1996): *Bosnia by Television*. London: BFI.

Graddol, D. and Boyd-Barrett, O. (1994): *Media Texts: Authors and Readers*. Clevedon: Multilingual Matters/Open University.

Hall, S. (1994), in Graddol, D. and Boyd-Barrett, O., *Media Texts: Authors and Readers*. Clevedon: Multilingual Matters/Open University.

Hall, S., Hobson, D., Lowe, A. and Willis, P. (1981): *Culture, Media, Language*. London: Hutchinson.

Hart, A. (1991): *Understanding the Media*. London, Routledge.

Hartley, J. (1999): *The Uses of Television*. London: Routledge.

Hebdige, D. (1988): *Hiding in the Light*. London: Routledge.

Herman, E. and McChesney, R. (1997): *The Global Media*. London: Cassell.

Hermes, J. (1995): *Reading Women's Magazines*. Cambridge: Polity Press.

Hillier, J. (ed.) (2000): *American Independent Cinema*. London: BFI.

Home Office (1981): *Broadcasting in the United Kingdom*. HMSO.

Home Office (1988): *Broadcasting in the Nineties*. HMSO.

Hooper, R. (1996): The United Kingdom, in *Media Ownership & Control*. The International Institute of Communications: London.

Kilborn, R. (1992): *Television Soaps*. London: Batsford.

Kitzinger, J. (1999), in Philo, G. (ed.): *Message Received*. Harlow: Longman.

Kuhn, A. (1985), in Cook, P. (ed.): *The Cinema Book*. London: BFI.

Lewis, L. (1993), in Brown, M.E. (ed.), *Television and Women's Culture*. London: Sage.

Lorimer, R. with Scannell, P. (1994): *Mass Communications: a Comparative Introduction*. Manchester: Manchester University Press.

McQuail, D. (1984): *Communication*. Harlow: Longman.

McQuail, D. (1992): *Media Performance*. London: Sage.

Morley, D. (1992): *Television Audiences and Cultural Studies*. London: Routledge.

Philo, G. (ed. for the Glasgow University Media Group) (1999): *Message Received*. Harlow: Longman.

Propp, V. (1968): *The Morphology of the Folk Tale*. Austin: University of Texas Press.

Shew, W. (1996): Survey for News International, in Hooper, R.: *The United Kingdom, in Media Ownership and Control*. London: International Institute of Communications.

Silverstone, R. (1999): *Why Study the Media?* London: Sage.

Taylor, P. (2000), in Gauntlett, D. (ed.): *Web Studies.* London: Arnold.

Todorov, T. (1976): The Origin of Genres. *New Literary History* 8(1).

Tunstall, J. (1977): *The Media Are American.* London: Constable.

Tunstall, J. (1993): *Television Producers.* London: Routledge.

Turner, G. (1992): *British Cultural Studies: an Introduction* (2nd edn). London: Routledge.

Van Zoonen, L. (1994): *Feminist Media Studies.* London: Sage.

▮ WEB SITES

I take the rather heretical view that one can waste a lot of time chasing ghosts across the Web. Sites sometimes change their addresses and can prove difficult to locate or access, even if you have been there before. Obviously the more information you can put in your search box the better. You also have to decide whether or not you want to confine your search to Britain. Depending on what academic level you are working at, there is, for example, some useful stuff on Australian university Web sites. If you are a student at university, then I strongly advise you to ask for help at your library/resources centre. There are many links to search engines and research facilities that you simply have to ask about (for example, bubl@bubl.ac.uk). So I am offering comparatively few Web sites for reference (all addresses were correct at the time they were accessed in early 2001).

I would advise you to start out with a reasonable search engine – try going to google.com.

In terms of companies (co.) and organizations (org.) it is fairly easy to raise most media organizations by name, and then search around their Web sites – e.g. bbc.co.uk or bfi.org.uk or Granada, and so on.

There are some universities that have useful sites, including book reviews, some reference material on specific topics, and links to other sites. The best one is at Aberystwyth (aber.ac.uk/media/functions/mcs.html or aber.ac.uk~dgc/media.html). There is a useful, if slightly selective, one at Leeds (www.theory.org.uk/). You could try Nottingham Trent (http://human.ntu.ac.uk). There is also http://www.ctheory.com/ and www.buvc.ac.uk (the British Universities Film & Video Council).

I have a weakness for www.the-bullet.com, which takes an independent look at media goings-on, and provides current information about take-overs, etc.

Also independent is the organization Campaign for Press and Broadcasting Freedom whose Web site is at: www.cpbf.demon.co.uk.

You can also try mailbase.ac.uk/lists/media-watch/ and cinemedia.org/welcomes/you.html.

There is www.imdb.com for you film buffs out there, as well as www.filmeducation.org for more serious film study, and www.empireonline.co.uk tied in to the popular magazine on films.

The media research organizations also have their own Web sites, though there is a limit as to how much is available – for example, www.brad.co.uk or www.abc.org.uk/electronic.

Index

Paradigm is a collection of signs that 'belong together' but that then need conventions to turn them into a working code. The alphabet is a paradigm of letter signs that need conventions to organize them into words (syntagms).

Preferred Reading refers to the way in which an article is so written or a programme is so constructed that the audience is subconsciously pressured into preferring (reading) one meaning into that material rather than any other meaning.

Propaganda refers to communication that is intentionally manipulated by a powerful source in order to project influential political messages. This source is also powerful enough to exclude alternative messages. It is a misuse of the term to call advertising propaganda.

Realism is a quality of a piece of communication, fictional or factual, that causes the reader or viewer to judge it to be more or less truthful or lifelike.

Regulation refers to the mechanisms, formal or informal, legal or economic, through which media production is controlled. (*See also* Censorship and Constraints.)

Representation refers to both the creation of a likeness of something through using signs and to the creation of meanings through those signs. Representations of people are constructed through image signs in the media. What those images mean or stand for is also represented.

Role is a particular pattern of behaviour that we take on because we see ourselves in a certain social position in relation to other people. Roles are also taken on because others assume we should do this. The positions are defined in terms of factors such as job or place in the family. So we talk about the role of daughter or the role of reporter.

Secondary Code is a particular code of signs and conventions that works on a level above the primary codes of speech, non-verbal communication, etc. The media are full of such codes, which belong to genres in particular, e.g. the news.

Semiotics refers to the study of signs, of sign systems and of their meanings.

Sign: anything can become a sign if we agree that it has a meaning. The particular meaning of a sign or set of signs is something that is agreed and learned through experience. Signs have no particular meaning of themselves, so gestures or elements of pictures become signs because we agree that they have a meaning.

Signification has two possible meanings. One refers to 'the signification' – what the receiver believes that a sign actually does mean, out of all the possible signifieds. The other refers to the 'process of signification' – the making of meanings through signs.

Signified is that part of the sign that is its possible meaning. In many cases the signifier could refer to a number of possible meanings.

Signifier is that part of the idea of sign that actually signals something – a wink, a camera angle, a word.

Socialization describes the processes through which a person becomes a participating member of society. It is learning to live with others. It includes the idea of acquiring beliefs, norms, values, conventions, and of ways of

Mass Communication is the general term for means of communication that operate on a large scale, i.e. in terms of the geographical area reached, the numbers of people reached, the numbers of pieces of communication that are reproduced.

Meaning is what you think it is! The meaning of communication, printed or broadcast, is what you believe it is trying to tell you. The meaning in a piece of communication is signified by the signs that make it up. The meaning that is intended by the sender of the communication may not be the same as the meaning that is decoded or 'read' by the receiver or audience.

Media Power refers to the power of media institutions, through ownership and control, to shape messages that, in turn, may influence the attitudes and behaviour of the audience.

Mediation describes the way in which the media come between the audience and the original material on which the programme or printed matter is based. The media provide their own version of this original material. In mediating it they change it.

Message is any item of information, of opinion, of value judgement that we believe we are being told through an example of media material.

Mode of Address refers to the way in which any media text 'talks to' the audience, to how it sets up a relationship with the audience through the way it 'talks'.

Moral Panic is a term that describes a collective response to events in society as shown through the media. The original work that helped coin the term was about news coverage of mugging. The suggestion was that the news people created a panic about mugging by reporting it frequently, and implying that it was a more serious problem than it really was.

Myth is a story or even part of a story that is not really true, but that says something about what a culture wants to believe in. Genres are full of myths about heroic deeds or even about ideas such as the 'American dream' that everyone can be a great success if they really want to.

Narrative refers to story making and story structure. The narrative of a programme or article is not just its storyline. It is also about how the story is organized and about how the understanding of the reader is organized by the ways in which the story is told.

Naturalization refers to the way in which the messages within much media material are made to seem naturally 'right' or 'true'. The messages that make up ideology are usually held to be naturalized, so that one is not aware that the ideology is there.

News Values are the news topics and ways of treating those topics that the news makers judge as important.

Opinion Leaders are those people in groups that we belong to whose opinions we respect, and that we are likely to agree with because of this. The effects of the media depend partly on these opinion leaders.

Opinion Makers are media figures such as the presenter who fronts a documentary series, who thus have the power to interpret information and represent views to the audience.

Glossary of Terms

The following is a list of terms used in this book, with a brief definition for each one. You may also come across some of them in your further reading, especially if you take on more 'difficult' books. For further references and information see O'Sullivan, *et al.* (1994).

Agenda Setting refers to the process by which the news media define which topics (the agenda) should be of main interest to the audience, by selecting these topics repeatedly for news material.

Anchorage refers to the element of a picture that helps to make clear (anchors) its meaning. In many cases it is actually the caption underneath the picture that does this.

Attitude, Attitude Formation refers to the hostile or friendly view that we hold towards a person or an issue presented in the media. Attitude formation refers to the ways in which the media shape our views on a given topic.

Audience defines the receivers of mass media communication (also readers and viewers). It may be measured in terms such as numbers, gender and spending habits.

Bias describes a quality of media material which suggests that it leans towards a particular view of a given issue when it should be more neutral. The term is often discussed in relation to news treatment.

Binary Oppositions refers to a frequent pattern in texts where characters, ideas or plot elements are set one against the other; the text is organized around the idea of opposites.

Campaign describes the organized use of advertisements and publicity across the media and over a period of time, in order to promote such things as sales of a product, the image of a company, the views of a pressure group or political party.

Censorship refers to the suppression or re-writing of media material by some person or committee that has power over those who created that material. The reasons for carrying out censorship are often based on religion (as in Eire) or political beliefs (China).

Channel is simply the means of communication. This general term could apply equally to speech or to television.

Code (*see also* Secondary Code) is a system of signs held together by conventions. Primary codes include speech made up from word signs, or visual communication made up from image signs.

Cognition refers to the mental process by which we recognize what is going on around us and then make sense of it in our heads. For example, when we decode a magazine for its meaning.

Consensus refers to the middle ground of beliefs and values agreed within a knowledge, influence how messages affect them; they may make dominant, negotiated or oppositional readings of texts.

3 BRIEF CASE STUDIES

- Some discussion of effects is related to specific issues and audiences, such as the effect of television on children, or the effects of violence on audiences.

3.1 The effects of television on children depend on many factors, such as the age at which they distinguish fiction from reality, and on the preconceptions that adults have about children.

3.2 There are many opinions offered about violence in the media and particular effects, but no direct relationship between media material and habitual violent behaviour has been proved. The media themselves often raise violence as an issue and perhaps cause anxiety about it. The most plausible effects proposed are long term and to do with attitude change and desensitization towards the depiction of violence. There have been many problems with research methods in terms of proving violence effects. Recent content analysis demonstrates that, in terms of acts of violence depicted on television, there are fewer than there used to be and fewer in Britain than elsewhere.

4 CONCLUSIONS

- Problems with research do not mean that the media do not affect us and that we should not be concerned. In terms of media effects, we need to be most concerned with possible effects on our attitudes, values and beliefs.

REVIEW

You should have learned the following things from this chapter on media effects.

- It is often proposed that the media affect our attitudes, beliefs and values, directly or indirectly.
- There has been a great deal of research into effects on the audience, but much of it is inconclusive or depends on certain conditions.
- There are many factors that may influence people's attitudes and behaviour. The media are only one of these. It is difficult to separate the media from those other factors when conducting research.

1 WHAT SORTS OF EFFECT

- Types of effect may be summarized as follows: short-term effects, inoculation theory, Two-Step Flow Theory, Uses and Gratifications Theory, Cultivation Theory, cultural effects, attitude change, cognitive change, moral panics and collective reactions, emotional responses and personal reactions, agenda setting, socialization, social control, defining reality, endorsement of the dominant ideology.

2 STUDYING EFFECTS

2.1 Types of research may be marked by quantitative or qualitative approaches. Methods of research notably include closed experiments, field studies, content analysis.

2.2 The media conduct a great deal of audience research of their own. Examples of organizations doing this are the Broadcasters' Audience Research Board (BARB) and the Audit Bureau of Circulation (ABC).

2.3 Problems surrounding effects research, and trying to prove effects, notably include the following: the number of variables to take account of, the context in which communication takes place, assumptions made by researchers, separating the influence of the media from other factors, the unrealistic nature of closed experiments, the quality of methodology and interpretation of field studies, the separation of content analysis from the audience.

2.4 A process-based critique of effects leads to the following conclusions: the status and credibility of the source of the message matters; media authority figures, known as opinion makers, also matter; the essential nature of the medium influences how the audience is affected; the degree of monopoly of information or of material in general possessed by the medium (owners) matters; the context in which the messages are received influences how they may affect the audience; opinion leaders in social groups may be part of that context; social conditions matter; events and issues raised by the media themselves are also part of the context in which the messages come through; the nature of the message matters; what is not said is as important as what is actually said; repetition has an effect; messages about subjects that are already in the media matter; the use of conventions of presentation affect the impact of the message; how the message is structured matters; the audience's powers of perception, their beliefs, their

So I am arguing that concerns are valid, research should continue, but that panicky and unfounded assumptions should be questioned rigorously, or even rejected.

It is fair to say that one should take account of the long-term and indirect effects of the media on ways in which we think about ourselves and about our society.

We are back to the meanings that we may construct by interacting with the media. These meanings are generated from the process that has been discussed throughout this book.

Media Studies is not simply about facts – who owns what or how newspapers are made – it is about the significance of those facts: how we think and how we live our lives. If it is about the production of meaning then it is also about the values by which we live and the beliefs that inform our actions, about the part the media may play in constructing and invoking these.

This seems to me to be a pretty good reason for making the media central to study. So, carry on …

Activity (20): Children, Reading and Effects

This activity should bring out points about how, in respect of ideas about media influence, there are assumptions made about effects and audiences that need to be questioned.

First, you need to TALK TO A NUMBER OF PARENTS AND/OR TEACHERS ABOUT CHILDREN AND READING. You will have to pick a particular age group of child. Try the following questions.

- What do they think that children read?
- What do they think children should read?
- Why do they think that children should read the kinds of material given in answer to the second question?

Second, you need to TALK TO SOME CHILDREN FROM THE AGE RANGE YOU HAVE CHOSEN.

- Ask them what they read and why.

See what you can learn from the similarities and differences between the answers given by adults and those given by the children. Do the answers tell you anything about the assumptions made by adults about children as children, as well as about their reading? Do the answers contain any assumptions about the effects of reading on children?